Praise for
A GUIDE TO THRIVING

"A breakthrough book that will reward the reader with a useful path forward. Grounded in science, this is a human-centered approach to changing our stories and our actions."

Seth Godin,
author of *The Song of Significance*

"Jon Rosemberg has written a book that is both a mirror and a lantern. *A Guide to Thriving* invites us into the deeply human journey of moving from survival to meaning—not with grandiose claims, but with humility, honesty, and heart. It's about reconnecting with what matters most and building a life from the inside out. Whether you're navigating loss, burnout, transition, or the quiet ache of feeling misaligned, this book meets you there—and gently walks you forward. Jon doesn't preach; he shares. And in doing so, he gives us all permission to breathe deeper, live braver, and believe in the possibility of thriving."

Dr. Marshall Goldsmith,
Thinkers50 #1 Executive Coach and
New York Times best-selling author of
The Earned Life, Triggers, and
What Got You Here Won't Get You There

"If you're ready to redefine success on your own terms, this book is a remarkable place to help you expand your options, ground your decisions, and align you with the people you care about."

Guy Kawasaki,
host of the *Remarkable People*
podcast and chief evangelist of Canva

"Jon Rosemberg reminds us of something we too often forget: we rise higher when we rise together. Whether in boardrooms or around dinner tables, *A Guide to Thriving* celebrates the extraordinary power of social connection as the engine of sustainable happiness and collective success."

Shawn Achor,
***New York Times* best-selling author of**
The Happiness Advantage* and *Big Potential

"In this deeply informed and intimate book, Jon Rosemberg guides us through and past the thicket of past-based emotions, beliefs, and body states that keep us imprisoned in survival mode. His well-lived and keenly observed experiences have led him, and thus the reader, to discover a path to genuine thriving—defined not as some external acquisition, but as inner peace, groundedness, and freedom."

Gabor Maté MD,
author of *The Myth of Normal: Trauma,*
Illness and Healing in a Toxic Culture

"Jon Rosemberg masterfully marries cutting-edge science with timeless wisdom in *A Guide to Thriving*. He demystifies personal transformation through the AIR (Awareness, Inquiry, Reframing) framework, making change both accessible and profound. The result is a guide that not only informs but inspires and empowers the reader to break old patterns and craft a life of greater purpose and meaning."

Chip Conley,
**Founder of MEA and *New York Times*
best-selling author**

"*A Guide to Thriving* is a profound and practical guide for anyone seeking to break free from old patterns and reclaim their innate power to grow. Drawing on the science of well-being and the wisdom of experience, Jon Rosemberg offers a structured and grounded framework that leads readers from merely surviving to truly thriving. This book provides a compass for a more meaningful, flourishing life."

Tal Ben-Shahar,
Founder, Happiness Studies Academy

"What's one thing humans need in an age of AI-everything? Balance, ballast, bearings. In this book Jon offers all three."

Neil Pasricha,
author of *The Happiness Equation*

"Plenty of books talk about 'thriving,' but this one actually shows you how. *A Guide to Thriving* reads like a blueprint for shifting from survival mode to truly living with purpose. Jon Rosemberg combines down-to-earth storytelling with solid science, making a case that we have more control over our lives than we think. It's refreshingly honest and aligns perfectly with the evidence-based approach to growth that many of us are seeking."

Jordan Harbinger,
creator of *The Jordan Harbinger Show*

"*A Guide to Thriving* is a compelling, science-backed road map to go from survival to thriving. Jon Rosemberg empowers readers to break free of limiting patterns and realize their full potential."

Scott Barry Kaufman,
host of *The Psychology Podcast*, Columbia Professor,
and author of *Transcend and Rise Above*

"Truly inspirational and timely, A Guide to Thriving is a beacon for those looking to turn pain into purpose. It arrives at a pivotal moment when the world is hungry for effective pathways to heal trauma and foster genuine well-being. Among many other paths, Rosemberg mentions his personal experience with the healing potential of psilocybin-assisted therapy. His message of reclaiming agency and embracing our full humanity echoes a global movement toward deeper healing and consciousness. This book will uplift and empower anyone ready to move beyond surviving into a life of possibility and wholeness."

Rick Doblin, PhD,
Founder and President, Multidisciplinary Association
for Psychedelic Studies (MAPS)

"A Guide to Thriving offers a profound and practical road map for moving from survival to growth. Jon Rosemberg's integration of personal narrative and science echoes key principles of Polyvagal Theory: that safety, agency, and connection are essential for thriving. His 'AIR' method—Awareness, Inquiry, Reframing—gently empowers readers to reshape old patterns and reclaim a life of meaning and resilience. This book is an inspiring guide for those ready to live more fully and authentically."

Stephen W. Porges, PhD,
Professor of Psychiatry, University of North Carolina
at Chapel Hill and Creator of the Polyvagal Theory

"Jon Rosemberg's A Guide to Thriving is a profound exploration of what it truly means to break free from merely surviving and step boldly into thriving. With clarity, compassion, and depth, Rosemberg offers actionable wisdom that aligns beautifully with my belief that leadership and life success hinge on our ability to consciously choose our responses rather than merely reacting. This book is essential reading for anyone committed to personal growth and leadership authenticity. It resonates deeply with the principles I've championed in *Any Dumb Ass*

Can Do It, reinforcing the power of intentional choices and the courage to face our truths. Highly recommended."

Garry Ridge,
USA Today best-selling author of
***Any Dumb Ass Can Do It* and Chairman Emeritus,**
WD-40 Company

"With warmth and insight, Jon Rosemberg reminds us that thriving is not about chasing happiness but about cultivating meaning every day. In *A Guide to Thriving*, he shows how even our ordinary days can become part of an extraordinary journey of growth and deep fulfillment."

Emily Esfahani Smith,
author of *The Power of Meaning*

"*A Guide to Thriving* is a powerful guide for anyone ready to break free from survival mode and live with intention. With deep psychological insight, personal vulnerability, and actionable tools, Jon Rosemberg equips readers not just to cope but to grow, heal, and lead lives of deeper meaning and purpose."

Michelle Gielan,
best-selling author of *Broadcasting Happiness*

"Jon Rosemberg distills an extensive body of scientific research into an actionable plan toward human thriving, your own thriving! Choices, practices, and core knowledge conspire to open the door to an enhanced way of living. Jon is a sort of coach, companion, committed friend on your road to realizing a more fulfilling and effective stance in living. You might find the you that you had sensed and hoped was possible all along."

Lisa Miller, Ph.D.,
Columbia Professor and NYT best-selling author of
The Awakened Brain* and *The Spiritual Child

"In *A Guide to Thriving*, Jon Rosemberg expertly shows that when we care for the human being behind the professional, it's not only good for people, but great for business. A must read!"

Erica Keswin,
workplace strategist, speaker,
and best-selling author of
Bring Your Human to Work, Rituals Roadmap
and *The Retention Revolution.*

"This book is a practical guide for life's tough moments. Rosemberg combines profound storytelling and rigorous science to help readers transform adversity into opportunity. His AIR method (Awareness, Inquiry, Reframing) is a life changer! Read it, live it, and thrive!"

Jon Gordon,
17x best-selling author of *The Energy Bus* and
The Power of Positive Leadership

"This highly readable book uses a multidisciplinary approach to show how we can cultivate growth and thrive, even in the most difficult times."

Lawrence Calhoun,
Professor Emeritus of Psychological Science at UNC
Charlotte and pioneer in the field of posttraumatic
growth (PTG)

"*A Guide to Thriving* is a much-needed user manual for the human psyche. In it, Rosemberg teaches how thoughts and emotions happen. This knowledge, ultimately, is the platform for positive change."

Dr. Robert Biswas-Diener,
author of *Radical Listening*

"*A Guide to Thriving* opens by inviting us to imagine circumstances that force the question: what truly matters? Jon Rosemberg offers the liberating reminder that thriving doesn't require escaping difficulty—it starts with the courage to envision the life you want and pursue it. With probing questions, stories, and practical exercises drawn from his coaching practice, he provides a clear map and method for charting a course toward a life you can truly embrace."

Michael F. Steger, PhD,
Director of the Center for Meaning and Purpose,
Colorado State University

"*A Guide to Thriving* is a powerful invitation to step out of survival mode and into a life of clarity, purpose, and possibility. With clarity and compassion, Rosemberg illuminates the unseen patterns that keep us stuck and offers both insight and tools to move beyond them. A rare blend of soul and science that is genuinely transformative. A must read."

Anita Moorjani,
New York Times* best-selling author of *Dying to Be Me

"Jon's remarkable book helps us to understand that there is another way to live our one precious life than to survive: we can thrive. He both teaches us the profound difference between the two and holds our hands so that we can take that journey. His book is everything you need: anchored in a map of the elements of thriving, it is personal, readable, compassionate, wise, and filled with practical suggestions. To accept his invitation is to reconnect you to yourself and to others around you, and remarkably, the world around you will benefit."

Lisa Lahey, EdD,
Harvard Graduate School of Education faculty,
co-author of *Immunity to Change* and
An Everyone Culture

"In *A Guide to Thriving*, Jon Rosemberg indeed provides a guide, not a list of directions or a recipe. Anchored by psychological science, deepened by thoughtful analysis, and brought to life with vivid examples, this book can help many find their personal route from survival to thriving."

Barry Schwartz,
author of *The Paradox of Choice*, *Why We Work*,
and co-author of *Practical Wisdom*

"Rosemberg's book is the culmination of years of coaching experience and personal growth. For him, positive psychology offers a path from ordinary, dead-end survival mode to thriving, and this book offers a vivid, memorable map to guide people along that path. This entertaining book offers plenty of inspiring stories about individuals learning to thrive, as well as insightful analysis based on ancient wisdom, modern research, professional experience, and the author's personal journey."

Roy Baumeister,
president, International Positive Psychology
Association and author of *The Science of Free Will*

"This book is both a guide and an invitation to thrive. Drawing on compelling personal and client stories, Rosemberg introduces a practical nine-element map that helps you move from survival mode to a life of greater agency, meaning, and well-being. Through tools grounded in neuroscience, emotional awareness, and the power of reframing, Rosemberg shows us how to break free from limiting patterns and reclaim control, even in challenging circumstances. With every chapter, you're reminded that thriving isn't a destination but an ongoing practice that honors setbacks as part of the journey. This is the kind of book you return to again and again—not just for insight, but for hope."

Louisa Jewell, MAPP,
Founder, Canadian Positive Psychology Association

"In a time when many people have given up on the very notion of thriving, this book is an opening to not only a better life but a better world. Using his compelling story as well as the stories of his clients, Rosemberg brings us an elegant, simple, and actionable way to change the way we interact with the world and with ourselves. Reading this book will encourage you to move toward thriving—and will give you a map to follow along the way."

Dr. Jennifer Garvey Berger,
author of *Unlocking Leadership Mindtraps: How to Thrive in Complexity*

"The amazing wisdom captured in this book derives from deep personal reflections, scientific discoveries, and professional experience helping people transition from merely surviving to thriving. Jon Rosemberg synthesized for you life's most important lessons in a highly engaging way. The book is not only informative but highly practical at the same time. If you are interested in personal growth and well-being, and in contributing to your family, peers, community, and society at large, read this book."

Isaac Prilleltensky,
Mautner Endowed Chair in Community Well-Being, University of Miami, co-author of *How People Matter*, co-editor of *How People Thrive*

"Instead of sugarcoating life's chaos, Jon embraces it. Raw, grounded, and fiercely insightful, this book is for anyone ready to trade burnout for boldness and survival for something a tad more human: thriving."

Ron Tite,
best-selling author of *Think Do Say*,
The Purpose of Purpose, and *Everyone's an Artist*

"Do more than survive—aim to thrive! Jon Rosemberg's *A Guide to Thriving* invites you to make choices to activate possibilities for your own or others' thriving. The book provides both a scientific foundation and map for thriving that gives you plentiful choices you can make to direct your experiences (and your life) toward thriving. The book recognizes our limits and our fallibilities, while also calling us to step beyond, and to try again to move out of surviving into a thriving mode. The book is both inspirational and practical with plentiful examples from Jon's life and from others' experiences that illustrate how to be agentic in charting a path toward thriving."

Jane E. Dutton,
Robert L. Kahn Distinguished University Professor
Emerita of Business Administration and Psychology,
Ann Arbor Michigan

"*A Guide to Thriving* is your playbook to reclaim control of your life. Jon Rosemberg masterfully breaks down the journey from merely surviving to truly thriving, making complex ideas simple, relatable, and actionable. It's like having a personal coach cheering you on every step of the way—highly recommended!"

Pat Flynn,
New York Times
best-selling author of *Lean Learning*

"Jon Rosemberg presents a powerful new model of flourishing in *A Guide to Thriving*—a research-grounded guide that anyone can use to navigate out of burnout and into experiences of curiosity, growth, and joy. A must-read for all who seek a way to navigate life's stormy waters, from a guide who has been there and can help you through it with clarity and compassion."

Stephanie Harrison, author of
The New Happy

"*A Guide to Thriving* is not just a book but a lifeline for anyone stuck in the illusion of high-functioning survival. With science, soul, and deep humanity, Jon Rosemberg offers a powerful framework to help us reclaim agency and design a life worth living."

Stefan Falk,
author of *Intrinsic Motivation: Learn to Love Your Work and Succeed as Never Before*

"This guide offers a renewed sense of possibility and the courage to step into a life that feels more whole. It's an invitation to be an active participant in your own journey, highlighting that thriving is a continuous process of self-discovery. By helping readers question the stories that keep them small and showing how to break through old patterns, *A Guide to Thriving* inspires readers to reclaim their agency and trust their capacity to adapt and overcome, even in the face of challenges. It truly is a book for anyone asking, 'Is this all there is to life?'"

Dan Tomasulo, PhD,
Academic Director, Professor of Teaching Spirituality, Mind Body Institute, Teachers College, Columbia University, and best-selling author of *Learned Hopefulness*

"*A Guide to Thriving* is like a user manual for your humanity— equal parts science, soul, and sanity. Jon Rosemberg takes you by the hand (and occasionally by the collar) out of survival mode and into a life that actually feels lived. Insightful, practical, and sneakily profound."

Jodi Wellman, MAPP,
author of *You Only Die Once: How to Make It to the End with No Regrets*

"A *Guide to Thriving* is both a deeply personal reckoning and a practical guide. Jon writes with the clarity of a teacher, the rigor of a researcher, and the soul of someone who has lived every word on the page. Through heartbreak, loss, reinvention, and resilience, he shows us that thriving isn't a destination, but a choice we make again and again. This book will stay with you long after you finish the last page"

Tamara Myles,
best-selling author of *Meaningful Work*

"A *Guide to Thriving* is more than a book—it's a trusted guide for navigating life's complexities. Jon's blend of hard science and heartfelt storytelling help you untangle the subtle traps that keep you stuck in survival mode, and offer practical tools to create meaningful, long-term change."

Cory Muscara,
author of *Stop Missing Your Life*

"A *Guide to Thriving* is a humble, heartfelt, and scientifically rigorous gem. After more than 20 years teaching in this field, I'm thrilled by Jon Rosemberg's fresh perspective and the practical tools I can now add to my toolkit. He seamlessly blends psychology and neuroscience with indigenous wisdom, spirituality, and rich coaching stories. For practitioners and wisdom-seekers alike, this book is an essential, hands-on guide to flourishing."

Emiliya Zhivotovskaya,
MAPP, MCC, CEO & Founder of
The Flourishing Center

"Jon's book is unlike anything I've read on well-being. A *Guide to Thriving* is both deeply personal and rigorously grounded in science, offering a rare combination of vulnerability, wisdom, and practical guidance. What sets this book apart is Jon's courage to share his own journey from survival to thriving, inviting readers to reflect, question, and ultimately reclaim agency in their own lives. Each chapter is a doorway to greater self-understanding and possibility, and the nine-part map he offers is simple and profound. Read the book to break through old patterns and step into a life of meaning, resilience, and ever-more authenticity. Yes!"

**Louis Alloro, M.ED.,
MAPP, Senior Fellow, Center for the Advancement
of Wellbeing**

"Jon Rosemberg possesses that rare and valuable gift: he can distill complicated scientific information into relatable terms and apply the science of well-being not merely as academic knowledge, but as a lived practice. *A Guide to Thriving* feels like conversations with a trusted friend, warmly guiding you on the essential journey from survival to thriving."

**Lyssa deHart,
LICSW, MCC, BCC author of *StoryJacking*,
the *Reflective Coach*, and *Light Up*, the Science
of Coaching with Metaphors**

"Jon Rosemberg and I both share a foundation in the science of Positive Psychology—but what he brings to life in *A Guide to Thriving* goes far beyond theory. With rare vulnerability and grounded wisdom, Jon offers a practical and heartfelt invitation to return to yourself. This book is a guide not just for feeling better, but for living better—on purpose, with presence, and with the kind of authenticity that leads to true transformation."

**Finnian Kelly,
founder of Intentionality and featured
mindfulness expert for National Geographic**

"For every successful hoop jumper and ladder climber who doesn't feel as good as they'd hoped, THIS IS THE BOOK! A *Guide to Thriving* is a heartfelt, thoughtful road map to help you shift from merely achieving to creating a life filled with meaning."

Sarah Vermunt,
best-selling author of *Careergasm: Find Your*
Way to Feel-Good Work

"Consider this your blueprint for thriving, no matter who you are. Jon Rosemberg delivers hard-won wisdom and actionable insights, making each page a catalyst for real change and growth."

Nick Sonnenberg,
best-selling author of *Come Up for Air*,
Founder & CEO of Leverage

"A *Guide to Thriving* is not just a book—it's a soulful, science-backed invitation to move from enduring life to truly engaging with it. Jon Rosemberg's writing is honest, human, and deeply reflective. Through compelling storytelling and grounded psychological insight, he walks us through what it means to break old patterns, reclaim our agency, and find meaning—especially when life feels most uncertain. As a leadership coach, I found myself nodding, reflecting, and pausing often. This book will meet you where you are—and gently walk you toward who you're becoming."

Manbir Kaur,
Executive & Leadership Coach, author of
Are You The Leader You Want To Be? and
Get Your Next Promotion

"*A Guide to Thriving* isn't a book about overhauling your life. It's about tuning into it. With relatable examples, insightful tips, and thoughtful questions, Jon helps you shift just enough to see—and feel—real change. He can do that because he's done the work. And it shows. Quick to read. Long in impact."

Chad Aboud,
Chief Commercial Officer of Goodlawyer and
TEDx speaker on How to Intentionally Design Your
Career and Life

"*A Guide to Thriving* is a compassionate, deeply personal, research-backed road map that will help readers question their mindsets, create healthy habits, and navigate life's left turns with confidence and agency. I was especially moved to learn about Jon Rosemberg's connection to MS, and how he and his family are actively applying the strategies he's developed to not just cope with a diagnosis, but to adapt and thrive. This book offers wise, approachable guidance from someone who gets it."

Ardra Shephard,
author of *Fallosophy: My Trip Through Life with MS*

"*A Guide to Thriving* took me by surprise. From the opening pages where author Jon Rosemberg draws you in with a personal story to the many other stories throughout the rest of the book, a compelling way to conceive of what it means to thrive in today's changing world of work is introduced, tested, and humanized over and over again."

Lisa Taylor, CEO,
Challenge Factory and author of *The Talent*
Revolution: Longevity and the Future of Work

"A *Guide to Thriving* is magnetic because it draws you into exploring concepts of surviving and thriving in stories and research. Jon shows that there really is a magnet that draws us toward thriving in ways that are within our reach in every moment. Let the book pull you magnetically through transformation toward thriving, not every moment, every day, just a little more each day."

Margaret Moore,
aka Coach Meg, Executive Coach,
Founder/CEO of the Wellcoaches Corporation,
and Co-Founder of the Institute of Coaching

A GUIDE TO
THRIVING

THE SCIENCE BEHIND BREAKING OLD PATTERNS, RECLAIMING YOUR AGENCY, AND FINDING MEANING

JON ROSEMBERG

WILEY

For general information on our other products and services or for technical support, please contact our Customer Care Department within the United States at (800) 762-2974, outside the United States at (317) 572-3993 or fax (317) 572-4002.

Wiley also publishes its books in a variety of electronic formats. Some content that appears in print may not be available in electronic formats. For more information about Wiley products, visit our website at www.wiley.com.

Library of Congress Cataloging-in-Publication Data is Available:

ISBN 9781394367931 (Cloth)
ISBN 9781394367948 (ePub)
ISBN 9781394367955 (ePDF)

Cover Design and Image by Molly Tuttle
Author Photo: © David Leyes

Printed and bound by CPI Group (UK) Ltd, Croydon, CR0 4YY
C9781394367931_031025

*To my sons, Jacques and Charles, and
my nieces, Anael and Nicole.*

Contents

Foreword

I FIRST MET Jon in our Master of Positive Psychology program at the University of Pennsylvania. He immediately stood out for his remarkable ability to distill complicated scientific information into relatable terms. More importantly, he had an incredible gift for connecting with everyone in our international cohort, making each person feel uniquely seen and valued. I often referred to Jon as a friend to everyone.

It's both an honor and a joy to write this foreword. I have watched Jon apply his expertise in the science of well-being and not just as academic knowledge, but as a lived practice. His journey from corporate leadership to entrepreneurship and purpose-driven work exemplifies the very transformation this book guides readers through.

What makes *A Guide to Thriving* exceptional is how Jon illuminates the path between survival and thriving through stories that feel like conversations with a trusted friend. The nine elements framework he presents offers a comprehensive roadmap for navigating life's challenges, grounded in rigorous research yet expressed with authenticity.

I take Jon's work seriously, not just because of his credentials or research knowledge, but because he truly embodies his message. When facing his own challenges, whether professional transitions or personal loss, Jon approaches them with the same compassionate curiosity he advocates for in these pages. His integrity, exemplified in the alignment between what he teaches and how he lives, lends depth to his work that purely theoretical approaches lack.

His presentation of AIR (Awareness, Inquiry, Reframing) that runs through these chapters provides a methodology that's both profound and practical. It reflects Jon's unique ability to make transformation accessible. As you encounter the stories of Emily, Simon, Deanne, and others throughout the book, you may recognize aspects of your own experience reflected with compassion and clarity.

This book will be especially valuable for those at crossroads in their lives, facing career transitions, relationship challenges, health concerns, or simply feeling that persistent sense that there must be more to life than just surviving. Jon offers both the conceptual framework to understand what keeps us stuck and the practical tools to move forward. In a world that often prioritizes quick fixes, he provides something more sustainable: a guide to lasting transformation that honors the complexity of human experience.

My hope is that as you read, you'll experience what I and many others have found in Jon's presence: a renewed sense of possibility and the courage to move beyond survival into thriving. Jon has a gift for meeting people exactly where they are while illuminating where they might go next.

As you turn these pages, I invite you to approach them not just as a reader but as an active participant in your own journey toward thriving.

With warmth and gratitude,

—Lara Merriken

Founder of LÄRABAR and co-founder of Anther

Preface

On January 4, 2023, I was feeling that sense of hope that comes with the new year when my phone rang. My best friend Nathan was on the other end, and his voice was brittle.

"I have stage IV liver cancer," he said, pausing just long enough for it to sink in. "And it doesn't look good."

When I asked him how he was holding up, I thought he might not answer. Then his breath caught, his words crumbled, and all he could say was, "I'm going to die."

I can still hear Nathan's voice, heavy with the pain of losing control. It's one thing to confront mortality on your own terms, and it's another to have it forced on you without warning. Over the next four months, separated by the thousands of miles between Caracas and Toronto, I watched him shift into survival mode and disconnect from the world as he sank into the depths of hopelessness. He stopped eating, and no matter how many times I texted or called him, he was almost impossible to reach. His life shrank.

The last words of the dying have a way of cutting through life's noise. Bronnie Ware, a palliative care nurse, spent years listening to her patients in their final days and compiled their greatest regrets.

Their responses weren't missed promotions, nicer cars, or bigger houses. They were:

> *I wish I'd had the courage to live a life true to myself, not the life others expected of me.*
>
> *I wish I hadn't worked so hard.*
>
> *I wish I'd had the courage to express my feelings.*
>
> *I wish I had stayed in touch with my friends.*
>
> *I wish that I had let myself be happier.*[1]

I've spent countless hours in boardrooms, across tables at late-night dinners, and in conversations with friends and clients who, despite their success, carry the unspoken burden of survival in many forms. Sometimes, that survival left space for thriving, but other times, it didn't. Along the way, I learned that thriving is something we create through intentional choices.

Nathan died four months to the day he called me. He lived with generosity and kindness, but in his last fight to survive, he built walls around him that even love couldn't break through. Watching him endure that final chapter of his life changed me profoundly. His struggle ignited a resolve in me to write this book and to support others in breaking through the defenses that keep us small. Even in times of crisis or loss, life can be more than mere survival.

Of course, thriving doesn't mean that everything is going well in life. Just two months after Nathan's passing, the love of my life, Adriana, was diagnosed with multiple sclerosis. Watching my wife confront a progressive disease that has an unclear path forward shook me to my core. There's a special kind of helplessness that comes with seeing someone you love face the unknown. It forces you to sit with uncertainty and to learn to live without answers. You want to fix it, to protect, to will it away, but you can't. So, you learn to stay present, to hold space, and to keep going.

As if 2023 hadn't asked enough, I watched with horror as the events of October 7th and their aftermath unfolded in Israel, Palestine, and the Middle East. Seared into my mind were the images of violence, families huddled in panic rooms, people taken hostage or fleeing, and entire communities reduced to ashes. What began as a single day of devastation became a war that left a trail of grief behind. Watching it from a distance is its own kind of anguish.

When life shatters our illusions of control, it's natural to slip into the primal instinct to survive. While we may have little control over what happens to us, we do have a say in how we respond. We can choose whether we stay walled in by terror or find the courage to break through survival and step into thriving.

■ ■ ■

For the first 40 years of my life, I lived in survival mode. I didn't recognize it then because it was all I knew, and I was convinced that simply enduring was the best I could do. As time passed, I began to see that the same patterns that made me feel safe also kept me imprisoned. In this book, I explore some of the limiting stories we all carry, where they came from, how they impact us, and what science tells us about what it takes to break them down. Thriving begins by dismantling these walls, brick by brick.

I come from a long line of survivors. My maternal grandparents endured the horrors of escaping the Holocaust, one fleeing Austria and the other Bulgaria. For them, every day was a battle for existence. My grandfather, a man of profound wisdom, a gifted violinist and painter with a deep appreciation for beauty and excellence, lost his entire family to the Nazi death camps. For him, survival was an act of defiance against a world determined to erase him.

My grandmother was equally remarkable and resourceful. In 1968, she boarded Pan Am Flight 217 for what should have been a routine trip home to Caracas. As the plane neared its destination, the shimmering lights of the city reflected against the hills, creating an optical illusion that deceived the pilots. The aircraft descended too soon and plunged into the Caribbean Sea. All 51 passengers and crew on board, including my grandmother, perished.

That day, my mother lost the anchor of her young life, and my grandfather was left to grapple with the sudden void left where his adored wife had been. Even after enduring genocide and war, fate still dealt devastating blows to them.

My father's family also knew displacement intimately. Fleeing the antisemitism and pogroms of Lithuania, they sought refuge in Cuba. At first, they found safety and hope. With grit and determination, they built a successful business and found a sense of stability. My grandfather's entrepreneurial spirit and my grandmother's kind-heartedness allowed them to create a thriving life surrounded by the vibrant culture of their new home.

That promise was short-lived when Fidel Castro rose to power and stripped them of their home, their business, and their community. They were forced to emigrate again, this time to Venezuela, where they were welcomed with open arms.

Venezuela, a land of warmth and opportunity, is also the place where my story began. I carry a strong sense of pride in having been born and raised in a nation whose resilience endures, seen in the millions who emigrated in search of safety and the millions who stayed, holding on to hope that the decades-long crisis will one day give way to something better. For years, Venezuela offered my family a haven, until that stability began to erode in the 1980s and ultimately crumbled with the rise of Hugo Chávez in 1999. What had once been a country of promise descended into chaos, anarchy, violence, and despair. The dreams of countless families, including my own, were suffocated.

Loss became constant, though some losses cut deeper than others.

A few days after my twenty-sixth birthday, my father was walking down the stairs in my childhood home, carrying my seven-month-old niece in his arms. He lost his footing and fell. In that split second, his instincts took over, and he twisted his body to shield the baby from the impact. She survived. He did not.

I spent that night with his lifeless body in a Caracas hospital, waiting for the Chevra Kadisha, the Jewish group responsible for preparing the dead for burial. It was the longest night of my life as time stretched endlessly through those painful hours. Grief has the power to suspend us in timeless pain.

Two years later, the ground gave way again when my business partner was shot three times and killed in an armed robbery, leaving behind two young children in a land gripped by lawlessness. Since staying in Venezuela was no longer safe, we had to leave to survive.

That's a lot of life packed into a few paragraphs. I share these stories because they carry the heartbeat of this book. While your journey is different from mine, we all share experiences of pain and struggle that influence how we move through the world. We all share a longing for safety and a yearning for the chance to thrive.

Adriana and I immigrated to Canada in search of a better life. Our sons were born here, and I see a new, bright future unfolding for my family. This country feels like a beacon of hope, a place where the cycle of fleeing can finally end, and where the roots of a thriving life can take hold for my family.

Surviving hardship leaves its mark. Focusing on survival teaches us to play it small and to prioritize safety above all else, and while those instincts can save us in times of turmoil, they can also keep us trapped in lives that feel far too narrow for our potential. For years, I approached life as though I were still fleeing, and worked hard to build security, to achieve, to prove that I could survive in the face of what I had left behind. Outwardly, I succeeded, but inwardly, I felt the same pain that I've heard in so many others: the sense that I was not truly living.

■ ■ ■

After moving to Canada, I threw myself into building a new life from the ground up. I was determined to prove that I couldn't only survive in this new country but also thrive. I worked my way through a series of increasingly senior roles at some of the world's largest companies. I led teams, managed multi-billion-dollar budgets, and climbed the corporate ladder with relentless focus. I was working toward the version of success I had long believed would finally make me feel whole.

In 2021, I stepped into what I pictured as my dream job as Chief Operating Officer at a tech startup experiencing double-digit growth month after month. It was everything I thought I wanted: status, power, and wealth. But less than a year in, success felt hollow, and I did something that terrified me: I walked away, convinced that I had been climbing the wrong mountain.

Few decisions in my life have asked more of me. Letting go of the identity I had spent years building felt like stepping off a ledge without knowing where I would land. In that uncertainty, I finally began to redefine what thriving could look like for me. I returned to graduate school, built a consulting company, and grew my coaching practice. I partnered with Lara Merriken, the founder of LÄRABAR, to create

Anther, a platform grounded in the belief that personal growth and collective thriving are deeply interconnected. These choices brought greater clarity into my life and aligned my professional efforts with the values that matter most to me.

As I reflect on my career, I realize that some of the most important lessons about thriving come from ordinary experiences on warehouse floors, in meeting rooms, through weekend emergency calls, in the thick of hard conversations, and in the moments after major decisions have been made. I've seen how so many of us wrestle with survival mode, which often shows up as unrelenting pressure and the weight of expectations. I've seen how often success comes at the cost of well-being.

Time and again, I've seen that transformation is rarely sparked by a single breakthrough. More often, it's forged through by a series of choices that accumulate over time. Growth asks us to look inward, make small shifts, and keep stepping into uncertainty. We're all capable of far more than we realize.

As part of my journey into the science of thriving, I earned a Masters of Applied Positive Psychology degree at the University of Pennsylvania, where I had the privilege of learning from some of the most brilliant minds in the field of psychology. I also completed a leadership coaching certificate at Georgetown University and the year-long professional training in Compassionate Inquiry, both of which deepened my ability to meet clients where they are and support their growth. These experiences taught me to approach thriving with curiosity, humility, and scientific rigor.

I'm writing this book for the version of me who, 10 years ago, was sprinting on a treadmill made of fear and ambition, not yet knowing there was another way. I'm writing it for the version of me who, 10 years from now, might forget. I'm writing it for the Nathans of the world, those facing the unthinkable and searching for a way to hold on to more than just survival. I'm writing it in memory of those who escaped horror, and those who continue to choose courage as they build new lives. I'm writing it for my children and nieces, so they might learn to thrive sooner in life than I did.

Most importantly, this book is for you, particularly for the times when you wonder, "Is this all there is to life?"

Let this be an invitation to learn how to break through, again and again, from mere survival to truly thriving.

Introduction

THIS BOOK IS about breaking through from survival to thriving. Not once, but over and over.

Survival mode is our emergency response system. It's designed to protect us in moments of real danger, but when it becomes our default, it can confine us to a life of constant vigilance and fear where the world begins to shrink, reduced to a series of threats we must endure. Thriving mode, in contrast, is a state of openness where curiosity, engagement, connectedness, and possibility guide us. When we're thriving, we find clarity, expand, meet challenges with confidence, and trust our capacity to adapt and overcome. Where survival mode makes us brace and react, thriving mode invites us to respond with agency and grow.

If you picked up this book, chances are you've felt trapped in a rut, searching for a way to break through the feeling that life is happening to you rather than with you. Maybe you're not sure what comes next, but you've started to sense that something needs to change. Perhaps the way you've been living no longer feels aligned with who you are or who you're becoming. This space can feel uncomfortable, messy, and even suffocating at times, but it's also where transformation begins by exploring important questions like:

What does it mean to truly live rather than merely exist?

How do we dismantle the walls we've constructed to protect ourselves, knowing they also confine us?

How do we step into a life that feels authentic and deeply meaningful?

How do we find the strength to confront the beliefs that limit our choices and reimagine a life guided by meaning?

From Survival to Thriving

As a fellow traveler on the journey of self-discovery, I've wrestled with depression, anxiety, and the persistent ache of not being enough, even in the midst of outward success. Along the way, I've come to understand that moving between survival and thriving is deeply personal and often requires us to pause and take a closer look at how we live. I've found that one of the most powerful ways to do that is by getting curious. That's why each chapter in this book ends with a series of questions, offered to support your exploration in your own way and at your own pace.

For example, in my coaching practice, the question "What can I do differently?" has become a compass for my clients as they uncover the hidden beliefs that limit them. It invites a shift from blame to possibility and creates space for new perspectives and choices. As we explore this question together, many begin to recognize patterns that once felt fixed and discover a greater sense of agency in how they respond.

These conversations have also been transformative for me. They have reinforced my belief that thriving is within reach for all of us, no matter where we begin. What my experience has shown me is that every person is inherently creative, resourceful, and wise, but accessing that potential requires a willingness to lean into the fullness of life, including the good, the bad, and everything in between.

Transitions in life often feel disorienting and heavy, like wading through thick mud. The harder we fight against it, the deeper we sink. At the same time, that mud can become fertile ground, a place where growth begins to emerge. Difficult moments push us to face what holds us back, and in doing so, they reveal strengths we didn't realize we carried. Over time, these strengths help us come through more resilient on the other side.

This isn't a book of magical solutions, and there are no quick fixes, prescriptions, or easy answers in these pages. Instead, it is an invitation to recognize the patterns that limit your life and to learn how to break free from them. Within each of us lives the ability to thrive, even in the face of life's most daunting challenges. That ability strengthens when we embrace discomfort and allow ourselves to be vulnerable without turning away. This book offers a map to guide you in questioning the stories that keep you small and stepping into a life that feels more whole.

A Map

In the chapters ahead, you'll find a map designed to help you navigate your own journey. Chapter 1 introduces the map, and each chapter that follows explores one of its nine elements in depth.

This map first came to me during my time at Georgetown University's Institute for Transformational Leadership, where I encountered a similar model that illuminated thriving as a multidimensional process. Inspired by what I learned there, I've since adjusted and expanded the elements, drawing from scientific research and wisdom traditions, including the Medicine Wheel, a sacred Indigenous framework that honors the balance of mind, body, emotions, and spirit.

Before you begin, consider that thriving isn't about checking off all nine elements of the map like a to-do list. Although they are intricately connected, you don't have to master all nine elements at once. Where you are in life will inform what resonates most, so think of each one as an open door to step through, knowing that different ideas may speak to you at different times.

Because the elements of the map are interconnected, when one is neglected, the others are affected, and when one is nurtured, the others are strengthened. This dynamic relationship between the nine elements reflects the complexity of our inner lives.

Navigating this map will help you discover some of the invisible patterns that guide your life and allow you to engage with them intentionally. Real change becomes possible when you gain enough distance to recognize these forces not as something you are inside of, but as beliefs you can observe and work with. This movement from being subject to these forces to seeing them as objects of reflection can be a powerful turning point in how you experience your life. With new-found awareness, you can begin to choose how you respond.

More importantly, thriving isn't a singular event but a continuous process, where each breakthrough reveals that transformation is less about reaching a final destination and more about getting to know yourself better. This ongoing process requires self-compassion and the courage to keep showing up, again and again.

An Invitation

As you move through these pages, you will encounter reflections and ideas drawn from science, philosophy, history, and real-life experiences. To protect privacy, the stories in this book have been anonymized and synthesized to reflect shared experiences rather than individual accounts.

This book is designed as a guide that you can choose to read cover to cover or explore by dipping into the sections that feel most relevant to you at any given moment. Each chapter stands on its own, so you can move through these pages in the way that best supports your journey.

There isn't a one-size-fits-all approach to thriving. While some ideas may resonate deeply, others may not, and that's okay. Take what feels meaningful to you, make it your own, and if something doesn't fit, let it go. My intention isn't to prescribe answers but to offer ideas and questions that will invite you to explore your own path.

In a time of so much upheaval, my hope is that this book offers a glimpse of what becomes possible when you embrace the boundless possibilities of thriving. After all, the world needs not only people who survive but also those who thrive and help others do the same.

Where do we begin? Right where we are, in the tension between survival and thriving. It's here, in this messy space between who we've been and who we're becoming, that transformation takes place.

Let's move toward thriving together.

PART

I

Foundation

1

From Survival to Thriving

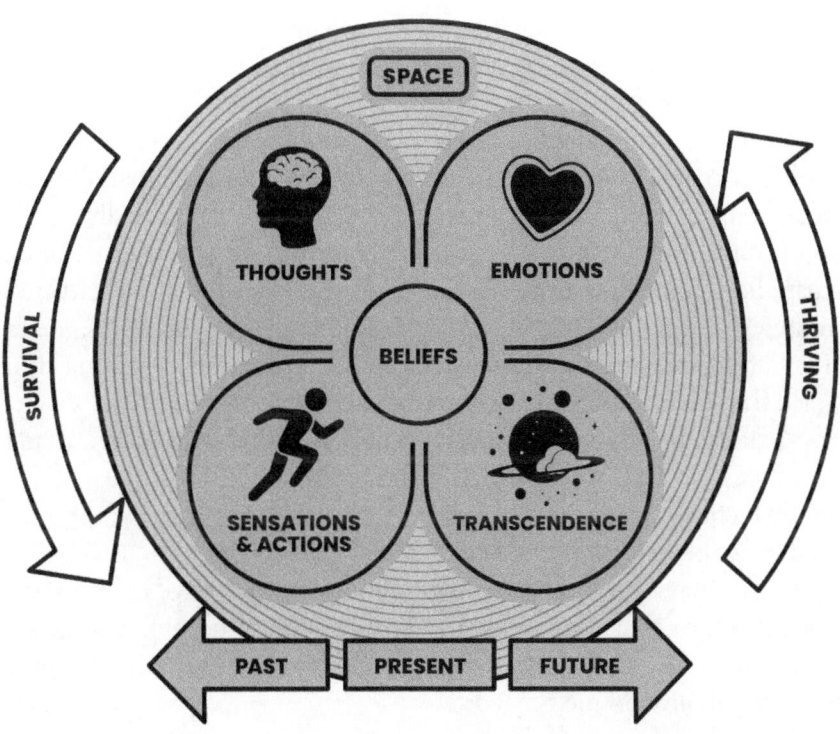

My FATHER'S ADVICE was clear: "Make yourself indispensable by taking on as much responsibility as you can." I took his words as gospel, and they became the foundation upon which I built my life. More responsibility meant better titles, and better titles meant more power.

More power meant more money, and more money meant more control. More control meant safety. If I worked hard enough, if I climbed high enough, if I earned enough, and if I won enough, I would finally become untouchable.

Working at one of the world's largest retailers, I was on my way to everything I ever wanted. Every morning, I woke up prepared to battle in the corporate world that rewarded my ability to outperform and outmaneuver. I was convinced I had cracked the system, but I was also cracking under it.

No amount of success alleviated the hum of anxiety, and no raise or promotion erased the exhaustion of always being in what I came to think of as survival mode. I carried a weight that no achievement could lift, and although many people assumed I was thriving, I wasn't sure how much longer I could keep going.

Then, one night, at 30,000 feet in the air, something cracked open.

I had recently stepped into a new role at one of Canada's most beloved retailers and was on a flight to Calgary, absentmindedly scrolling through Netflix, when I clicked on *Nanette*, a stand-up special by Australian comedian Hannah Gadsby. At first, the show delivered sharp wit and humor, but as it unfolded, Gadsby stopped telling jokes and started speaking about suffering and the weight of existing in a world that demands that people make themselves smaller to survive.

A tightness gripped my chest, and my throat closed. Then, to my own shock, a single tear slipped down my cheek.

One tear.

It was the first time I had cried in 30 years.

Until then, I had spent my life building walls to prove I always had it together. In that airplane seat, though, something broke through, freeing the sadness and the loneliness trapped inside the hard shell I had built all around me.

I closed my laptop, pulled out my phone, and started typing a letter to the company's CEO. The words poured out faster than I could filter them. I wrote about *Nanette* and how vulnerability was not weakness but courage. What the CEO had always tried to communicate to shareholders, employees, and customers finally clicked: we were a company that stood for something greater than what we sold. We could lead with meaning instead of just market share.

When I landed, I hit send.

She replied soon after, and it was clear our values aligned. Slowly, I started leading differently. Work started to feel more meaningful, and I was having fun like never before. I also started struggling in ways I was not prepared for, because the more I uncovered, the more I realized how little I knew about how to live in thriving mode. I had to learn more.

Looking back, I see it clearly: I had been sprinting for years without realizing I was on a treadmill. I had spent decades mistaking exhaustion for achievement, thinking the finish line would make everything better, but it never did.

If you feel overwhelmed, burned out, stuck, or constantly on edge, you may be trapped in survival mode. Life in this state becomes an endless cycle of reactivity, where you stay guarded against every perceived threat and shrink yourself to stay safe. It can be draining, confining, and prevent you from fully thriving. When we're operating in survival mode, we're dominated by scarcity and self-protection, making us more likely to behave selfishly or destructively.

If you feel open, energized, flexible, and deeply connected, you're likely experiencing thriving mode. In this state, life expands, uncertainty becomes less threatening, and curiosity guides your way forward. Thriving mode is empowering because challenges transform into opportunities, and you get to access your boundless capacity for creativity and collaboration.

Survival Mode

Imagine walking in the woods when a low growl stops you in your tracks. Before your conscious mind can identify the sound, your stomach tightens into a knot, your heart pounds, your muscles tense, and your breath quickens. For our ancestors, this automatic response was essential for survival. They couldn't afford hesitation because a rustle in the bushes might be the wind or a saber-toothed tiger. In moments of real danger, this efficient evolutionary feature can save our lives, but it also sacrifices nuance for speed.[1]

In today's world, unless we're directly exposed to violence, most of the threats we face are psychological rather than physical: an impending deadline, a rude comment on social media, a tense conversation with a friend, or a perceived slight from a colleague. Nonetheless, left unchecked, the brain and body react as though survival is on the line.[2]

In a classic example of what experts refer to as *evolutionary mismatch*, the ancient circuitry that once saved us from danger remains wired to interpret anything uncertain or unfamiliar as potentially life-threatening.[3] Imagine receiving an abrupt email from your boss asking for a meeting ASAP. Without any context, your brain begins to fill in the blanks. "What did I do wrong? Is my job on the line?" Thoughts spiral into worst-case scenarios. This is survival mode in action, a state evolved to handle dangerous physical threats, now misapplied to an ambiguous situation.

In survival mode, our brains amplify perceived dangers and ignore signals of safety in the environment. This state of hyper-alertness can lead to what psychologists call *negativity bias*, the tendency to focus on negative or threatening information while overlooking neutral or positive cues.[4]

Picture yourself scrolling through social media and fixating on a single critical comment, even though it's surrounded by dozens of positive messages. Our brain zeroes in on the perceived threat, amplifying its importance and discarding any evidence of support and affirmation. While such a narrow perspective can be useful in life-or-death moments, a critical comment isn't a tiger in the bushes, even if our brain reacts like it is.[5]

When we face distressing situations, our brain's natural response is to protect us by shifting into survival mode. An internal alarm system gets triggered, and stress hormones flood our bodies to activate the well-known fight, flight, or freeze response.[6] This reaction can be life-saving by sharpening our senses and preparing us to face or escape danger. However, we can become stuck in survival mode when the alarm never fully turns off once safety is restored. Prolonged survival mode can cause shrinkage in the part of the brain responsible for sorting memories and recognizing that something is in the past, making it challenging to tell the difference between a present threat and an old memory.[7]

Survival mode may manifest in daily actions, such as the relentless impulse to do more or as an overwhelming urge to shut down. It may show up as irritability with others, procrastination on important tasks, or numbing with distractions or substances.

Over time, survival mode can become a pattern. We begin to loop through the same thoughts, emotions, sensations, and actions, stuck in an endless pursuit of safety even after the threat has passed. These conditioned responses, while once protective, can have long-term negative consequences and erode our well-being.[8]

The first step in breaking free from survival mode is recognizing when we're in it. From there, we can take deliberate steps to move toward thriving by leaning into the nine elements described in this book.

Survival mode can be strangely attractive. Pushing ourselves to the edge can offer a temporary sense of certainty, especially in a world that often feels unpredictable. The urgency and thrill of productivity can give the impression that we're doing something meaningful, but what feels like control may also be fear in disguise.[9]

Early in my career, I worked as a buyer for Sears, managing the paper purchases for the iconic Sears Catalog. When I first took over, I was determined to prove my worth. Fueled by ambition and a need for approval, I immediately jumped into action, convinced I could save the company millions. My colleagues had nicknamed me "pit bull" for my aggressive negotiation style, and I was determined to live up to the title. I started cold-calling paper mills across the country and launching into bold demands on the price per ton. I remember thinking, "This will impress everyone."

The people on the other end of the line sounded confused. One even said, "I think you might want to check with your team first." But I didn't stop.

Deep into my quest, my phone rang with the general counsel of Sears on the other side. "What do you think you're doing?" he asked. Nobody had mentioned that the price negotiations had already been finalized at a conference in Miami, held once a year. Driven by the need to prove myself, I acted impulsively and left everyone scrambling to clean up my overzealous attempts to make a difference. My brain, perceiving my new role as a potential threat to my reputation, had overridden rational thinking and plunged me into survival mode. After that phone call, I experienced my first panic attack, which led me to 12 weeks of group therapy and my first steps toward caring for my mental health.

Being in survival mode narrowed my options, amplified my emotional responses, and pushed me to act before I reflected. Recognizing patterns like these is the first step toward breaking free from their grip.

Thriving Mode

In thriving mode, we feel grounded and present. This state is marked by a deep sense of alignment between who we are and how we move through the world. When we're thriving, we respond to life with creativity rather than reactivity. We allow ourselves to experience a fuller emotional spectrum without feeling overwhelmed. We feel safe enough to be curious, connected enough to care for others, and resilient enough to grow from the challenges we face.[10]

Imagine being at a dinner party with close friends, laughing and savoring delicious food. The atmosphere is warm and inviting. Your body is at ease, your mind is open, and your heart is full. This moment of simply being is thriving mode in action.

Thriving feels like stepping off the proverbial hamster wheel and into a wide-open field. Where survival mode narrows our focus to manage threats, thriving mode widens our lens to engage with more possibilities as the brain and body operate in harmony. In this expansive state, we can navigate life with more intention.[11]

For most of us, thriving isn't automatic but something we learn.[12] It begins with awareness, expands through curiosity, and invites us to reframe our beliefs so we can cultivate the habits and environments that support our growth. It's a state that requires the courage to ask, "What if?" and the resolve to find out.

When we're thriving, we see others as partners and we're more likely to approach relationships with openness and extend empathy.[13]

Contrary to popular belief, thriving can coexist with adversity. Rather than signaling the absence of challenges, thriving means engaging with them constructively and, by doing so, emerging stronger and more fulfilled on the other side. It's less about avoiding difficulty and more about growing through it.

As a child, my mother would take us to the market on Saturdays to pick out fresh calamari. My sister and I then spent hours cleaning them before breading and frying them, filling our entire home with the smell of the sea. Since neither of my parents sought out the kitchen, cooking became a space where I could experiment and learn.

Years later, when I enrolled in culinary lessons, that sense of wonder expanded. Cooking felt like magic because simple ingredients could transform into something extraordinary. I still treasure the memory of the first time I made boeuf bourguignon, searing the beef and watching the red wine darken into a velvety sauce. I remember the kitchen coming alive with the scent of simmering herbs and garlic, making me feel like I was conjuring joy from scratch. Since then, cooking has become a form of presence for me, a practice where thriving turns into something I can share with others.

On most Fridays, I keep this ritual alive by leaving work early to step into my kitchen, where the world slows down. The rhythm of chopping and tasting pulls me into a state of flow. The aromas, the warmth of the stove, and the anticipation of welcoming friends and family feel deeply grounding. We light the Shabbat candles, sit around the table, and for a few hours, the difficulties of the week fade away. With time, I've come to recognize these moments as thriving, when my presence and connection to others reflect what's possible, and I'm no longer stuck in survival mode.

What I didn't realize at first is that moments like these also light up a part of the brain that supports exactly this kind of expansion: the *prefrontal cortex*. The prefrontal cortex allows us to reflect on our actions, plan for the future, and solve complex problems.[14] While this part of the brain gives us the ability to build cities, write poetry, send people to the moon, and map the human genome, it tends to be less active when we're in survival mode. In other words, thriving often emerges when we engage this part of the brain.[15]

Perhaps no other evolutionary trait has affected the trajectory of the human species as profoundly as the prefrontal cortex's capacity for problem-solving. The development of language, the harnessing of fire, the invention of the wheel, agriculture, and the printing press are all triumphs of this part of the brain.[16]

Throughout history, humans have moved beyond survival to achieve groundbreaking progress through imagination. Enduring the isolation of the plague years, Isaac Newton developed the laws of gravity and motion. During the COVID-19 pandemic, scientists across the globe collaborated at unprecedented speed to develop lifesaving vaccines.[17]

Penicillin emerged from Alexander Fleming's willingness to stay curious about a mold inhibiting bacterial growth, rather than dismissing it. Perhaps Fleming's choice to engage with uncertainty reflected a shift into thriving mode that turned a random occurrence into a medical revolution.[18] Today, penicillin is one of many medical breakthroughs contributing to the doubling of global life expectancy, which rose from approximately 32 years in the early 1900s to 71 years by 2021.[19]

Thriving mode represents the pinnacle of human potential and comes alive when we turn unexpected opportunities into deliberate innovation. By understanding the conditions that foster thriving, we can intentionally support our own growth and the growth of those around us.

A Map with Nine Elements

Looking to help others transition from mostly surviving to mostly thriving, I created a map that reflects how thriving isn't a one-time change but a process that unfolds across nine interconnected elements that define who we are and how we engage with the world. This map is my own, but it incorporates insights and wisdom from several other models, including a framework developed by Georgetown University's Institute for Transformational Leadership, the Medicine Wheel from Indigenous traditions, ideas from philosophy, and research-backed approaches from neuroscience and multiple schools of psychology.

The full map appears below. At the beginning of each chapter, the map highlights the topic of each section, just as Survival and Thriving are highlighted in the map at the beginning of this chapter.

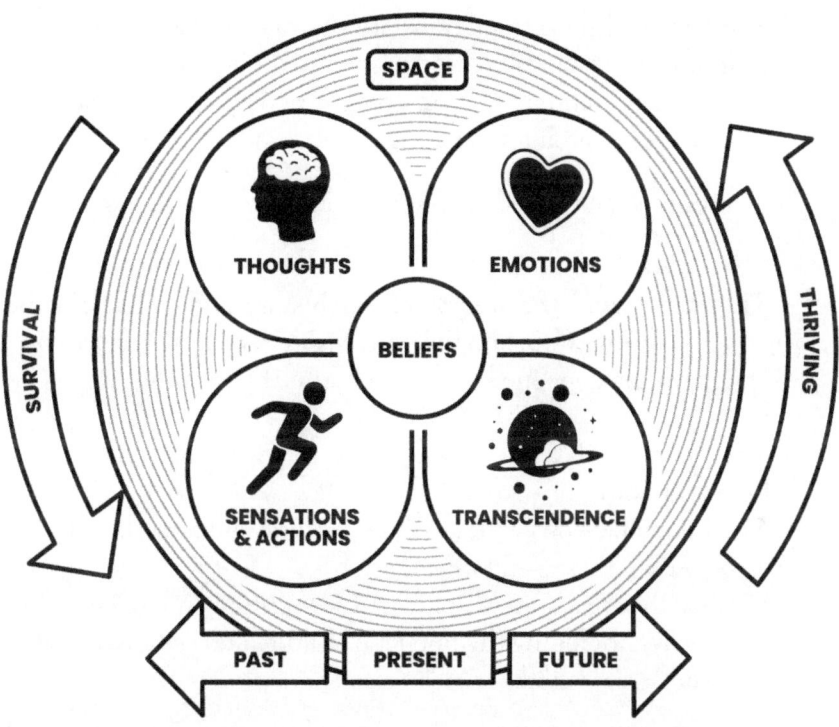

- *Beliefs* sit at the core of the map because they influence our perception of what's possible and define our sense of identity, consciously and subconsciously. They ripple outward and influence every other element of the map, including how we interpret our thoughts, emotions, sensations, actions, transcendence, and even our relationship with time and space.
- *Thoughts* both emerge from and feed our beliefs. While we can't choose every thought that arises, we can influence the ones we give power to by managing our internal dialogue.
- *Emotions* are messengers that reveal what matters most to us. While we may not be able to control when they surface or the form they take, we can choose how we respond to our feelings.
- *Sensations* and *Actions* are paired together because it's through sensing and acting that we engage with our bodies and make experience tangible. Sensations provide signals that guide our

awareness, while actions translate that awareness into tangible changes within ourselves and the world around us.

- *Transcendence* connects us to something beyond ourselves and supports our search for meaning.

The remaining elements reflect the way our lives unfold across time and space.

- The *Past* carries the weight of our history and influences the attachments we form and the patterns we repeat. While we can't change what happened, we can rewrite the meaning we assign to it.
- The *Present* calls us to show up fully, to engage with life as it is, here and now.
- The *Future* beckons with hope, possibility, and uncertainty, created by our choices and imagination.
- Finally, the *Space* in which our lives unfold influences us in many ways, including the impact of culture and systems on what we believe is possible.

The Journey from Survival to Thriving

The distinction between survival mode and thriving mode reflects a fundamental difference in how we experience and approach life. *Survival*, as a noun, denotes a prolonged state in which we endure and do what's necessary to keep existing. It's a baseline state of functioning, focused primarily on minimizing risks and conserving resources. While *surviving* is a crucial short-term response, it can evolve into an ongoing, heightened state that we remain unknowingly stuck in for years. Throughout this book, when I refer to *survival mode*, I'm describing the extended state in which we may appear functional on the outside but internally struggle to find balance and meaning.

Thriving, by contrast, conveys dynamic engagement. When we're in *thriving mode*, we lean into life with a willingness to grow. Notice the subtle grammatical difference between a noun (survival) and a verb (thriving): survival can become a stagnant state in which we feel stuck, while thriving describes an active state we consciously practice. Thriving mode, therefore, emphasizes agency and intentionality.

Surviving has its place. It's essential in situations when we need to react quickly to danger, but many of us spend more time in survival mode than necessary. Even after the immediate distress has passed, we can remain on high alert, bracing for a threat that's no longer there. Over time, this state becomes so familiar that we forget what it feels like to be safe.

Thriving mode doesn't require us to radically alter our life circumstances. There's a Zen proverb that captures this idea: "Before enlightenment, chop wood, carry water. After enlightenment, chop wood, carry water." The tasks of life remain the same, but our relationship to them changes fundamentally when we're thriving. Instead of simply enduring, we begin to approach everyday experiences with openness and see challenges as opportunities to discover meaning.

The journey from survival to thriving is far from linear. Instead, it's shaped as a continuous spiral, sometimes rising and sometimes falling.[20] Progress doesn't unfold in tidy, predictable steps, and neither does regression. One day, we may find ourselves ascending toward thriving, only to be pulled back into survival the next day by old patterns. Even though external forces, such as a sudden loss or an unexpected opportunity, can steer the spiral in either direction, we're not powerless. We can use downward spirals as invitations to confront what's unresolved and let upward spirals propel us into thriving. Every twist in the spiral is a chance to break through.

Although the survival-thriving spiral is personal, it's rarely disconnected from the larger systems we navigate. In many modern societies, especially in the Western world, thriving can seem like a purely personal responsibility, even though our families, communities, workplaces, institutions, and broader culture heavily influence it. Many systems are designed to prioritize stability over transformation, and some are invested in maintaining familiar patterns, even when they limit thriving.[21]

While we work toward creating more supportive social systems, we can also begin by turning inward. The journey starts with knowing ourselves. Before we can make intentional choices or create structures that support collective progress, it helps to understand the personal patterns that influence our thoughts, emotions, sensations, and actions. At any moment, we can pause, reflect, and reframe our perspective toward choices that serve us better.

Change is built into us. Our brains are flexible and capable of rewiring at any stage of life thanks to *neuroplasticity*, the brain's ability to reorganize itself by forming new neural connections.[22] Neuroplasticity explains why someone with a history of chronic stress or anxiety can, over time, develop greater emotional regulation. It's why trauma survivors, with the right support, can heal and regain a sense of control. Every time we choose how we respond, we're rewiring the circuitry of our brains.[23]

Agency: The Power of Choice

Agency is our capacity to be active participants in our lives by making intentional choices, guided by the belief that those choices matter and have an impact. Being intentional means recognizing that in any moment we have more than one way to respond to life's changing situations. It's the ability to see viable alternatives where none seemed to exist before. Agency is the antidote to helplessness because it allows us to see challenges as opportunities rather than insurmountable obstacles.[24]

The transformation from survival to thriving is a way to reclaim our agency. In survival mode, we often feel trapped, as if we're at the mercy of external forces. Our vision of the world constricts, we perceive our options as limited, decisions seem predetermined, and our sense of control diminishes. Alternatively, thriving mode allows us to recognize that even in the face of uncertainty, we retain the capacity to influence our future.

This power of personal agency becomes particularly clear when we examine how people respond to adversity. Two individuals might face a job loss or a difficult medical diagnosis in profoundly different ways. While one might remain stuck in survival mode, consumed by a sense of despair, the other might choose to harness resources to navigate the challenge, learning and growing in the process.

Many of the behaviors we develop in survival mode are *adaptive* in the short term but can become limiting or *maladaptive* over time.[25] For instance, withdrawing from certain relationships can protect us from emotional pain, but prolonged social isolation can lead to loneliness and depression. Adaptive patterns can help us respond to challenges and improve our chances of thriving, and maladaptive patterns can hold us back and create obstacles to our well-being. Our ability to rec-ognize and modify these patterns is an expression of agency, as it allows us to discern whether a behavior is causing harm (maladaptive) or whether it is time to choose a different response that supports our growth (adaptive).[26]

Intentional learning is a powerful tool for cultivating agency.[27] It requires seeking out experiences that challenge us and then extracting meaningful lessons from them. Going back to school in my 40s became a deliberate part of my intentional learning process. Re-entering an academic environment after years in the workforce brought discomfort as I adjusted my routines and reconnected with my identity as a stu-dent. It was challenging to sit in the learner's chair again after being the person others turned to for answers for so long. At the same time, it was a profound gift to remember what it feels like to be stretched by new ideas. Intentional learning can be challenging but it expands our perspective, pushes us to question our assumptions, and to develop new skills and habits.

It's worth noting that, for some, survival mode is a lived reality. War, systemic oppression, financial instability, and chronic trauma can make thriving feel out of reach. Still, humans can take extraordinary steps toward thriving.

In the early 2010s, in the besieged Syrian city of Daraya, a group of young men risked their lives to build a secret underground library by salvaging books from bombed-out buildings. Over time, the library grew to hold thousands of volumes and became a refuge where people gathered to learn.[28] Stories like this one show that even during a crisis, agency can become a means to express the human spirit's relentless pursuit of growth.

Thriving calls for a clear-eyed acknowledgment of our circum-stances and a willingness to engage with them. It involves using our agency to seek out support during difficult times and taking steps toward positive change.

The first step toward thriving is learning to recognize when we're in survival mode so we can access the resources and develop the skills to move toward a more meaningful life. Recognizing when survival mode has taken hold gives us the power to pause and choose a more intentional path. It's a simple idea in theory, yet profoundly complex and transformative in practice.

While survival mode is the brain's natural response to perceived danger, thriving mode is a state we can learn to access more consistently over time. The goal isn't to eliminate survival mode, as it exists to protect us, but to develop strategies so that thriving becomes our baseline rather than a fleeting experience we stumble into by chance.

We can't always change life's circumstances, but we can choose how we respond to them. This concept is central to many schools of philosophy, including Stoicism, which emphasizes the distinction between what is within our control, such as our attention and effort, and what is not, like external events.[29] By focusing on what we can influence, we reclaim our agency and find freedom even in difficult situations. Cultivating agency doesn't require life-altering decisions. It can be practiced in everyday life through the small choices we make.

Recognizing Survival and Thriving Modes

Recognizing the common signs of survival mode gives us a chance to use our agency to make intentional changes to move toward thriving[30]:

- Mind racing with worst-case scenarios, fixating on potential threats, or feeling trapped in all-or-nothing thinking.
- Feeling tense, defensive, irritable, disconnected, or completely shut down.
- Feeling an overwhelming need to act immediately or make quick decisions without taking time to pause and reflect.
- Tight chest, shallow breathing, clenched jaw, headaches, or persistent exhaustion despite rest.
- Procrastinating on tasks, avoiding difficult conversations, or feeling powerless to take action.

Alternatively, recognizing the common signs of thriving gives us a chance to strengthen our ability to return to thriving mode even when challenges arise[31]:

- Mind open and clear, able to explore possibilities, generate ideas, or view challenges with curiosity and optimism.
- Feeling calm, balanced, energized, or deeply connected with self and others.

- Feeling comfortable slowing down, reflecting thoughtfully, or responding intentionally rather than impulsively.
- Body relaxed and grounded, breathing deeply, experiencing restful sleep, and feeling physically refreshed and alert.
- Actively engaging with tasks, openly addressing challenging conversations, or feeling confident in your ability to navigate uncertainty.

AIR: Awareness, Inquiry, and Reframing

Each chapter ends with questions designed to help you recognize survival mode and enter thriving mode. These are organized into a framework I developed called AIR, which stands for *Awareness, Inquiry*, and *Reframing*. AIR offers a simple and powerful way to shift from reaction to intention and from fear to possibility.

In survival mode, it can feel like we're underwater, barely able to catch a breath, and thriving often begins by simply remembering to come up for AIR. Awareness, Inquiry, and Reframing offer a way to pause, surface, create space, and explore new paths forward.

Awareness is the first step because, without it, we remain at the mercy of reactive patterns.

Awareness: What mode am I in right now?

- *Am I physically safe right now?*
- *Am I in survival mode right now? Is this state really necessary, given what's going on?*
- *Am I in thriving mode right now? What habits, choices, or relationships are supporting me?*

The second step is Inquiry, which helps us recognize the outdated patterns that keep us in survival mode, often influenced by past experiences when certain beliefs first formed. Inquiry creates space to explore what drives our conditioned responses and begins to loosen their grip.

Inquiry: What beliefs, perceptions, or assumptions are driving my reactions?

- *What old pattern may be playing out?*
- *What am I believing right now? How well is it serving me?*
- *What else might be true?*

The final step in AIR is Reframing, which helps replace old patterns with new, intentional ones that move us toward thriving. Reframing our thoughts can create a radically different experience expands our understanding of what's possible.

Reframing: What can I do differently to move toward thriving?

- *What's the most empowering way to view this situation?*
- *What choice would reflect who I'm becoming, not just who I've been?*
- *What is one small experiment that I could try to move toward thriving mode?*

The AIR questions at the end of each section invite you to begin the work of transformation. In the next chapter, we'll explore the first of the nine elements: beliefs, the sometimes visible and sometimes invisible scripts that influence how we see ourselves and move through the world. This is your opportunity to create a turning point, to choose a life beyond mere survival and step into one of thriving.

PART

II

Transformation

2

Beliefs
The Architecture of Reality

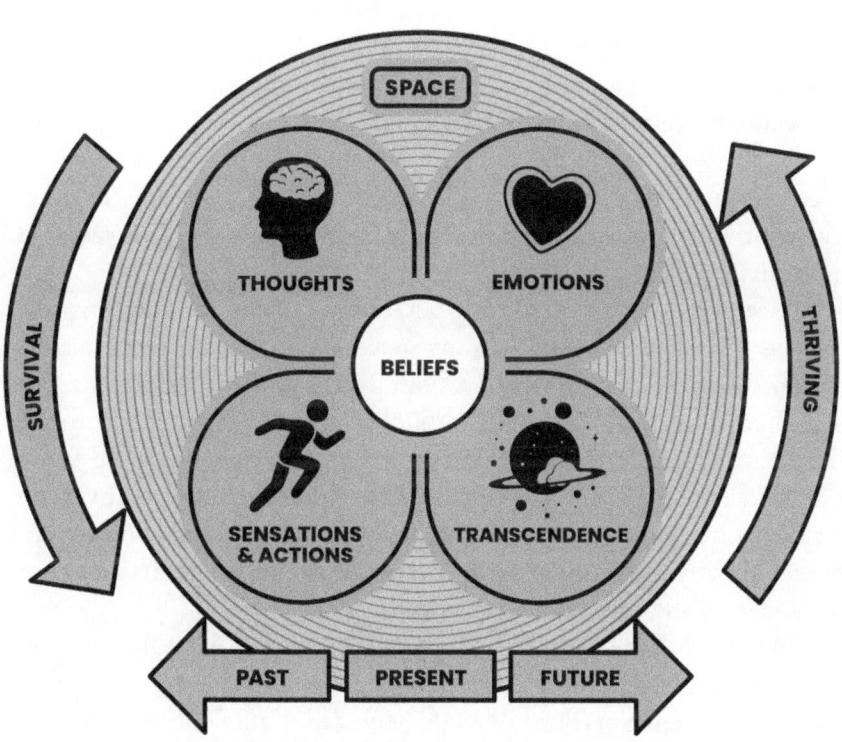

Beliefs guide our lives. In this chapter, we'll explore how the ones we hold, often without question, can either support our growth or stand in the way. Sometimes, it's necessary to challenge and change our beliefs to make room for something new.

Where Does My Sense of Worth Come From? Meet Emily

From the outside, Emily's life was a shining example of success. She was a senior executive at a prestigious consumer packaged goods company, admired for her strategic brilliance and tireless work. She came to coaching because her organization believed she was ready for the C-suite and wanted to further develop her leadership skills.

Emily never missed a detail, from perfectly formatting her Power-Point slides to remembering every team member's birthday. Her office was impeccably organized, with color-coded binders and a single orchid she watered every Monday morning.

In our sessions, a different story emerged where no achievement ever felt sufficient. In spite of every accolade, she lived with the gnawing fear that the world would find her not good enough. She was stuck in survival mode.

As she and I discovered together, the core belief driving this feeling was: "My value depends on my success." This belief was forged in childhood, when love felt conditional on a perfect performance. In one of our sessions, she recalled proudly showing her parents the 93% she'd earned on a difficult math test. Her mother's smile faded as she glanced at the paper. "What happened to the other seven points?" she asked. "You're capable of more, Emily. Don't settle." Emily nodded and retreated with the promise to try harder next time. Achievement was the currency she used to buy acceptance.

Emily's breaking point came during a routine Monday morning meeting. Her team presented their numbers, each one striving to match the perfection they knew she expected. Emily felt a tightness in her chest and the beginning of a headache. As the meeting ended, her assistant handed her another report to review, and the words blurred on the page. Back in her office, Emily shut the door, sank into her chair, and pressed her hands against her face. For the first time, she let the thought form fully, "I can't keep this up." What she didn't dare admit, even to herself, was the terrifying belief that without relentless striving and achieving she'd lose her identity.

During our next session, I asked, "Emily, what would happen if you stopped believing that your worth depended on your success?"

Emily recoiled and her shoulders tensed, "I . . . I don't know," she said finally, hesitating. I felt that the question had touched something raw.

For perhaps the first time in our work together, I watched her sit with discomfort. Her shield of continuous perfection cracked just enough for her to acknowledge that measuring her value by success had been the belief guiding many of her decisions for years.

Though Emily didn't answer my question at the time, confronting it was the first step toward a life guided by something other than the persistent need to prove her worth. Choosing to question that belief, even momentarily, was an act of courage and the beginning of a journey of transformation.

Beliefs Define Reality

All of us live by beliefs. Some were handed down to us, and others we created ourselves, often without questioning where they came from or whether they still serve us.[1]

Beliefs color what we see, how we feel, and the choices we make. Some empower us, and others hold us back. Research by Jer Clifton at the University of Pennsylvania suggests that when we believe the world is dangerous, our attention locks onto threats and reinforces our fear. When we see the world as abundant, our sense of possibility expands.[2] We can use agency to reinforce beliefs that support our growth and challenge the ones that don't.

The influence of our beliefs extends far beyond perception. In one study, participants drank identical milkshakes but were given different information: one group believed they were drinking an indulgent, high-calorie shake, while the other believed it was a low-calorie option. Even though the milkshakes were the same, those who thought they were indulging showed a sharper drop in ghrelin, the hormone that signals hunger. In other words, their bodies responded not just to the actual ingredients in the shake but also to what they believed they were consuming.[3]

Other studies have shown that participants who receive a placebo instead of a painkiller experienced real pain relief as their brains release natural opioids. Belief, not fact, influenced their body's response.[4]

Think of the once widely held belief that low-fat diets guaranteed health. For decades, people consumed processed fat-free foods, and to compensate for the loss of fat, manufacturers increased sugar content. Eventually, research overturned the assumption and showed that healthy fats, like those found in avocados and nuts, promote physical health, while excessive sugar intake has been linked to increased risks of obesity and metabolic diseases.[5] Our beliefs can evolve when we're confronted with new information.[6]

Even in relationships, our beliefs serve as the lens through which we view the world. Researchers at the University of Maryland showed that on days when people saw the world as a better place, they felt more satisfied in their relationships and viewed their partners more positively. The way we see the world guides the way we move within it.[7]

Think about some of the sweeping belief changes that have occurred in society over our lifetimes. They usually begin when people like you and me dare to question what we've always taken for granted.

For years, many believed intelligence was fixed, meaning some people were naturally gifted, while others were not. This idea defined school programs and career paths until Carol Dweck, a psychologist studying motivation and achievement at Stanford University, noticed that students who believed their abilities could improve with effort consistently outperformed those who thought intelligence was innate.[8]

Initially, her findings were met with skepticism. Education systems had long operated under the assumption that intelligence was inherited and that you either had it or you didn't. But study after study confirmed her findings, and the belief in fixed intelligence began to unravel. Her research led to what is now known as *growth mindset*, the belief that talent and intelligence are not just set at birth but are also influenced by persistence and learning.[9] Schools changed their focus from talent to effort, companies built cultures that rewarded perseverance over raw ability, and individuals who once feared failure began to see it as part of the learning process.[10]

The journey to change our beliefs is rarely quick or easy. It asks us to let go of narratives that may have defined our identity for years. At Harvard, sociologist Lisa Lahey and psychologist Robert Kegan call this self-protective resistance our *immunity to change*, a system of beliefs that unconsciously shields us from discomfort, even as it sabotages our growth.[11] And yet, the rewards of rewriting beliefs can be profound: the freedom to live more authentically, to reclaim our agency, to align our values and our actions, and to create ripples of change that inspire others.

Beliefs, no matter how deeply entrenched, can evolve when we question them and find the courage to persist through the discomfort of transformation. Beliefs can trigger survival, but they can also activate thriving.[12]

The Science of Belief

Beliefs are intricate patterns of thought, emotion, and sensation that help our brains make sense of the world.[13] They act as mental shortcuts by filtering our experiences and guiding our decisions, often without our conscious awareness.[14] But what if some of these shortcuts are deceiving us? What if the beliefs you hold most tightly are holding you back?

Not all beliefs carry the same weight. Some, like dogmas tied to religion or ideology, feel immovable because they're rooted in belonging. Other everyday beliefs are absorbed in childhood through comments from others and experiences we never thought to question. These beliefs feel personal but are not always deliberate. As we grow, it's wise to ask whether they still serve us.[15]

The prefrontal cortex, often referred to as the brain's executive center, is responsible for reasoning, problem-solving, and decision-making. This region plays a key role in how we examine and update our beliefs. When we pause to reflect and entertain new perspectives, the prefrontal cortex helps us step back from automatic reactions to choose a more agentic path.[16]

Beliefs are not purely products of rational thought. The *amygdala*, an almond-shaped structure deep within the brain, imbues them with emotional weight, particularly when they're tied to experiences involving fear or threat.[17] When emotionally charged beliefs are challenged, the brain's threat detection system triggers a survival mode response. This is why conversations about politics or religion can quickly escalate into heated arguments, even among close friends or family. These emotional imprints make certain beliefs feel intensely personal, even sacred, and difficult to dislodge because questioning them can feel like questioning who we are.[18]

Belief perseverance is the human tendency to cling to initial beliefs, even in the face of overwhelming evidence to the contrary. Think of that friend who swears by a particular diet, convinced it's the secret to health and longevity. We might show them scientific research debunking some of the diet's claims, but they double down, insisting the studies are flawed. They might even claim that big diet lobby paid for the studies, so they're not credible.[19]

Brain imaging studies reveal that challenges to core beliefs activate threat-detection regions like the amygdala. These studies confirm why we respond defensively rather than rationally when confronted with opposing evidence. Our brains are wired to protect our beliefs because they help us navigate a complex world by giving us a sense of certainty and control.[20]

Emily knew she was smart and logical, a problem-solver and a fixer. But when it came to her worth, logic had no sway. No matter how much she achieved, the feeling of unworthiness would not budge. Questioning the belief that her value depended on success had once felt like questioning gravity. Now, the cost of holding onto it was beginning to outweigh the benefits it used to offer.

Science as a Model of Questioning Beliefs

Scientific progress throughout history has been made through the questioning of existing beliefs. Unlike rigid ideologies that demand conformity, like cults, science moves forward by testing assumptions and refining ideas. The greatest scientific breakthroughs in history often come from those willing to challenge prevailing wisdom. In fact, scientists who agree with their peers rarely leave a mark on their field. Careers in science are built on challenging the status quo and providing evidence that redefines established paradigms. This willingness to dissent drives innovation and makes science a dynamic force for dis-covery. Constructive dissent ensures that progress is a collaborative effort driven by the pursuit of knowledge rather than the preservation of authority.

Science is based on the fundamental belief that knowledge is tem-porary. No theory is sacred, and what we accept as true today can be revised tomorrow as new evidence emerges. In good science, there are no absolute truths, only the best understanding available at any given moment.

Before the germ theory of disease, the prevailing belief was that diseases were caused by "miasmas" or bad air. This notion influenced medical practices and public health policies for centuries. When Ignaz Semmelweis and later Louis Pasteur proposed that microorganisms were the true culprits, they faced fierce resistance. Semmelweis was ridiculed and ostracized for suggesting that doctors should wash their hands to prevent the spread of infection.[21]

The scientific community eventually embraced germ theory as overwhelming evidence accumulated, and this paradigm shift revolu-tionized medicine, saving countless lives and improving public health worldwide.[22]

Science leads us to some good news: beliefs are not set in stone. Thanks to neuroplasticity, the brain has a remarkable ability to reor-ganize itself by forming new neural connections. Every time we chal-lenge an old belief, question an assumption, or adopt a new perspective, we rewire our brains. However, change doesn't happen overnight; it requires conscious effort, repetition, and support from others.[23]

Between Belonging and Becoming

Belief change is rarely a solitary process and is deeply influenced by the people around us. In other words, our social bonds can either reinforce old patterns or create space for transformation. To replace outdated beliefs with ones that serve us better, we often need to manage our need to belong.[24]

Beliefs tend to function as the social glue that holds groups together. Shared narratives about the world, such as religious tradi-tions and social norms, have helped humans build cohesion and cooperation. These shared beliefs created a sense of collective identity, which in turn enhances survival.[25]

The human need to connect with others can make it difficult to question limiting beliefs. We've all had times when we held back to fit in, when we downplayed dreams, kept quiet our opinions, or chose not to share ideas for fear of rejection. When belonging is conditional on aligning our beliefs with those of the group, our psychological safety can feel threatened, setting off a survival response.

Extreme examples reveal how powerful the need to belong can be. The tragic story of the People's Temple, led by Jim Jones, began with a vision of social justice and equality. While the ideals offered a sense of belonging, over time, members were isolated from their families, subjected to manipulation, and coerced into accepting Jones's claims of divine authority. In 1978, this chain of events culminated in the Jonestown massacre, where more than 900 people died in a mass murder-suicide.[26]

Social groups can also create fertile ground for transformation, opening spaces where our authenticity is celebrated and where we're safe to explore our identities. In Alcoholics Anonymous, individuals struggling with alcohol use disorder find a community anchored in mutual support, where shared experiences become the foundation for healing. These groups show that when belonging is guided by compassion, it can be a powerful catalyst for positive transformation.[27] The delicate dynamic between belief and belonging can either keep us in survival mode or help us step into thriving mode.

Throughout human history, isolation often meant death because belonging to a group offered protection from predators and access to shared resources, especially in the face of threats.[28] As Neil Theise describes in *Notes on Complexity*, the survival of an ant colony depends on collective effort, where each ant plays its part. Many of us have all marveled at the remarkable coordination in a line of ants, each one following the trail left by those before it. Except that the colony's survival doesn't depend only on those who follow the established path.[29]

Divergent ants, those that stray from the familiar routes, are essential for the colony to survive and thrive. These explorers leave the safety of the established trails and venture into the unknown in search of new sources of food. When they return, they bring back the discoveries that sustain the entire colony. Without them, the colony risks starvation once resources along known routes are depleted.

Human societies move forward when there's a balance between conformity and divergence. Like those pioneering ants, people who stray from the well-trodden paths may risk alienation, but they may also return with discoveries that nourish the collective.

For more than a decade, I've been part of a WhatsApp group chat with many of my childhood friends. We discuss a wide range of topics, from sports to world events to the meaning of life. Recurring debates about gender always bring out strong reactions. One friend put his viewpoint this way: "Men are men, women are women." His entrenched position that women and men play different roles in our societies is a belief defined by centuries of social norms.

For a long time, I shared that belief. It was what I grew up around, what I heard at school, at home, in the jokes we told, and the expectations we never questioned. But as I was exposed to more perspectives and started discovering the science behind gender, I began to see things differently.

What if the differences between men and women aren't as rigidly separated as we were taught? Today, chromosomes are often cited as the definitive markers of sex, but biological reality is more nuanced. Some individuals possess atypical combinations of sex chromosomes, such as XXY, XYY, or XO, that don't fit neatly into the binary categories of XX or XY.[30] Additionally, there's considerable biological diversity among individuals of the same sex, including variations in anatomy, hormone levels, gonadal development, and reproductive function.[31] Learning about these complexities changed my belief: it's more useful to view each brain and body as unique, influenced as much by lived experience as by genetics and hormones.[32]

Questions about sex, gender, and other foundational elements of identity are rarely just about science because they cut to the heart of belonging. For many, their lived reality collides with the expectations of their family, friends, or community. This tension can become a daily struggle that impacts their choices and the stories they tell themselves about who they're allowed to be.

For Emily, belonging had to be earned. She believed that if she worked hard enough and met every expectation, she would secure her place in the world. This manifested in the way she constantly anticipated rejection, rewriting texts repeatedly before hitting send, and shifting her tone to fit whoever she was speaking to. She had mastered the art of being who she thought others wanted her to be.

The Cost of Inauthenticity

The need to belong can raise a profound dilemma between authenticity and belonging. When these two forces align, we experience the liberating sense of being fully seen and accepted for who we are. In that space, we can thrive. Unfortunately, we often learn early in life that authenticity and belonging don't always go hand in hand because revealing our true selves can jeopardize the attachments we depend on for love and safety.

Picture a kid who loves to draw wild, colorful creatures like unicorns with dragon wings or tigers with rainbow fur. One day, this kid eagerly shares a creation with a caregiver only to be met with a dismissive comment: "That's silly. Why not draw something real?" The child, yearning for approval, might start drawing everyday things instead, even if doing so stifles their creativity.

To avoid the pain of rejection or isolation, we begin to edit ourselves and suppress our authenticity to fit the expectations of others. In the moment, this self-erasure feels like self-protection, and in small amounts, it may be useful, as it helps us stay connected. But over time, that self-protection can lead to long-term suffering if we find ourselves in toxic relationships, unfulfilling careers, and identities that feel hollow. Contorting ourselves to belong can strain our well-being.

For years, Emily believed that her value was tied to achieving, first in the home she grew up in and then in her workplace. Although this belief drained her physically and emotionally, she refrained from challenging it, fearing alienation in a family and culture that worshiped productivity. The cost of suppressing her true needs left a constant undercurrent of dissatisfaction that led her close to burnout.

Inauthenticity is far from painless. The more we hide our true selves to belong, the more we fracture our inner world. When we finally gather the courage to embrace authenticity, as Emily eventually did, we face a tremendous risk: losing the very connections we contorted ourselves to preserve. In such moments of vulnerability, the familiar pull of staying small wrestles with the call to grow. Can we bear the discomfort of being seen as we truly are? Without the courage to face this unease, we risk remaining stuck in the cycle of suppression that creates more suffering for ourselves in the name of survival.

Belief perseverance and the need for belonging often make it difficult to challenge familiar beliefs, even when they feel restrictive or outdated.[33] In our sessions, the question "What would happen if you stopped believing that your worth depended on your success?" became an anchor for Emily.

With each conversation, Emily challenged her beliefs. At first, making changes felt unnatural, and she worried about disappointing colleagues or being seen as less dedicated. She started small, leaving the office on time a few days a week and resisting the urge to check her inbox every few minutes. She practiced pausing before saying yes and began delegating in meetings. Slowly, agentic choices began to replace self-doubt with confidence that she was enough, even when she wasn't working herself to the point of exhaustion.

Emily's journey was anything but easy. By setting boundaries at work, she risked alienation from colleagues who continued to buy into the culture of nonstop productivity. Ultimately, her decision to prioritize her well-being led to a more authentic sense of belonging, opening more space to connect with those who valued her for who she was, not just for what she produced.

In thriving workplaces, families, spiritual groups, or communities, questioning is an essential part of the collective journey. However, not all environments welcome dissent, and not everyone has the freedom to walk away. Sometimes we stay because we need a paycheck, or because we love the people, or because leaving would mean losing something we're not ready to let go of. Even when leaving isn't an option, we can still use our agency to seek small moments that help us stay aligned with who we are.

Changing a Belief Using AIR

Emily's transformation took time. It was an intentional process of unlearning and rebuilding that required agency and the steady application of the AIR method.

Awareness: Emily became aware of her inauthenticity by pondering, "What would happen if I stopped believing that my worth depends on my success?" She began to notice how this belief informed every corner of her life, from her extended work hours to the guarded way she interacted with others.

She started by cautiously trying out other ways of behaving. One morning, instead of diving straight into emails, she took 10 minutes to journal her thoughts, something she hadn't done since college. When her sister invited her to have a coffee together, Emily put her phone inside her purse to be fully present. These moments felt like acts of rebellion against her old beliefs. Slowly, she began to feel more peaceful.

At work, she tested new approaches that seemed impossible before. When her team asked for her input on a project, she resisted the urge to take over and instead asked, "What do you think?" Their ideas surprised her, not because they were good (they were), but because nothing fell apart when she stepped back. This gave her permission to let go, one decision at a time.

Inquiry: Emily reflected on questions like, "How is this belief serving me? How is it hurting me? Is it true, or have I simply accepted it as truth? Am I relying on outdated narratives?" Pondering this last inquiry allowed Emily to trace her belief to her childhood, where praise was contingent on achievement. As an adult, she began to question: "Why should my worth be measured by the approval of others? What would it look like to define my value on my own terms?"

She also tested this belief by listing times when imperfect work led to positive outcomes. Slowly, she built a repertoire of evidence that her worth was not tied to perfection.

Reframing: Emily began to create more adaptive beliefs to replace the old ones, like "My worth is inherent and unchanging." She repeated it like a mantra and posted it as a daily reminder on her bathroom mirror.

Based on her reframed belief, she chose to close her laptop and stop checking her phone at 7 p.m. At first, it was painful, like walking away from a fire instead of extinguishing it, but gradually she began to adapt, using those reclaimed hours for joyful activities, like reading novels or joining her sister for impromptu baking sessions. She noticed her laughter returning to the office and in conversations with friends. Warm moments, once drowned out by the noise of survival, became her new markers of success.

Working on new beliefs can feel fragile, like a sapling struggling to take root against the pull of old habits. But through consistent practice and evidence that supports a new story, new beliefs can grow stronger until they become our new default.

When Emily began to believe that her worth was not tied to her achievements, she no longer shielded herself with defensiveness and perfectionism. Instead, she started to listen without pre-emptively crafting a response and to acknowledge mistakes without spiraling into shame.

Once, after admitting a mistake to a colleague, she expected judgment but was met with understanding. "That's all right, Emily," said her colleague. "We've all been there, and we'll all be there again." It was a small moment that felt monumental.

The rigid walls of self-criticism began to crumble, making room for more genuine relationships. She became more present and no longer felt trapped in the endless loop of "I'm not doing enough." Her interactions with her team transformed from transactional check-ins to meaningful conversations. She became more approachable and empathetic toward her colleagues, and this newfound openness created a more collaborative space for everyone, eventually leading to her promotion to the C-suite. Her authenticity was magnetic and drew people in, making her a more effective leader.

Ripples in the Pond

Changing a belief might seem like a small shift, but its impact can be profound and far-reaching. When Emily redefined her sense of worth, her transformation rippled outward, affecting her team, family, friends, and community. Her transformation created a new reality that encouraged others to examine their own limiting beliefs.

One afternoon, a colleague told her, "I've noticed you seem different lately. Lighter or maybe just . . . more at ease?" Inspired by Emily's calm, he had taken his first guilt-free mental health day. For years, Emily had believed her stress was hers alone to bear. Now, she realized that by changing her own narrative, she had given others permission to do the same.

This is the power of belief change: it starts within, and it doesn't stay there. By changing our beliefs, we transform how we interact with the world, and in doing so, we have a profound impact on it. Questioning long-held beliefs is no small feat.

This ripple effect happens in society on a broader scale when collective beliefs evolve to pave the way for new laws and cultural norms. Decades ago, many people believed seat belts were unnecessary. It took years of research, public education campaigns, crash data, and stories from survivors to challenge that belief. Today, buckling up is second nature to most drivers and passengers. It's a small behavior anchored in a big belief: that safety matters and prevention is powerful.[34]

In our coaching sessions, Emily practiced small steps to ease her stress, like grounding herself in the present moment and using gentler self-talk. Although it felt uncomfortable at first, these moments built resilience and softened the grip of survival.

The path to thriving requires the courage to challenge our beliefs, supported by environments where it feels safe to explore and make mistakes. By fostering this kind of space within ourselves and our communities, belief changes become possible and potentially liberating. We can practice this in everyday conversations by pausing to listen without rushing to provide answers, and by asking questions to understand rather than to challenge.

Paradoxically, we gain greater resilience and flexibility by recognizing the fleeting nature of our beliefs. When we cling too rigidly to what we believe in, we become so brittle that we risk shattering when reality challenges it. Holding our beliefs lightly allows us to view them as lenses rather than truths carved in stone.

Emily cultivated this safety by intentionally surrounding herself with supportive people and reframing her missteps. "Instead of seeing them as proof I'd failed," she shared, "I started calling them experiments." Over time, these deliberate choices created a buffer against her old fears and gave her the strength to question entrenched patterns.

Using AIR to Explore Beliefs

To explore your beliefs, consider starting here: "Do I believe I'm enough as I am?" In my work with clients, this belief has surfaced more often than any other. It may take different forms and be tied to career achievement, financial stability, relationships, or physical appearance. You can use the AIR approach to explore any beliefs that may be keeping you in survival mode.

Awareness: Recognizing a Belief in Action

- *Are my daily choices determined by what I believe?*
- *Are any of my beliefs limiting or exhausting me?*
- *Do I ever feel discomfort when I go along with the group?*

Inquiry: Questioning a Belief's Validity

- *If I had to put a personal belief into a single sentence, what would it be?*
- *Where did this belief come from? Whose voice echoes in my mind when I think about it?*
- *How might this belief be limiting me?*

Reframing: Exploring New Beliefs

- *What would a new belief sound like?*
- *If I lived as if this new belief were true, how might my life change?*
- *What is one small experiment I could try to put this belief into action?*

3

Thoughts
The Stories We Tell Ourselves

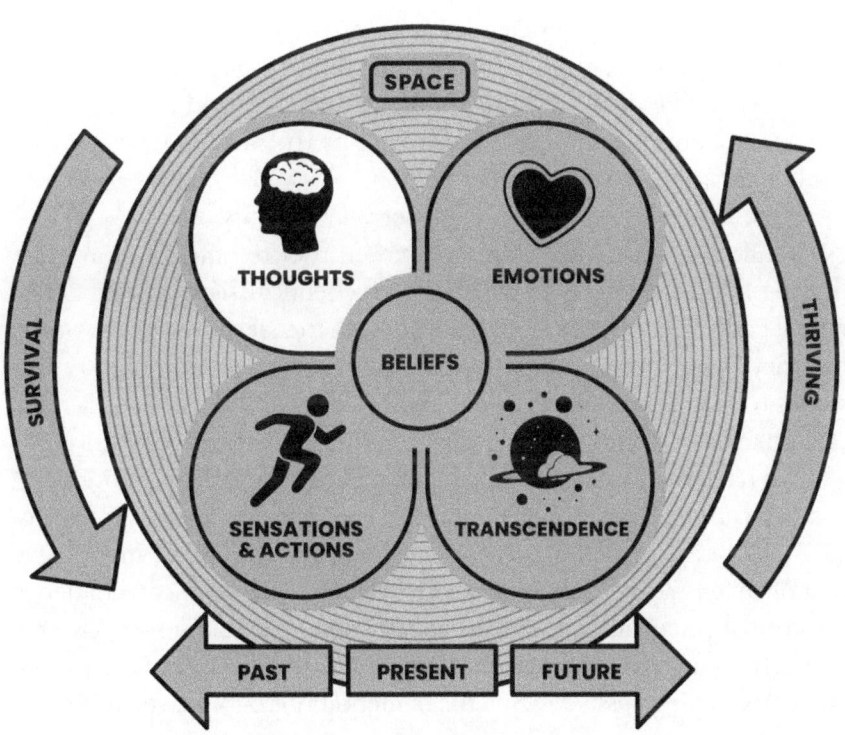

THE MIND IS always speaking. Even in silence, our inner voice narrates our days and searches for meaning in every encounter. These thoughts can feel like irrefutable truths, but what if they're not?

In this chapter, we'll dive into the world of thoughts, the most accessible expressions of our beliefs. Where do they come from? When they keep looping in unhelpful patterns, how can we challenge and adjust them to better serve us?

By understanding our thoughts, we reclaim our agency and take the first step in rewriting the stories we tell ourselves. That skill can open a door from survival to thriving.

The Dual Power of Thoughts

Depending on how we engage with them, thoughts can lead us into downward spirals of despair or offer hopeful insights when we face complexity. The dual power of thoughts to distort and to clarify is at the heart of our internal experience. It's why the same mind can create doubt or spark inspiration.[1]

Here's a liberating idea: *You are not your thoughts.*

While thoughts wield immense power, they're nothing more than fleeting brain states and transient electrochemical signals firing across neural pathways. They're the mind's attempt to make sense of the world, but they're not necessarily reflections of objective reality. They're like stories told around a campfire, colored by context and past experiences. And, like most stories, they're subject to interpretation and revision.[2]

We have the capacity to step back from the thoughts our minds create. We can see them not as immutable truths but as flexible creations. This realization is profoundly freeing. It means the inner monologue that once felt like an unalterable script can be edited. We can challenge the critical voices and reframe disempowering ideas that no longer serve us. Each time we do, we reclaim a little more agency over our lives. We move from being passive recipients of mental noise to active authors.[3]

Which Thoughts Deserve My Attention? Meet Simon

Simon reached out on the recommendation of a board member at his company. When I first started coaching him, it became clear that his inner critic had taken the driver's seat in his everyday life.

One morning, a thought came to him uninvited as he caught his reflection in the mirror: "You're falling behind." He couldn't quite trace its origin. Perhaps it was the emails piling up in his inbox or his calendar blocked with back-to-back meetings. Whatever the trigger, the thought followed him and lingered as an unwelcome guest throughout his day.

By the time the afternoon rolled around, the thought had become darker: "You're falling behind. You'll never catch up." Many of us experience this pattern: a single intrusive thought gains momentum and spirals into a larger conviction of inadequacy.

Simon called himself a "pursuer of excellence," a trait that served him well in his early career as an architect when he earned praise through precision and avoiding mistakes. He once spent an entire weekend adjusting the angle of sunlight in a render for a client presentation, convinced the shadow placement could evoke just the right feeling of calm sophistication. While it worked, it also left him too exhausted to enjoy the celebration dinner with his team.

Simon's work was frequently recognized in industry journals, and his name had become synonymous with elegance and originality. As his reputation grew, so did the pressure. Simon rarely spoke about it, but what he truly wanted was to create something enduring, a legacy that would remain long after he was gone.

The relentless pace of his practice left little room to rest and left him in a constant state of exhaustion. As Simon shared in one of our sessions, "Architecture used to light me up, and now it just feels like a nonstop juggling act." The joy he once felt in sketching out a vision or seeing a project come to life was now overshadowed by the dread of not meeting expectations.

There was a time when Simon would stop mid-meeting to sketch an idea. Now, his sketchbook sat mostly untouched. Even small setbacks, like a delayed permit or a missed email, seemed to carry the potential for disaster. When the day's noise subsided, his mind filled the silence with incessant catastrophic thoughts.

Simon once shared a moment that haunted him: his son had shown him a new drawing full of color and life. Exhausted from the day, he offered a distracted "Looks great, buddy," before retreating from him. Simon couldn't even remember what color the drawing was, and that realization hit him hard. The recollection of the disappointment in his son's eyes caused him lingering pain. Later, he realized, "I'm so tired and on edge all the time that even when I'm with my son, I feel like my mind is elsewhere and I can't enjoy it." Simon's preoccupations were robbing him of meaningful relationships with those he loved.

In one of our sessions, Simon shared that, at home, after a long day at work, he would often collapse onto the couch, his mind a storm of "You're falling behind. You'll never catch up. You don't have what it takes." Simon's thoughts twisted to exaggerate his flaws and amplify his anxiety. What began as a passing thought quickly took root and sprouted into fears far larger than reality. He felt paralyzed by a sense of impending doom. Caught in survival mode, Simon's thinking magnified his stress and narrowed his perspective. A small part of him longed to walk away and to start over where no one knew his name.

The Unreliable Narrator

Our brains generate thoughts from the moment we wake until we drift to sleep. Neuroscientists estimate that we experience more than 6,000 thoughts each day that flow in clusters. Using advanced brain imaging, researchers have coined the term *thought worms* to describe the trails of neural activity that trace how one thought twists into the next.[4]

Most of these thought worms pass unnoticed and flicker at the edges of our awareness. But some take hold and influence our emotions, sensations, actions, beliefs, and even our sense of identity. They become narratives that feel personal because they're tinted by our unique memories. As these thought worms burrow, we tend to believe they reflect reality.[5]

The catch is that our brains often lie and distort because the mind's primary job is not to make us happy but to keep us alive.[6] To this end, the brain takes shortcuts as it scans for danger and fills in gaps. In pursuit of safety, it leans toward the negative, focusing on what could go wrong and interpreting ambiguity as a threat. This negativity bias has been crucial for human survival over the course of evolution, but it can also tether us to survival mode and keep us from thriving.[7]

As we've seen, in survival mode, the brain's focus narrows. It becomes hypervigilant and attuned to immediate threats, whether real or imagined. This is a feature, not a bug. The challenge is that the brain sometimes struggles to distinguish between actual danger and perceived threats. Learning to pause and ask whether a response is truly needed or whether we're safe enough to quiet the reaction is a powerful skill that supports our shift into thriving mode.[8]

Psychologists call the tendency to create coherent narratives from incomplete or inaccurate information *confabulation*. It's the mechanism that allows us to look back on a disjointed series of life events and craft a cohesive story about who we are.[9] This storytelling impulse can be empowering when we're in thriving mode, consciously constructing narratives that enable us to see challenges as opportunities and setbacks as stepping stones. But the same impulse to confabulate can also fuel distortions that keep us stuck in survival mode.

A breakthrough moment for Simon in our sessions was realizing how often he confabulated, unconsciously stitching together unrelated events into stories of inadequacy that amplified his stress and eroded his confidence. A colleague's brief pause during a meeting became a tale of disapproval. A routine revision request by a client translated into evidence of professional incompetence. Even neutral facial expressions sparked the thought, "They must think I'm not pulling my weight." Believing his self-critical confabulations, Simon over-prepared for meetings and second-guessed his decisions. In survival mode, confabulations can corrode agency and reinforce self-doubt.

Simon's journey from survival to thriving involved identifying negativity biases, confabulations, and the distortions they created. I reminded him that the thoughts we have about ourselves are just the mind's attempts to make sense of an ambiguous world. That helped him learn to challenge the inner stories that were keeping him in survival mode.

The Limits of Logic

For centuries, Western culture has worshiped thought and reason. From the Enlightenment to the Scientific Revolution, rationalism became the engine of progress. Descartes famously declared, "I doubt, therefore I am—or what is the same—I think, therefore I am." This emphasis on inquiry and logic cemented reason as the supposed foundation of human existence and propelled science and technology forward to create the world we live in today.[10]

Except reason, for all its brilliance, has its limits. It simplifies what is complex and measures only what is measurable.[11] Emotions, sensations, spirituality, and intuition are all essential and don't fit neatly into logic's framework. When rationalism is over-emphasized, we risk reducing the richness of the human experience to data points. We attempt to think our way out of discomfort and may end up trapped in endless thought loops.

Reflection allows us to thoughtfully engage with our experiences, gain perspective, and find insight. It's intentional and often leads to growth.[12] *Rumination*, by contrast, is a loop in which a concern circles around in our minds repeatedly without resolution, like a song stuck on repeat. Rumination masquerades as problem-solving, but spinning the same thought over and over rarely serves us. Research shows that rumination amplifies stress rather than alleviating it.[13]

Today, we often measure success in numbers like profits, net worth, performance metrics, calories burned, and social media engagement. Rationalism's gift is precision, but when it becomes the only tool, life shrinks to what can be counted. A world governed solely by logic is a world drained of color. Reason is essential for navigating complexity, but it can also blind us to the richness found in emotion and intuition.

Thriving benefits from balancing the sharpness of reason and the depth of feeling. The mind needs the wisdom of the body. Some of the greatest breakthroughs in history, like Einstein's theories and Michelangelo's sculptures, were not just feats of intellect but also of imagination.

For Simon, this balance was key. His analytical mind had driven him forward, but it had also sharpened his inner critic until every perceived failure became a personal indictment. When he reconnected with what first drew him to architecture, the love of form and space, he found a deeper well of motivation.

Thinking Traps: The Brain's Shortcut to Survival

Our brains take natural shortcuts for quick decision-making. Some of these shortcuts distort the narratives we create about ourselves so predictably that psychologists call them *thinking traps*.[14]

Thinking traps often work without our conscious awareness. Before we realize it, they turn minor challenges into seemingly insurmountable obstacles.[15] Let's explore four of the most common thinking traps and the ways they color our thoughts: catastrophizing, all-or-nothing thinking, mind reading, and confirmation bias.

Catastrophizing: Imagining the Worst

Catastrophizing involves taking a minor setback and inflating it into a full-blown disaster. It's like looking at a small crack in a windshield and convincing ourselves that the entire car is about to fall apart. Instead of interpreting manageable imperfections, the brain projects worst-case scenarios.

Research shows that catastrophizing leads to an amplified perception of pain and exaggerated stress responses. Catastrophizing sends our nervous system into survival mode.[16]

For someone applying for a new job, catastrophizing might show up as thinking, "They probably hate my resume. I'll never get an interview. I'll be unemployed forever." Catastrophizing turns uncertainty into certainty of disaster, like when a child comes home late from school and a parent immediately assumes something terrible has happened, fueling unnecessary panic.

For Simon, a client's request for revisions was an indication of professional doom. His mind spiraled: "They hate the design. They'll cancel the project. My reputation will be ruined." A single email could quickly snowball into a narrative of total failure.

Catastrophizing traps us in a loop where every challenge feels like a crisis. Simon's brain went into overdrive, his heart raced, his breathing became shallow, and his thoughts whirled through worst-case scenarios, effectively sidelining rational thought and problem-solving. Catastrophizing and survival mode are mutually reinforcing.

The irony of catastrophizing is that it leaves us less capable of handling the very challenges we fear. When Simon eventually sat down to address the client's feedback, he was exhausted and struggled to think creatively.

Had Simon been operating in thriving mode, he might have recognized his catastrophizing thoughts and found a way to stop them. He might have seen the revisions as an opportunity to refine and elevate his work. Instead, survival mode kept him fatigued and locked in self-doubt.

All-or-Nothing Thinking: The Tyranny of Perfection

The all-or-nothing thinking trap reduces complex situations into binary extremes: success or failure, good or bad, perfect or worthless. Cognitive therapy pioneers Aaron Beck and colleagues identified all-or-nothing thinking as one of the key thinking traps underlying anxiety and depression.[17] This thinking trap can make setbacks feel decisive. Thus, missing one workout means abandoning a fitness goal entirely.

For example, when I first sent the manuscript of this book to an editor, I braced myself for feedback but secretly hoped for a glowing review. Instead, the editor suggested many, many revisions. My initial reaction was, "If it's not perfect, maybe I'm not cut out for this." After sitting with it, I realized the feedback was an opportunity to refine and strengthen my work. If I had let all-or-nothing thinking take over, this book might never have reached you.

Simon once said, "To me, a design is either a masterpiece or a total failure. There's nothing in between." Even after completing major projects, he struggled to celebrate success. He focused on minor flaws, convinced that nothing short of perfection was acceptable. Even when clients were thrilled, he couldn't take pride in his work if he spotted a single imperfection. A missed deadline wasn't just a scheduling hiccup, but confirmation that he wasn't suited for his role. Simon was unable to appreciate progress or incremental victories. Over time, this thinking trap shattered his joy and eroded his motivation.

All-or-nothing thinking may also lead to avoidance by convincing us that if it can't be perfect, it isn't worth starting. This trap paralyzes us and keeps us stuck in a cycle of procrastination.[18]

Simon had a breakthrough when he recognized this pattern beyond the workplace. He recalled how often he would start something, only to abandon it midway, like the CrossFit membership he stopped using after a few weeks and the guitar lessons he never finished. Each unfinished attempt confirmed the belief "if I can't do it perfectly, I might as well not do it at all."

Had Simon been operating in thriving mode, he might have recognized that growth often comes through imperfection and that success occurs on a spectrum. Only for him in survival mode, there was no middle ground.

Mind Reading: Filling in the Gaps

Mind reading occurs when we assume we know what other people are thinking, often jumping to negative conclusions.[19] In survival mode, people fall into this trap when their brains are constantly scanning for social threats, like rejection or judgment. The irony is that we humans are notoriously bad at mind reading.[20]

A study showed that people consistently overestimate how well they understand what others are thinking, particularly in ambiguous situations. In one experiment, participants were tasked with inferring a partner's emotions based solely on nonverbal cues. They guessed correctly only 20% of the time, which is no better than chance. Despite this, they rated their confidence in their guesses as high. This disconnect stresses the dangers of assuming we know what others think.[21]

In my career, I can't count the number of times I misread a manager's neutral tone as dissatisfaction. Convinced I had fallen short, I spent countless hours redoing work that was already acceptable. Looking back, I can see how those moments of overcompensation intensified my own feelings of inadequacy and created more stress than the situation warranted.

During a team meeting, Simon noticed that a colleague seemed distracted. His mind immediately filled in the gaps: "She's bored. She doesn't respect my ideas."

Had Simon been in thriving mode and recognized that he was falling into the trap of mind reading, he might have asked his colleague what she thought about the idea he had been presenting. She might have said, "I was jotting down notes so I wouldn't forget one of the points you were making." Instead, by assuming the worst, he unwittingly cut himself off from a relationship and deprived himself of useful feedback. Mind reading tends to amplify social isolation.

Confirmation Bias: Seeking What We Expect to See

Imagine a detective who, upon arriving at a crime scene, decides on a suspect and then seeks only evidence that confirms that suspicion, ignoring any clues that might point elsewhere. This is an example of a common thinking trap known as confirmation bias, where we see what we expect to see and ignore what we don't expect to see.[22]

In relationships, confirmation bias can create emotional distance. Because Simon was exquisitely sensitive to criticism, he tended to focus on moments that reinforced his self-doubt while overlooking acts of kindness or support. Over time, this bias chipped away at his confidence, weakened his connections with colleagues and clients, and left him increasingly lonely.

Confirmation bias strengthened the stories that kept Simon in survival mode, turning his mind into an echo chamber that amplified his insecurities. Even when colleagues or clients offered praise, he barely registered it. Compliments were dismissed as politeness, and every minor critique felt like proof of his belief that he was defective.

To make matters worse, every time Simon brushed off positive comments as insincere, his brain reinforced the narrative that he was an imposter who "didn't have what it takes." Even when a client publicly praised his work at a conference, he fixated on the one detail he wished he had done differently. His focus on perceived flaws became a self-reinforcing cycle.

Had Simon been in thriving mode, he might have identified his confirmation bias and embraced a more balanced perspective. He could have recognized his strengths and achievements while seeing areas for improvement as opportunities for growth. Confirmation bias distorted his reality and kept him tethered to thoughts that held him back.

Spotting the Traps in Action

These thinking traps don't necessarily operate in isolation. In Simon's case, a single ambiguous event could trigger a cascade of thinking traps. Recognizing and acknowledging the power that they have was a turning point in his journey toward thriving.

For example, Simon shared in one of our sessions that he had received an email from his client with a short message: "We need to talk." His first thought was, "They're disappointed in me," a classic case of mind reading, in which his brain assumed it could intuit the client's emotions. Then came "They'll probably cancel the project," a textbook example of catastrophizing, where his mind leaped to the worst possible scenario. His brain then began looking for confirmation by replaying past meetings and filtering out moments of praise to fixate solely on instances of tension. By the time the meeting came, Simon was exhausted and had already convinced himself he was failing. Turns out, the client simply wanted to discuss an administrative matter.

Simon's experience also reveals how these traps connect thoughts to beliefs. The spiraling thoughts "You're falling behind," or "You'll never catch up" were intimately tied to his core belief: "I don't have what it takes". Left unexamined, thoughts stemming from thinking traps reinforce the beliefs that keep us stuck. But once we see them for the mental habits they are, we become more agentic and able to create space for different thoughts and even new beliefs.

Engaging with Thoughts Differently

The first step to breaking free from unhelpful thoughts is recognizing that they're just thoughts; temporary mental events, not objective truths.[23] By learning to observe them without judgment, we create distance that allows us to link thoughts together differently.[24]

Once we gain distance from our thoughts, we also gain the power to inquire into them and reframe them. The Stoics understood this well. Marcus Aurelius wrote, "You have power over your mind. Not outside events. Realize this, and you will find strength."[25]

Our thoughts are influenced by genetics, life experiences, culture, and much more.[26] Rising automatically, they may whisper fears of failure or scream warnings of dangers that may not exist. While we can't control the thoughts that emerge, we can cultivate the agency to choose how we engage with them.

Austrian neurologist and psychiatrist Viktor Frankl, reflecting on his harrowing experiences as a prisoner in the Nazi concentration camps, articulated this idea beautifully: "Everything can be taken from a man but one thing: the last of the human freedoms—to choose one's attitude in any given set of circumstances, to choose one's own way."[27]

Frankl's words emerged from the darkest corners of human suffering. In the camps, Frankl faced the reality of a life reduced to its most basic struggle for survival. The prisoners were starved, beaten, dehumanized, and forced into conditions designed to crush the body and spirit. But in an environment where despair seemed inevitable, Frankl recognized that some people found a way to maintain their humanity.

He observed something extraordinary about those who endured: though they had no control over the brutal realities surrounding them, they discovered their agency as the power to choose how to relate to their suffering. For Frankl, this realization became a lifeline.[28]

On a bitterly cold morning, Frankl was forced to march for miles to a worksite. Every step was agonizing. As he walked, he closed his eyes and imagined his wife's face. The pain receded, and he felt a warmth that transcended the horrors around him. His body remained imprisoned, but his mind was free and soared to a place of love.

Frankl learned that between the external horrors he faced and his internal reaction, there was a moment of agency. So he made choices, such as offering a kind word to a fellow prisoner, standing tall during roll calls, and resolving to bear the day's pain with dignity. He made a choice between letting hopelessness consume him and finding meaning, however small, in his suffering.

Most of us face challenges that are far less extreme, but they're significant to us: a health scare, a car accident, a harsh comment from a boss, or a failed project. These moments may trigger automatic thoughts of despair that, when left unchecked, can trap us in survival mode. But as Frankl tells us, between the event and our reaction, there's a space where we have a choice.

Agency unlocks the ability to decide whether to believe the thought that says, "I'll never recover from this failure," or to challenge it. It's where we can choose to align our response with our values. The more we practice pausing in that space, the more expansive it becomes and the more we respond with intention rather than impulsive reaction.

Changing Thoughts Using AIR

Awareness was the first step in Simon's journey toward freedom. We practiced that whenever the thought "I don't have what it takes" surfaced, he would pause and mentally label it as self-doubt. This simple act of naming the thought helped him see it for what it was: a passing mental state, not an ultimate verdict on his worth.

Inquiry became an important part of our sessions. When Simon experienced a thought that tended to start his downward spiral, like "I'm falling behind," he challenged it with questions, like "Is this really true? What evidence do I have for and against this statement?" He imagined what he might say to a friend experiencing similar doubt. This gentle act of inquiry loosened the grip of the thought and began to unravel the limiting beliefs beneath it.

The space between thought and response became a refuge for Simon. He learned to pause, to breathe, to consider his options, and then to choose. As we worked together, he began to recognize how his reactive thoughts kept him tethered to survival mode. By observing and challenging these patterns, he started moving into thriving mode. Each small victory brought him closer to the clarity he was seeking.

Reframing largely involved Simon understanding what was really needed in his current situation. One evening, he caught himself redrawing the same line on a floor plan for the fifth time, adjusting, tweaking, and perfecting. Then, almost defiantly, he hit save and closed his laptop with a wry smile. "Good enough," he thought, surprising even himself.

The transformation was not without its struggles. Simon admitted that he still felt a pang of inadequacy every time he compared himself to his younger self. But over time, he weakened the power of his negative thoughts until they could no longer hijack his reality. He moved from a life dominated by doubt to one guided by agency.

Ripples in the Pond

As Simon sat across from me, he reflected on the changes he had noticed within himself and in his interactions with the people around him.

"It's funny," he said, "I didn't expect this work to have the impact it has." Conversations with his team had become less defensive and more open. Where he used to brace for criticism, he now found himself leaning into feedback with curiosity. "You know," Simon said, "I've realized that the way I show up affects the energy in every room I walk into. When other people start picking up on that, it becomes contagious."

Simon's shift in presence also changed the way he led at work, evolving from a top-down directive style to one that's more collaborative and curious.

"I used to think asking for help would make me look weak," he said. "But lately, it's been the opposite. When I admit I don't have all the answers, it seems to bring the team closer, like we're solving the problem together instead of me just directing from above."

He also recalled a team workshop where everyone sketched ideas on sticky notes and posted them on the whiteboard. One note stood out and, normally, he might have brushed past it, but instead, he paused and asked, "Who wants to tell me more about this?" What followed was a perspective no one had considered, a fantastic idea that restructured the entire project.

The path from survival to thriving is not linear. We adjust the thoughts that move through our minds by continuously observing, questioning, and reframing them over time. Each new challenge invites us to confront the unreliable interpreter within and offers us a chance to break free from old patterns to embrace more empowering perspectives.

In one of our final sessions together, Simon said, "It's amazing. I don't feel stuck in my thoughts the way I used to be. Back then, I was terrified of failing. Now, I'm more interested in growing together, with the team." It was a powerful moment. The fear that once kept him guarded had softened into curiosity. In changing how he worked, he changed how he related to himself, his colleagues, his family, his friends, and his community.

"One night, my son brought me another drawing. You know how much he loves to draw. This time, I looked at his drawing. Really looked. I asked him about the characters, and he just lit up, telling me all these wild stories about them."

He paused, his voice catching slightly. "It hit me then. How much more present I've been with him. Life isn't just about me anymore." Simon said that the next day, he signed up for a membership at the local art museum to enjoy with his son on slow Sunday mornings. A new ritual and a way of telling him: I'm here, and I want to share this with you.

He also described how even mundane moments, like pouring his morning coffee, felt different now. Instead of mentally racing through the day's to-do list, he found himself more energized to enjoy the little things. He started walking regularly to take in the architecture around him, something he loved doing years ago. Even Simon's dog, an excitable retriever, experienced the change. Where Simon once hurried through walks, distracted by his phone, he now lingered, watching her chase after squirrels and feeling the crispness of the morning air.

This journey requires the curiosity to examine our thoughts. It also demands self-compassion and gives us an opportunity to hold space for our imperfections. Growth isn't about becoming flawless but about becoming whole.

When we begin to challenge our internal narratives, the ripple effect can extend to entire communities. Internal shifts can transform entire cultures. In this way, thriving becomes contagious by fostering spaces where people can express and experience kindness.

Simon couldn't help but think back to the man he used to see in the mirror, the one who had felt so weighed down by thoughts of falling behind. Now, the reflection staring back was different. He felt lighter, as though he'd finally caught up with himself.

Using AIR to Explore Thoughts

You can use the AIR approach to explore any thought patterns that may be keeping you in survival mode.

Awareness: Recognizing Unhelpful Thought Patterns

- *When an unhelpful thought arises, do I automatically believe it?*
- *Do I notice recurring thoughts that drain my energy or create stress?*
- *Is there a pattern in my thinking that keeps me stuck in fear?*

Inquiry: Questioning the Validity of Thoughts

- *If this thought pattern were a story, what title would it have?*
- *Where did this thought pattern originate? Who or what influenced it?*
- *What evidence do I have that an intrusive thought is true? What evidence suggests otherwise?*

Reframing: Creating New Thought Patterns

- *Given that this thought pattern offers one perspective, what other perspectives could I use to view situations like this?*
- *What thought would be more empowering in this moment?*
- *What's one small action I can take to disrupt this thought pattern and create a new one?*

4

Emotions
The Compass Within

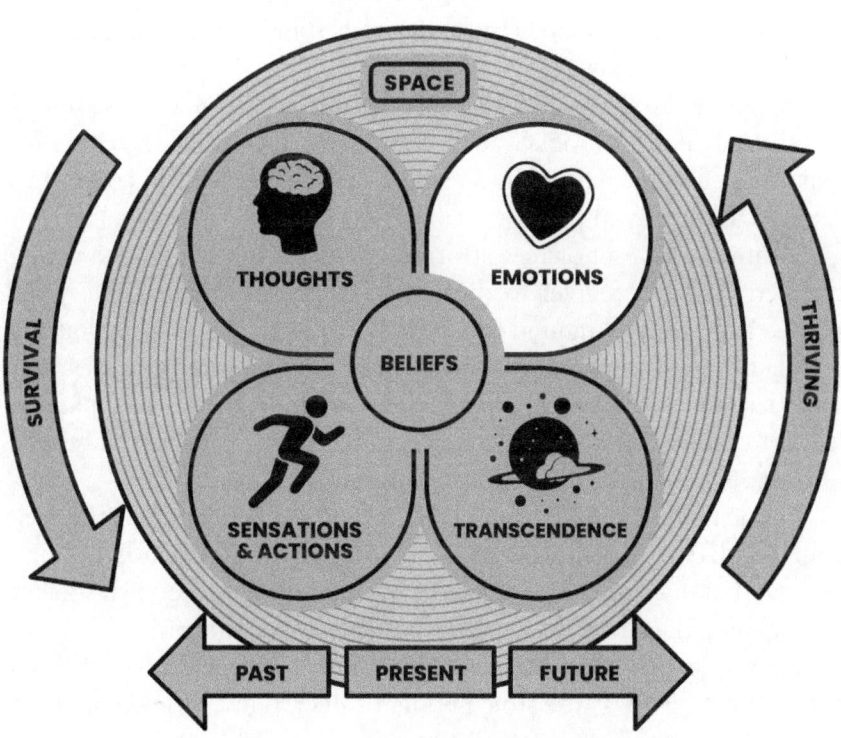

SOME EMOTIONS ARRIVE gently like a breeze, while others crash in like a storm. Either way, they have a profound impact on the way we interpret the world and who we believe ourselves to be. In this chapter, we'll explore the vital role emotions play in the journey from survival to thriving.

What Are My Emotions Trying to Tell Me? Meet Deanne

When Deanne first joined the Zoom room, her voice was steady and her tone resolute. "I don't do emotions," she said almost defiantly. "They're a distraction. People who get caught up in them make mistakes." She delivered the line with the confidence of someone who had lived by that belief for a long time. It wasn't the first time I had heard such a declaration, especially from someone in a high-stakes profession like the law.

As she spoke, I noticed the slight hesitation before each sentence and the way her eyes looked away from the camera as if searching for something. I wondered if she was perhaps looking for the courage to keep a mask firmly in place.

Deanne was a renowned attorney, a wife, a mother of two young children, and a caregiver for her aging parents. On the surface, she seemed to have it all figured out. She could easily switch from drafting ironclad legal documents to managing her kids' bedtime routines. Her calendar was a model of precision, balancing client calls, parent-teacher conferences, and doctor's appointments for her father, whose early-onset dementia was progressing faster than expected.

From the outside, Deanne's life looked like she could give a masterclass in balancing acts. On the inside, it was a house of cards. Deanne told me that even as she ticked off every item on her to-do list, she felt the creeping question: "Why doesn't this feel like enough?"

Each role Deanne performed demanded something different from her. At work, she was the stoic problem-solver, praised for keeping her cool under pressure. At home, she was the dependable anchor, carrying her husband and kids through the toughest times. With her parents, she was the dutiful daughter, making sure their needs were met. But when Deanne needed someone to lean on, she didn't know how to ask.

Words heard in childhood from her father echoed in her mind: "There's no room for feelings when there's work to do." She remembered standing in the garage with the sharp scent of motor oil hanging in the air, watching her father under the hood of their aging sedan, as her mother's angry voice rang out from the kitchen, a familiar backdrop to their unfinished battles. Deanne wanted to ask him for guidance about an upsetting experience at school. Instead, she clenched her fists and swallowed the lump in her throat. She understood the lesson that emotions were a problem to be managed, not something to be expressed.

Deanne was too young to understand the weight of his words but old enough to carry them into adulthood. She learned early that survival meant being useful, productive, efficient, and composed. Now, as she juggled the demands of her work and family, she felt that emotions were a luxury she couldn't afford.

Deanne didn't come into coaching ready to confront her feelings. Her focus was on becoming a better leader and growing her client base. She was driven to excel, but beneath her focus on outcomes stirred an unease she struggled to name. "It feels like a knot in my chest I can't untangle," she admitted, "but I know it's there for a reason."

Despite her success, Deanne carried the familiar emptiness that comes with living in survival mode. The victories at work no longer brought satisfaction, and the demands of caregiving for her dad, even though rooted in love, were taking a toll on her health. Even her cherished role as a mother felt like another item on an endless to-do list. Some nights, when the house was quiet, a question meandered in her mind: "If I had made different choices in life, would I feel free from the weight I'm carrying now?"

Deanne had long seen emotions as liabilities to be suppressed. But emotions are powerful messengers that can offer guidance, even when they arrive wrapped in discomfort. They can alert us to threats and opportunities.

To understand what her emotions were trying to tell her, Deanne needed to stop pushing them away.

The Brain Constructs Emotions

Where do emotions come from? For centuries, emotions were believed to be hardwired reflexes triggered by specific stimuli.[1] Charles Darwin argued that emotions were innate and shared across all cultures. The *hardwired* perspective gained traction in the 20th century when psychologist Paul Ekman identified six basic emotions (happiness, sadness, fear, anger, surprise, and disgust) that he claimed were universally recognizable in human facial expressions.[2]

Recent studies suggest a more extensive spectrum of emotions. Psychologists Dacher Keltner and Alan Cowen at University of California, Berkeley, identified up to 27 distinct emotional states, including awe, contempt, disgust, nostalgia, surprise, anxiety, and envy.[3]

Neuroscientist Lisa Feldman Barrett's research at Northeastern University suggests that emotions are not hardwired reflexes at all but *constructed* experiences actively created by our brains in a never-ending effort to make sense of the world. Responding to physical sensations, such as sweaty palms or quickened breath, our brains form interpretations based on context, memory, and culture.[4] The same physical cues might signal fear during a tense conversation or excitement before a long-awaited reunion.

While we often think thoughts create emotions, reality is far messier. Emotions can surface before we're even aware of them and can be informed by a complex tangle of conscious and unconscious processes.[5] The bodily response may be nearly identical across situations, but the brain's interpretation influences what we come to feel and the meaning we make of our experience.[6]

Mood is the background feeling that lingers over time. It informs what we feel, influences how we think, and colors how we see the world. Mood is like our inner weather; it can make everything feel brighter or darker.[7]

While emotions and moods may feel persistent, they're more fluid than we often realize. Researcher Jill Bolte Taylor at Harvard found that emotions rise and fall in about 90 seconds. After that, any lingering distress comes not from the initial trigger but from the thoughts we attach to it. We replay the moment, connect it to memories, assign meaning, and knowingly or unknowingly sustain the emotion beyond its natural course.[8]

Emotions Happen in the Body

Before we even put them into words, emotions take form as sensations. They're embodied experiences that the brain later organizes into meaning.[9] For example, tightness in the chest often accompanies sadness or grief. Clenched jaws and tense shoulders might reflect suppressed anger, and an unsettled stomach could hint at anxiety or fear. In some people, unacknowledged emotions emerge as physical tension, an ever-present knot in the shoulders, tension in the jaw, chronic back pain, or headaches.[10]

We can learn to notice these signals and ask, "What is my body trying to tell me?" Rather than push sensations aside, we can tune into them to unlock valuable insights into the tremendous complexity of emotions, including those we may not even realize we're feeling.

We have far more agency in designing our emotional landscape than we realize. The physical sensations that accompany our emotions can act as clues and help us decode what's happening beneath the surface. Recognizing sensations in our body is the first step toward understanding that our emotions, while undeniably powerful, are not fixed or unchangeable.[11] Emotions offer us instant evaluations of whether something feels safe or threatening, fulfilling or lacking. They also prepare us to act and push us toward what we need or away from what might harm us.[12]

Cultural Influences on Emotions

Our environments profoundly influence the way we understand and express what we feel. In Western cultures, openly displaying joy and pride is acceptable because these feelings reflect personal success. At the same time, sadness and anger are frequently suppressed because they reflect vulnerability or seem unprofessional.[13]

Contrast this with collectivist cultures in East Asia, where the social harmony of the group takes precedence. People there might suppress anger and frustration to avoid disrupting group harmony. Displays of joy or pride might be tempered to avoid drawing attention, reflecting the cultural value placed on modesty.[14]

Even within cultures, there are variations influenced by language, gender, age, occupation, social status, and so much more. In societies where anger is perceived as a sign of strength and sadness is viewed as a weakness, men are encouraged to display anger and discouraged from showing sadness. Women, on the other hand, are more likely to suppress anger, seen as unfeminine, and feel more comfortable expressing sadness, which is socially accepted. Over time, these norms determine how emotions are individually experienced. As a result, a man might not even recognize his own sadness, unconsciously converting it into anger, while a woman might feel uncomfortable feeling a spark of rage.[15]

Cultural expectations around emotion often lead us to experience *secondary emotions*, determined not by the situation itself but by how we process or react to our initial feelings. For example, a woman experiencing anger in response to an injustice may turn that emotional energy into guilt or shame because expressing anger feels culturally inappropriate. While these secondary emotions can help us navigate social rules, they can also mask our feelings, leaving us disconnected from what we're truly experiencing.[16]

Instrumental emotions are often expressed to influence others, like when a person exaggerates sadness for reassurance or uses anger to assert control. While sometimes helpful and not always intentional, these patterns can become habitual and strain relationships when others sense they're being manipulated.[17]

How we learn to express emotions is also influenced by cultural norms.[18] In recent decades, cultural changes in the Western world have begun to challenge traditional expectations. This evolution is making space for men to embrace vulnerability and express emotions like sadness and allowing women to assert anger without being labeled as aggressive. While these evolving norms reflect a growing recognition of the value of emotional authenticity, there's still a long way to go. Deeply ingrained stereotypes and biases continue to guide how expressions of emotion are judged.[19]

The rise of social media has made emotional authenticity even more complex. While these platforms create new opportunities for vulnerability, they also encourage curated expressions of emotions. True emotional authenticity requires aligning what we outwardly express with what we genuinely feel inside.[20]

Suppressing Emotions Has a Cost

Suppressing emotional sensations can feel like trying to hold a beach ball underwater. The harder we press, the greater the resistance, until eventually, it bursts to the surface in unexpected ways. A tight chest or a clenched jaw, when left unacknowledged or misinterpreted, can escalate into chronic tension or even physical illness.[21]

When we consciously or unconsciously suppress or misinterpret feelings, we disrupt the brain's ability to construct coherent emotions. This disruption makes it harder for the brain to regulate the body effectively, leading to greater dysregulation that can keep us stuck in survival mode. Over time, the body pays the price, with elevated blood pressure, disrupted sleep, pain, or a weakened immune system.[22]

Researchers have found that people who regularly bottle up their feelings are more likely to experience depression and anxiety. The mental energy it takes to keep everything under wraps can leave people feeling drained and detached.[23]

While pushing emotions aside might seem helpful in the moment, suppressing them may disrupt the biological balance among the parts of our brain that regulate our feelings and responses.[24] In essence, the prefrontal cortex, responsible for emotional regulation, has a harder time managing signals from the amygdala, which acts as an emotional alarm system. This imbalance can leave us feeling constantly on edge, with stress responses that linger far longer than they should.[25]

I experienced this struggle firsthand. Until the recent death of my close friend Nathan, I found it nearly impossible to cry. I was 26 when my father passed, and I couldn't shed a tear. Instead, anger surged to the surface with an intensity that scared me.

A few days after my father's funeral, I was driving back from yet another tense meeting with my uncle about the family business. As I gripped the steering wheel, the rage hit me like an erupting volcano. My hands trembled, my vision blurred, and I could feel a blistering heat rising in my chest and arms. It was as if the sheer force of my fury could shatter all the glass around me. I pulled over abruptly onto the shoulder and screamed at the top of my lungs, holding the wheel as if it were the only thing keeping me from falling apart.

In the weeks after the loss of my father, I had to move back to my childhood home to help my mother navigate a world suddenly devoid of her partner. I resentfully stepped into my father's role in the family business, where I had to engage in legal battles with my uncle and his family, who were intent on taking as much as they could from my father's estate. I was in a constant fight to protect what my father had built, carrying the crushing weight of both responsibility and betrayal. The days blurred together in an endless cycle of problem-solving and sheer survival. There was no room to process my grief for my father.

Relief came unexpectedly in the form of SSRIs, or selective serotonin reuptake inhibitors, commonly prescribed to treat depression and anxiety. I recall sitting in the doctor's office, reluctant and defensive but desperate for anything to keep my head above water. The medication didn't solve everything, but it created a crack in the wall I had built to numb myself. It gave me space to start feeling again, to face the grief that I had buried.

Even as I write this, crying doesn't come easily to me. But the work I've done to recognize and honor my emotions softened the sharp edges of my rage. Slowly, I've learned to sit with the sadness I once avoided, to let it speak what it must. I've found that when I let myself experience my emotions, they tend to clear a path.

The world around us often tells us what we're allowed to feel and how we're allowed to express it. For me, anger was acceptable, but sadness was forbidden. Challenging that rule meant reclaiming a part of myself I had long denied.

Emotions Are Not Obstacles

Like me, Deanne had learned to treat emotions as obstacles to be avoided. She believed that emotions were dangerous because they could derail her focus and expose her vulnerabilities. In her line of work, this belief had served her well. She could walk into a boardroom and argue her case with clinical precision, never letting her opponents see her sweat. She could sit across from clients in crisis and provide clear, actionable advice without being swayed by their anxiety.

Over time, however, Deanne's unacknowledged emotions emerged as physical sensations that she could no longer ignore. She began experiencing migraines, first occasionally and then with increasing frequency, that forced her to push through days clouded by throbbing pain. Deanne interpreted signals from her body as just stress, but her patience at home was wearing thin, and she found herself snapping at her kids for minor infractions and then retreating into silence, overwhelmed with exhaustion and guilt.

Her husband, Daniel, had always admired her strength, but lately, he had been voicing concerns about her distance. "I feel like you're here, but you're not *here*," he said one night after a particularly tense argument. Deanne didn't know how to respond. How could she explain that she felt terrified to let even one emotion slip through because then the whole facade might crumble?

One evening Daniel asked her, "Do you even care how I feel anymore?" Deanne told me his words felt like a low blow. She opened her mouth to answer, but no words came. In the silence that followed, she became acutely aware of how far she had drifted from the life she wanted to build.

Deanne's pain was bleeding into the relationships she valued most. Hurt people hurt people, not intentionally, but because unprocessed emotions inevitably find their way out, often harming the very relationships we most wish to protect.

As we explored her story, it became clear to Deanne that her avoidance of emotions was about much more than just maintaining control. It was also about protecting herself from the vulnerability she dreaded might undo her.

Emotional Agency

Emotional agency is the ability to actively engage with our emotions rather than ignoring them or letting them control us.[26] Emotional agency starts with the ability to notice emotions as they occur and to consider where they come from and what they tell us about ourselves in the current context.[27]

"You're making me angry." It's a phrase many of us have said or thought at some point. The words *you're making me* suggest that our emotions are directly caused by someone else's actions, and we're passive recipients of their influence. But people can respond in very different ways to the same situation, which invites us to look a little more closely.

What if no one can *make us* feel anything?

Understanding emotions as constructed experiences means recognizing that the brain informs what we feel before we're even aware of it because it filters events through the lens of our beliefs.[28] When we realize this, we gain the ability to step back and respond with agency rather than react on autopilot. Emotional change happens when we become aware of what we feel and choose to transform it. This requires facing emotions and putting them into words. Over time, painful emotions can transform as new meanings emerge.[29]

Emotional agency invites us to take responsibility for our emotional lives and to see our feelings as valuable sources of insight rather than fixed truths. We have the power to challenge the narratives that keep us stuck and choose perspectives that serve us instead.

Whether in relationships or at work, emotional agency offers a bridge from survival to thriving. When we practice it, we stop feeling at the mercy of our emotions and start constructing them with intention instead.

Early in our work together, Deanne frequently spoke about the frustration she felt toward her husband Daniel for what she perceived as his lack of support. "He makes me so frustrated. He knows how much I'm juggling, and he still asks if I've scheduled dinner with friends or picked up the dry cleaning. It's like he's deliberately adding to my stress."

Deanne often referred to her feeling as frustration, a word that felt relatively safe and socially acceptable. As we explored her feelings further, it became clear that beneath this polite label laid anger that was sharp, unrelenting, and raw. Naming it for what it was didn't come easily to her.

We don't always see our emotions clearly. Often, what we feel on the surface is a secondary emotion that masks something deeper. For Deanne, anger was primary, and frustration secondary. Even beneath the anger was a sadness she hadn't fully acknowledged. Understanding these layers helped her see her emotions as guides to knowing herself better.

Deanne also began to understand that emotions were most useful to her when they were neither pushed aside nor allowed to take over. Too little anger left her needs unheard, while too much risked harming the relationships she cared about. Fear worked in a similar way; ignoring it led to burnout, but being consumed by it kept her stuck. Over time, she realized that emotions had a natural range within which they could guide her rather than control her.

In our coaching sessions, I encouraged Deanne to consider alternative explanations for Daniel's behavior by asking a series of questions: "What might Daniel's requests reveal about his feelings or needs? How do you think he views your role in the relationship? What else could explain why he asks these things? How might his behavior reflect the way he seeks connection or support?"

At first, Deanne resisted these questions. "I don't want to excuse his behavior," she said. But the next time Daniel asked about a household task, she paused. Instead of reacting immediately, she allowed herself to explore what she was truly feeling. The anger subsided as she began to see his questions as subtle bids for connection.

Eventually, Deanne's growing emotional agency transformed her relationship with Daniel. What once felt like frustration became a doorway to partnership, and moments of tension opened space for understanding. She started recognizing similar opportunities to explore her emotions in other areas of life.

Shifting Our Emotional Reality

Our brains are meaning-making machines, constantly interpreting the world around us.[30] A study at Stanford University explored what happened when participants were taught to reinterpret stressful situations as challenges to overcome rather than threats to their well-being. The results were striking. Those who embraced this mindset shift reported lower levels of anxiety and anger, performed better under pressure, and even experienced a sense of calm in situations that would normally overwhelm them.[31]

We can reframe events and change the meaning we assign to them. When we do, we often transform their emotional impact.[32]

Imagine sending a text message to a friend and not receiving a reply for several days. Instinctively, the survival brain might leap to conclusions: "They're ghosting me. Maybe they're upset." Anxiety or frustration builds, and the silence feels personal. What if, instead, we paused to reframe by asking, "What else might be going on?" Perhaps they're overwhelmed with work or simply forgot to respond. The power of reframing lies in recognizing what we don't know and allowing space for other possibilities to change our perspective and soften our emotional response. The situation remains the same, but its emotional impact transforms.

The first step of emotional agency is naming what we're feeling. Psychiatrist Dan Siegel calls it *name it to tame it,* a practice that works like turning on a light in a dark room, signaling to our brain that we're safe.[33]

As the skill of naming feelings evolves, we start to perceive emotions more precisely. Instead of simply feeling bad, we might identify sadness, frustration, anger, or guilt. Each label offers a distinct perspective that points us toward more tailored responses. Sometimes, we see that we're feeling more than one emotion at a time, like the joy that a child is graduating combined with the sadness that they're moving away from home. The simple act of naming emotions creates a vital pause that allows us to move from the reactive state of survival into a thoughtful space more characteristic of thriving.[34]

Facing Emotions Using AIR

Awareness: We started small. Each week, Deanne practiced identifying and naming her emotions, using simple phrases like "I feel sad" or "I feel angry."

Inquiry: One day, I invited Deanne to look at her long-held belief that emotions were mere distractions. "What might it feel like," I asked, "to consider that your emotions aren't working against you? How could they be signals, trying to guide you toward something important?"

Deanne exhaled sharply. "I don't see the point of analyzing my feelings," she said. "I just need to get things done." The thought of sitting with her emotions felt like a waste of time. For a moment, she looked away as if debating whether to push back or lean in. After a few moments, her expression softened, though some skepticism lingered. Then, she quietly muttered, "But how would I even begin to figure that out?"

Reframing: Over time, she started to see useful patterns: how her anxiety spiked when she felt out of control, how her sadness intensified when she neglected her own needs, and how her joy surfaced in unexpected moments, like sharing laughter with her father during a rare moment of clarity in his dementia.

Each small step brought Deanne closer to knowing herself better. She had spent years pushing her feelings down, unaware of the toll this was taking on her body, like the tight knot she frequently felt in her chest. As she learned to name what she was feeling, the knot began to loosen, bringing an unexpected sense of freedom. Psychiatrist Bessel van der Kolk, in *The Body Keeps the Score*, describes how emotions that go unexpressed often linger in the body long after the mind believes it has moved on.[35]

"I always thought that talking about my emotions would make me feel worse," Deanne once told me, her voice lighter with relief. "But instead, I feel like I've let go of a weight I didn't even know I was carrying." As she noticed patterns in her emotions, she started to reframe them as meaningful signals pointing to important information about herself. For Deanne, emotional agency became a breakthrough that transformed her inner world and her relationships.

Facing Emotional Challenges with Curiosity

A critical email arrives from your boss. The words sting, and your mind instantly jumps to, "This is so unfair! I've been working so hard, and they don't appreciate everything I've done!" Anger rises like a tsunami.

While a reactive response is like tossing dry wood onto a fire, an intentional choice is like adding water. Instead of firing off a defensive reply or spiraling into self-doubt, situations like these invite us to wonder, "What's really happening here? What am I truly feeling?" These questions can reveal what lies beneath the surface, like fear about not meeting expectations or a longing for acknowledgment.

Curiosity is an agentic ally in recognizing and diffusing the intensity of our emotions. It also gives us clarity to see the bigger picture: "This feedback is an opportunity to learn and get better." Or we might reach a different conclusion: "This criticism feels unfair and unfounded." Curiosity allows us to make meaning out of our feelings while opening a path to respond with intention rather than react from a place of helplessness. For instance, acknowledging that anger stems from a sense of injustice can enable us to channel it constructively, like initiating a courageous conversation or setting clear boundaries.[36]

Naming our emotions and meeting them with curiosity can shift how we experience setbacks, especially in our closest relationships.[37] Imagine sharing exciting news with someone you love, only to be met with a distracted or lukewarm response. The first feeling might be disappointment or frustration, wrapped in the thought, "They don't care about me." If we pause and turn inward with curiosity, we might notice sadness stirred by a longing for connection and acknowledgment. That insight can soften our perspective and invite us to reframe the moment. We might think, "Maybe they're caught up in something hard," or recognize that our sadness reveals how much their support truly matters to us. When we sit with what we're actually feeling, we begin to understand our needs more clearly and with greater compassion.

When we ask, "What else could this mean?" we create space for reframing, and we can choose responses that reflect who we want to be. The difficulty of the moment remains, but curiosity can change what feels like a dead end into a path forward. When we reframe, we activate the parts of our brain responsible for logic and empathy while calming our survival response, a transformation that allows us to engage with life proactively instead of reactively.[38]

Emotional Toolkit

When we take responsibility for our emotions, we reclaim our agency. External events, like a loss we didn't anticipate, a strained relationship, stress at work, or someone cutting us off in traffic, might still challenge us but no longer control us.

Becoming aware of our emotions by naming them, inquiring into them, and reframing them is a powerful tool in our personal toolkit. Each time we apply them, we hone our ability to respond to life's twists and turns with bravery, an essential step on the way from survival to thriving.

For Deanne, leaning into emotional agency was life-changing. The emotions that she once dismissed as dangerous distractions revealed themselves as expert guides. Her anxiety, instead of being an ever-present shadow, became a reminder of her care for the people and roles that mattered most to her. Her anger, previously smoothed over as frustration, spoke of her desire for a richer partnership with her husband. Even her sadness, long buried under stoicism, emerged as a testament to her capacity for love. Exploring the uncharted territory of her emotions helped Deanne realize that her feelings offered insight into the life she truly wanted to live.

Using her toolkit, Deanne began to change her emotional responses. Situations that once provoked defensiveness or withdrawal became openings for change. She paused to ask: "What is this emotion trying to tell me? What unmet need or unspoken value lies beneath it?" She started to respond with curiosity instead of judgment.

Over time, Deanne realized that she didn't have to suppress her emotions; instead, she had to unlearn the beliefs about emotions she had absorbed in childhood, including the notion that feelings were liabilities and distractions. Letting go of that story is ongoing work, but it created space for growth.

Ripples in the Pond

As Deanne embraced emotional agency, her relationships began to transform. One evening, Daniel was preparing dinner, something he rarely did. Watching him move around the kitchen, she felt a sense of appreciation she hadn't noticed before.

"Thank you for this," she told him. Daniel smiled at her. "Your support is important to me . . . I'm still learning how to ask for help," she added, surprising herself. Her words opened a door to communicate in ways they rarely did. Having the vulnerability to name her own needs was key to letting others show up for her.

Emotions deepen our bonds and fuel our motivation. Studies show that emotions are contagious.[39] Deanne hadn't realized how much her emotional distance influenced the atmosphere in her home and at work. The stress she carried created tension between her and the people she interacted with. But as she developed emotional agency, her growing openness softened conversations. Her willingness to acknowledge her emotions gave Daniel and their children unspoken permission to do the same.

One night, as she tucked her daughter into bed, Deanne said, "You know, I felt angry earlier when you didn't pick up your room. I was mean to you because I'm really tired. I'm sorry. It's not your fault." Her daughter looked at her with wide eyes and whispered, "I get upset when I'm tired too." The moment brought tears to Deanne's eyes. She saw that the lessons she was learning rippled outward.

Even her work evolved as she connected more authentically with her team, colleagues, and clients. At first, she feared seeming less capable in a profession that valued detachment. Letting go of emotional suppression felt like stepping into unknown territory.

As Deanne embraced her emotions, she found that authenticity enhanced her leadership instead of eroding it. She also became more attuned to the emotions of others. She noticed that empathy diffused tense negotiations, and her willingness to acknowledge uncertainty inspired trust in her team. She became a more grounded and confident leader precisely because she was no longer hiding her feelings. Instead of losing her edge, she sharpened it, and this helped her grow her practice beyond her wildest expectations.

In survival mode, fear, anger, and shame narrow our focus and keep us trapped in cycles of defensiveness and reactivity. In thriving mode, we respond intentionally. When we draw on the full range of our emotions, we can connect with others and resourcefully embrace challenges as opportunities for progress.

Using AIR to Explore Emotions

You can use the AIR approach to explore any recurring emotional responses that may be keeping you in survival mode.

Awareness: Recognizing My Emotional Patterns

- *Do I tend to suppress, ignore, or downplay certain emotions?*
- *Are there physical sensations in my body that might be carrying unprocessed emotions?*
- *Is there a particular emotion I find difficult or uncomfortable to express?*

Inquiry: Questioning My Emotional Narratives

- *What messages did I receive about emotions growing up?*
- *How do I interpret the emotions of others differently from my own?*
- *If my emotions could speak, what would they be trying to tell me?*

Reframing: Cultivating Emotional Agency

- *What might my emotions be pointing me toward?*
- *How can I practice expressing emotions in a way that feels both authentic and safe?*
- *What's one small experiment I could try to engage with my emotions rather than resist them?*

5

Sensations and Actions
The Wisdom of the Body

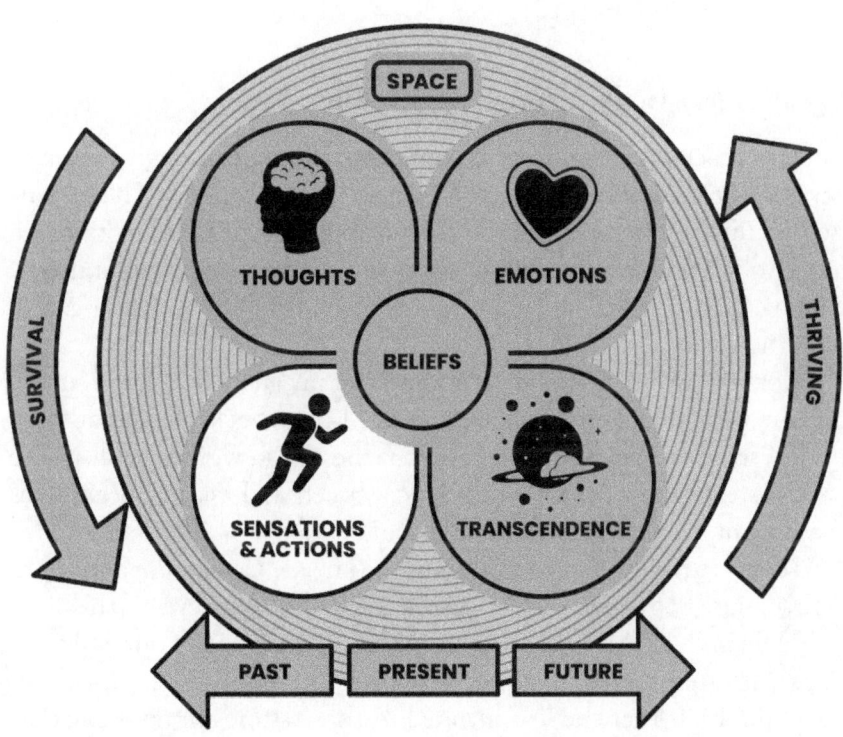

THE BODY IS an active participant in the way we process information. Long before the mind can understand, the body has already begun to respond. The connection between mind and body is constantly active, whether we're aware of it or not.

In this chapter, we'll explore the role the body plays in unlocking the power to thrive. To move beyond survival mode, it's helpful to tune into the sensations in our bodies and ask what stories our brains are constructing out of them. Building intentional habits around bodily awareness can transform fleeting insights, like noticing our shoulders tense every time we open our inbox, into lasting change. By cultivating bodily awareness, we honor the body's ability to translate thoughts and emotions into actions that influence our lives and the world around us.

What Is My Body Trying to Say? Meet Jon

Robyn's space was bright, with sunlight streaming through oversized windows and illuminating raw cement walls and ceilings. The air carried a faint, soothing scent, maybe lavender. From the first time we met, Robyn greeted me with a warm smile, her voice calm and welcoming. She handed me a cup of tea, its earthy aroma rising gently with the steam.

Robyn and her setting invited me to let my guard down and simply be. She wasn't concerned about whether I had checked off items on a to-do list, like other therapists and coaches I had worked with in the past. Instead, she worked with physical touch and asked, "What does that feel like?" or "What do you notice?"

I came to Robyn for coaching because I needed a different approach. As a somatic bodyworker, she engaged the body as a gateway to healing.

"The body doesn't lie," Robyn told me during one of our early sessions. "It often points us toward what needs attention before we can name it." I felt that she was attuned to those stories in my body that I couldn't put into words.

As a man, the idea of exploring feelings and sensations in my body was a little suspect. I had been taught to control vulnerability, not lean into it. I wanted to feel at home in my own body, but I had spent so long over-focusing on my mind and intellect that I didn't know where to begin. As Robyn worked, her hands pressed into the places in my body where I held tension I hadn't even noticed.

Robyn understood that the body is a repository of priceless information, an idea now supported by neuroscience. The concept of mind-body connection isn't new, even if it felt revolutionary to me. Eastern practices like Chinese medicine and Ayurveda have understood the body and mind as unified systems for centuries. These traditions contrast sharply with the Western tendency to separate mind and body.[1]

Robyn's techniques included breathwork, body scanning, Reiki, energy work, osteopathy, and craniosacral therapy. Her methods taught me to perceive physical cues accurately and use them to distinguish between real threats and false alarms.

Robyn frequently asked me to slow down and tune in. She showed me that the body holds wisdom. Where others encouraged me to strategize my next career move, Robyn invited me to explore the tightness in my jaw or the knot in my stomach. She taught me to see these physical sensations as messengers that revealed long-buried information. By gently guiding my bodily awareness, she allowed me to rewrite that narrative. Feel first, then choose differently.

At first, I resisted her. It was unnerving to feel so seen. I was used to deflecting vulnerability with sharpness or humor. But Robyn didn't try to outwit me or prod me into revelation. Instead, she created a space where the only voice that mattered was the one I had suppressed beneath years of living in survival mode. Session by session, resistance gave way to trust.

"What do you notice?" she asked once after I had recounted a particularly frustrating incident with my boss at work.

"What do you mean?" I asked.

"In your body. What do you notice right now?"

Her question caught me off guard. I realized I hadn't even thought to check. To ask my body how it felt seemed almost absurd.

Until then, I had treated my body as a useful machine. Growing up, my mother was a clinical psychologist trained by Joseph Wolpe, one of the pioneers of behavioral therapy. She taught me that behavior alone was the catalyst for change.[2] This early conditioning left little room for me to listen to my body's signals.

I had built a life that looked successful from the outside, but inside, I felt like a stranger to my own experience. So many of us, especially men, are conditioned to see discomfort and pain as a test of strength rather than a message, as something to be silenced rather than understood. Robyn prompted me to listen to my body.

The Body Speaks; Are We Listening?

We experience physical sensations every moment, such as an aching back after a hectic day or a lump in the throat when holding back words. These bodily signals are raw data. The brain makes sense of them by drawing from past and present experiences to create emotions and thoughts.[3]

Just as the body speaks and the mind translates, the mind speaks and the body responds. A single thought can send a rush of heat to the face or soften tense muscles. When we recall a painful memory, our shoulders may tighten as if bracing against the past. When we tell ourselves we're safe, breathing may deepen.[4]

I had ignored these signals for years. My body buzzed with an undercurrent of tension, constantly braced against invisible threats. To survive, I had to be vigilant, so I tightened my jaw and forced my way forward. Any pain, no matter how small, was an unwelcome guest and a heavy burden. When it was unbearable, I sought refuge in medication or numbed myself with alcohol.

Robyn helped me break through my body-mind disconnection with questions and bodywork that led me to uncover invisible forces holding me back. The body's wisdom is profound, and when we ignore its messages, it will find other ways to be heard. Sometimes it whispers through restless sleep or a lingering tightness we can't shake. Other times, it roars through illness or burnout. Robyn invited me to stay curious and to sit with the discomfort. Much like Deanne's work with emotions in the previous chapter, tuning into my bodily sensations taught me new information about myself and created space to step into thriving mode.

Instead of fixing problems, somatic work creates awareness of experiences stored in the body, from traumas to triumphs and everything in between. These embodied memories can either trap us in survival mode, keeping us stuck in loops of tension and avoidance, or propel us into thriving mode, opening us up to growth.[5]

The shift from survival to thriving requires courage to sit with what hurts, both emotionally and physically. The body is indeed one of our greatest teachers. Not the idealized body we see in social media or advertising, but the felt body, the aching body, the alive body that holds our pain and our potential.

Senses as the Gateway to Experience

Robyn once told me, "Your body is the first language you ever spoke. Long before words, there were *sensations*."

From the moment we take our first breath, the body becomes our primary interface with the world. Our senses of sight, sound, taste, touch, and smell are miraculous. They allow us to perceive the hues of a sunset, hear the rustle of leaves, savor the richness of a meal, feel the texture of a loved one's skin, and breathe in the aroma of freshly baked bread.[6]

As extraordinary as our senses are, they only take in a sample of reality. We can't detect as many odors as a dog can, nor use echolocation like a bat. Even within the range of what we can see, hear, smell, taste, and feel, the sensory systems in the brain act as curators that edit the information we take in, actively deciding what's relevant and what can be ignored. The brain turns overwhelming complexity into a refined and coherent narrative of reality.[7]

Through *sensory compression*, our senses prioritize what matters most for our immediate survival, such as detecting predators or finding food.[8] This explains why in survival mode, our perception shrinks to the most immediate, high-priority information, such as the sound of approaching footsteps or a burning smell. While that tunnel vision ensures we stay alert to threats, it can also restrict our experience when it becomes our baseline. Conversely, thriving mode broadens our view of the world and allows us to perceive stimuli that attune us to beauty and connection, like the song of a bird or the warmth of the sun.[9]

The limitations of our senses become especially evident through *sensory illusions*, such as the famous invisible gorilla experiment, where participants were instructed to count basketball passes in a video.

Because their visual systems were focused on ball passes as the most relevant information, most participants completely missed seeing a person in a gorilla costume walking through the scene.[10] Similarly, auditory illusions can trick our sense of hearing, like the Shepard tone, which creates the illusion of a rising or falling pitch without ever truly ascending or descending.[11]

Even as our senses deceive or limit us at times, they remain invaluable. Touch, for example, is the first language of connection, with skin-to-skin contact with a newborn offering profound developmental benefits.[12] A hand extended in friendship can convey what words sometimes can't, and a hug can soften grief more than any condolence card. Research shows that gentle touch from medical caregivers can reduce pain and anxiety in patients,[13] and the warmth of a pet curled up on their lap can provide a profound sense of solace to people navigating loneliness. Too often we undervalue the power of sensory stimulation.[14]

Proprioception

Proprioception serves as our internal compass by guiding our physical navigation through the world. This ability enables us to sense the position and movement of our bodies without conscious effort. In action, this awareness allows us to reach for a glass without knocking it over, walk down the stairs without watching every step, or navigate dimly lit rooms without colliding with furniture.[15]

Beyond physical coordination, proprioception profoundly influences our sense of groundedness.[16] This embodied confidence is integral to the journey from survival to thriving as it allows us to find balance, even when our lived experience feels uncertain. When we feel grounded in our bodies, we're more able to find connection in our relationships and choices. We stand taller and inhabit the world with a sense of presence.[17]

By contrast, survival mode shifts the body's focus toward threat detection, deprioritizing proprioceptive functions like balance and coordination. When proprioception is disrupted, we may feel clumsy, as if we've lost our footing. Proprioception can often be restored through grounding exercises like breathwork and movement practices

like yoga, tai chi, or Feldenkrais, a method that builds bodily awareness through movement.[18]

Interoception

Interoception is the brain's capacity to sense the body's internal state.[19]
It's how we know we're hungry or thirsty and how we notice the need
to stretch after sitting too long. It encompasses everything from the
rhythm of our heartbeat to the churn of our stomach and the way our
lungs expand and contract with each breath.

Standing backstage before giving a big presentation, you might
notice your pulse racing and knots in your stomach. This awareness is
interoception in action, our ability to perceive and interpret our body's
signals, in this case, as we prepare for a challenge. Stepping outside
after the presentation, you might feel your shoulders loosen and your
heartbeat steadying. Noticing relief that the challenge is over is also
interoception at work.

Often called the sixth sense, interoception provides a continuous
stream of feedback about our physical condition.[20] Interoception is an
internal sense that develops long before we have words to describe our
experiences. Since babies don't understand hunger as a concept, they
cry because their bodies signal discomfort and demand attention.
Similarly, babies feel soothed when held because their nervous systems
are calmed by the rhythmic pressure and warmth of an embrace.[21]

This capacity to sense our internal state is fundamental for thriving. Neuroscientists have identified the *insula* as a key brain region
involved in processing interoceptive signals.[22] This area acts as a bridge
between the body and the mind by translating physical sensations into
conscious feelings. For instance, the insula helps us recognize the
pounding of the heart as anxiety or excitement, which adds context to
turn sensations into emotions and thoughts.[23]

Research shows that people with sharp interoceptive awareness
are often better equipped to handle stress. They notice the early signs
of becoming overwhelmed and take steps to manage their mood.[24]
Disruptions in interoception can cause people to misinterpret or
ignore bodily signals, resulting in a disconnect between their physical
experiences and the emotions and thoughts that accompany them.

This disconnect is often linked to conditions like anxiety, depression, or eating disorders.[25]

Interoception also guides the way we connect with others by helping us respond to shared human emotions.[26] Those with strong interoceptive skills tend to be more attuned to the nonverbal cues of those around them. We feel empathy when someone sighs deeply or when their shoulders slump under the weight of tension. Interoception allows us to bridge the gap between our inner world and theirs. When we understand our own bodily signals, we're better equipped to understand other people.[27]

Perhaps most importantly, interoception helps us distinguish between survival and thriving. When our bodies are in survival mode, interoception alerts us to the signs of stress, such as shallow breathing or clenched muscles. In thriving mode, these signals change to reflect a state of ease and balance, such as deeper breathing or relaxed shoulders. By leaning into this often-overlooked sense, we can recognize when to pause and when to push forward, when to defend and when to explore.

Through bodywork with Robyn, I strengthened my interoception by learning to notice the tightness in my jaw when I felt resistant and the tightness in my throat when I held back emotions. Listening to my body became a way to move through life with more awareness and intention.

Neuroception

The term *neuroception* was first introduced by psychologist Stephen Porges to describe the body's unconscious scanning of the environment for cues of safety or danger. It explains why a child instinctively reaches for a caregiver's hand in a crowded place or why we calm down when entering a cozy room. It's also why we might feel uneasy in a workplace meeting where voices are tense or when someone's body language signals aggression, even if no direct threat is present.[28]

Through neuroception, our nervous system continuously interprets the world around us and assesses whether it's safe or threatening. For instance, unpredictable behavior may be perceived as a threat and trigger a survival response of fight, flight, or freeze.[29]

Fight is a form of active resistance to perceived danger, often expressed through defensiveness or confrontation. *Flight* is an escape response that emerges as distraction or restlessness, making it difficult to remain fully present. *Freeze*, the most evolutionarily primitive response, shows up as passivity, numbness, or disengagement, a state of immobilization in which we're physically present but emotionally withdrawn. Fight, flight, and freeze responses activate specific regions of the brain and nervous system and trigger physical changes in our bodies.[30]

Since stress responses are essential for our survival in moments of urgency, the goal isn't to eliminate them but to cultivate bodily agency. By tuning into the nervous system's cues, we gain the ability to recognize when we're drifting to an unnecessary emergency response state and consciously guide ourselves back to equilibrium. A flexible nervous system is capable of meeting life's demands and returning to balance once the pressure eases.[31]

The Mind in the Body

The body and the mind are inextricably linked and constantly influencing one another in a bidirectional relationship. This connection consists of a vast internal web of interactions involving the nervous system, the heart, and the gut. While it was once believed that the brain issued commands and the body simply obeyed, we now know the conversation flows both ways.[32]

The *nervous system* has two primary branches. The *central nervous system*, located in the brain and spinal cord, is the control room that processes information and sends commands.[33] The *peripheral nervous system* extends outward throughout the whole body like a field team. It delivers sensory information back to the brain and carries out its instructions.[34] Together, the two branches of the nervous system create a loop of communication that keeps us alive and functioning.

The *vagus nerve*, the longest cranial nerve in the peripheral nervous system, functions as a bidirectional communication channel by constantly transmitting signals between the brain and the body.[35] Running from the brainstem through the heart, lungs, and digestive system, the vagus nerve acts as a communication superhighway. Research shows that up to 90% of its fibers transmit signals from the body to the brain.[36] This highlights the profound interdependence between our physical state, our thoughts, and our emotions. Think of that flutter in the stomach before a big decision or the tightness in the chest after hearing bad news as messages using the vagus nerve to travel from our bodies to our minds.[37]

The *limbic system*, a key part of the central nervous system, is often called the emotional brain because it processes emotions and motivation and governs our fight, flight, or freeze response. When danger looms, whether a swerving car or the pressure of an overwhelming deadline, the limbic system floods the body with cortisol and adrenaline. While this response is vital for our survival, it can also trap us in a loop of stress and exhaustion when it becomes chronic.[38]

Beyond pumping blood, the *heart* plays a role in the mind-body connection through a network of approximately 40,000 sensory neurons, sometimes referred to as the *heart brain*.[39] Studies show that emotions like gratitude and compassion can create coherent heart rhythms that positively influence our mental well-being. Conversely, states like anger or anxiety can create erratic cardiac rhythms that intensify stress.[40]

The *gut*, sometimes called the *second brain*, has more than 100 million neurons and a vast community of microbes that influence much more than digestion. The microbes play a crucial role in producing neurotransmitters that affect our emotional well-being.[41] Astonishingly, the gut produces about 90% of the body's serotonin, which plays a major role in mood regulation.[42] Disruptions in this system can ripple into conditions such as irritable bowel syndrome, anxiety, and depression.[43]

For too long, many of us have learned to treat the body as a vessel that carries out the mind's commands, privileging logic and intellect while ignoring the voices of our physical selves. Now, science affirms what ancient practices have long known: the body and mind are partners in our experience of the world.[44]

The Autonomic Nervous System

The peripheral nervous system includes the *autonomic nervous system*, which oversees essential involuntary functions such as digestion, heartbeat, breathing, and plays an important role in managing how we respond to stress. This system operates through two distinct branches: the *sympathetic nervous system*, which mobilizes us for action, and the *parasympathetic nervous system*, which supports rest and recovery.[45] Every day, we move back and forth between these two states as we respond to life's many demands.

When the sympathetic branch is activated, a built-in emergency response sets off a rapid chain of events designed to prepare us for immediate action. Cardiac rhythm accelerates, breathing becomes quick and shallow, and pupils widen to absorb as much information as possible. Blood flows to the muscles, priming us to fight, flee, or freeze.[46] Although this response evolved to help us survive immediate threats such as predators, natural disasters, or even physical attacks from other humans, the same response can often be triggered by modern stressors, like difficult conversations or social media comments. In other words, the ping of a text message can have the same impact as the roar of a tiger.[47]

In contrast, the parasympathetic nervous system, also known as the rest-and-digest system, is responsible for maintaining our bodily functions in balance. Following the sympathetic system's response to a stressful event, the parasympathetic branch acts like a brake, helping the body recover by slowing the heart rate and stopping the release of cortisol and adrenaline.[48] With the parasympathetic system in control, our bodies perceive that it's safe to relax and recharge.

The parasympathetic branch also manages *homeostasis*, the body's process of maintaining balance to support repair and growth. Like a thermostat that adjusts to keep a room comfortable, homeostasis is a continuous process of fine-tuning in response to external changes. If the temperature rises, the cooling system activates. If it drops, the heat turns on. In the same way, the parasympathetic system makes subtle adjustments to keep internal conditions within healthy ranges to ensure the body can function with ease and vitality.[49]

The Window of Tolerance

Psychiatrist Dan Siegel coined the term *window of tolerance* to describe the optimal nervous system state in which we feel calm and capable of meeting life's demands.[50] It's a space of balance, much like a room kept in the right temperature range. Inside this window, we can think clearly and adapt to challenges without feeling overwhelmed.[51]

Outside the limits of our window of tolerance, survival mode manifests in two distinct ways. The first is *hyperarousal*, a state of heightened activation often driven by the sympathetic nervous system, in which we feel anxious or overwhelmed. The second is *hypoarousal*, linked to a parasympathetic freeze response, where the world dulls, and we feel disconnected or shut down.[52]

When chronic stress pushes us beyond our window of tolerance, the nervous system can get caught in survival mode, swinging between hyperarousal and hypoarousal. The racing thoughts, irritability, and heightened alertness of hyperarousal can give way to the numbness and disconnection of hypoarousal.[53] This dysregulation often places immense strain on our physical and mental health.

In contrast, thriving mode keeps us within our window of tolerance, allowing us to approach life's challenges with intention and flexibility. In this state, we can pause, reflect, and choose how to respond rather than react. Research shows that we can enhance our ability to stay in the window of tolerance through mindful bodily practices that support nervous system regulation, such as breathwork and meditation.[54]

In stressful moments now, I hear Robyn's voice gently prompting, "What do you notice?" That simple question has become my anchor and guides me back into balance when my nervous system veers toward hypo- or hyper-arousal. This question is a powerful prompt to awaken bodily awareness, interrupt the survival loop, and reclaim our agency.

Building Resilience Through Flexibility

I used to assume strength meant being in control, but somatic bodywork taught me that real strength comes from flexibility. It comes from being able to face challenges and move smoothly between states of sympathetic arousal and parasympathetic calm.[55] In many ways, the challenges I've faced throughout my lifetime have contributed to my current flexibility.

Biosphere 2 is a sealed ecological experiment in Arizona, where trees grew at an accelerated pace inside a dome shielded from storms

and unyielding winds. Their branches stretched high toward the artificial sky, but as they reached maturity, they collapsed under their own
weight. Initially baffled, scientists eventually understood that, without wind to challenge them, the trees developed shallow roots and
soft trunks. What should have been a sanctuary for growth had instead
created fragility. It turns out that resilience isn't born in comfort but
in resistance. In other words, we grow stronger not by dodging life's
storms but by learning to bend so that when the winds come, we
don't break.[56]

We can build resilience by developing bodily agency, the ability to
notice high-alert responses typical of sympathetic arousal and intentionally change our internal state toward calmness. Neuroscientist
Richie Davidson's research at the University of Wisconsin-Madison
suggests that while most people that while most people experience
similar levels of arousal, what distinguishes resilient individuals is how
quickly they recover.[57] Grounding exercises and movement practices,
such as mindful walking, stretching, Qi Gong, or even dancing, signal
safety to the body and help restore balance. Simple sensory experiences, such as listening to music or soaking in a warm tub, can also
calm the nervous system by supporting a sense of ease.[58]

Relationships can also play a role in regulating the nervous system
after a stress response activation. For instance, *co-regulation*, the process through which two or more nervous systems stabilize one another,
has a profound impact on our ability to regain balance.[59] A warm hug
or the reassuring tone of a trusted friend's voice can signal safety and
help our bodies become calm. Likewise, we can offer the same help to
the people around us.[60]

Our Vehicle to Navigate the World

Unlike the mind, which can spiral in thought and rumination, the
body doesn't overanalyze. Instead, it acts.

The body is the bridge between thought and action, between
intention and reality. Every idea must pass through it to take form in
the world. A musician doesn't create in the mind alone. The body
must lift the instrument and press the keys or strum the strings.
Through motion, the body influences reality.

Throughout history, cultures have revered movement. The Olympic Games, started by the ancient Greeks, embodied *arete*, the pursuit of excellence in mind, body, and spirit.[61] Indigenous traditions use movement as a living archive of history and identity. In Native American *powwows*, dance connects the present with the past.[62] In West African traditions, drumming and dance create a rhythmic dialogue that binds individuals to the collective.[63]

In religious traditions, movement can bridge the physical to the divine. The whirling dervishes of Sufism spin in meditative prayer, seeking transcendence through motion.[64] Zen Buddhist walking meditations transform each step into mindfulness.[65] Hasidic Jewish traditions practice *shuckling*, a rhythmic swaying that harmonizes physical presence with spiritual devotion.[66]

The body also remembers. The way we carry ourselves tells the story of how we have moved through life. Slumped shoulders might speak of burdens long borne, or a spring in our step might signal hope.[67]

In survival mode, movements tend to be tight and reactive, and posture shrinks as the body braces against perceived threats. Thriving mode shows up differently, with the body expanding, gestures becoming fluid, arms opening to embrace, and steps feeling more grounded.[68]

The Life-Changing Power of Habits

Whether conscious or automatic, repeated movement becomes a habit. Just as a muscle strengthens with use, so do our patterns of behavior. These patterns live in the body, determined by repetition, and reinforced over time. Uprooting them requires not only willpower but retraining the nervous system to find safety in new practices.[69]

Habits simplify our lives by reducing the mental load of constant decision-making, thus creating space for creativity and innovation.[70] In ancient Japan, samurai warriors developed disciplined rituals like tea ceremonies and calligraphy, practices designed to cultivate inner mastery and character through repeated physical actions.[71]

If movement is the spark, habits are the fire that keeps burning, sustained and strengthened through repetition. While we may unknowingly train ourselves into habits that keep us stuck, we also have the power to create habits that set us free.

Journalist Charles Duhigg's work shows that habits follow a predictable loop: *cue, routine, reward.* We often think of cues as external, like passing by a bar or seeing a drink on television, each sparking the urge to have a drink. However, cues can also be internal, arising from within the body and noticed through interoception, like a quickened heartbeat or a tightening in the chest signaling that a craving is about to surface. In this way, the body can register cravings before the mind crafts a justification. Lasting change often begins by learning to use interoception to notice and tolerate the bodily signals that trigger our habitual routines.[72]

I invite you to pause for a moment and consider your daily habits: exercise routine, interactions with others, hobbies, watching television, or time spent on social media. Are they lifting you toward the person you want to become or anchoring you to old patterns that no longer serve you?

In survival mode, habits often form unconsciously to protect us against discomfort. Stress-snacking to escape anxious thoughts might provide temporary relief, or endlessly scrolling through social media can offer a distraction from difficult sensations, thoughts, and emotions.[73] These habits may have a purpose in the moment, but they rarely meet deeper needs or support lasting well-being. Thriving mode invites us to approach habits with intention and to transform them from reactive coping mechanisms into deliberate acts of self-fulfillment. By aligning our habits with our values, we craft a life that reflects who we truly want to be.

Since habits are formed through decisions made repeatedly, each choice retains the power to design our lives,[74] as described in this proverb of unknown origin:

Sow a thought, reap an action;

Sow an action, reap a habit;

Sow a habit, reap a character;

Sow a character, reap a destiny.

Nelson Mandela maintained a disciplined routine that reflected his identity as a leader and a freedom fighter during his 27 years in prison. He exercised daily, read voraciously, and wrote letters to allies and adversaries. His habits were acts of resistance and declarations of hope that reminded him and those around him that transformation was possible, even under the most oppressive conditions. Mandela's habits reinforced his commitment to justice and his belief in the power of reconciliation. He emerged from imprisonment as a thriving visionary capable of guiding a fractured nation toward healing.[75]

During a particularly difficult period in my career, I began a simple morning ritual: a few moments of mindful breathing, followed by jotting down three things I was grateful for. Over time, this habit of practicing gratitude became an anchor and helped me navigate uncertainty by bringing often-overlooked gifts into clearer focus.

Even during life's most challenging circumstances, we have the power to influence our destiny, one small action at a time. This perspective can fundamentally transform how we approach change.

Ripples in the Pond

Before we explore how AIR can be used to work with our habits, it's worth considering the powerful ripple effects that even small changes can set in motion. In his *Foundations of Positive Interventions* course at the University of Pennsylvania, James Pawelski expanded on the previously cited proverb, adding two powerful lines that illuminate the connection between personal growth and societal evolution:

> Sow a destiny, reap a culture;
> Sow a culture, reap a society.[76]

Collective habits can change entire societies. Take, for example, the sugar boycotts carried out by abolitionists working to end slavery in the 18th and 19th centuries. At this time, change was not solely in the speeches of reformers. It lived in kitchens and teacups of the British and American families who challenged the institution of slavery by refusing to buy sugar produced by enslaved laborers. Picture a family gathered around a modest kitchen table with a pot of freshly brewed tea, but no sugar. The lack of sweetness can be put into words: "This is how we stand for what's right." Individual families refusing to buy sugar coalesced into a powerful groundswell of public opinion.

This collective momentum contributed to the abolition of the transatlantic slave trade in 1807 and, eventually, the dismantling of slavery itself.[77]

Rosa Parks's refusal to give up her seat in 1955 in Montgomery, Alabama was a pivotal act of resistance in the ongoing Civil Rights Movement. That action was a one-time event, but the Montgomery Bus Boycott that followed was a change in the habits of thousands of individuals willing to disrupt their daily routines. Instead of taking the bus to work, people walked miles and organized carpools. Churches became gathering places where people came together after work to share stories and prayers, turning ordinary evenings into acts of extraordinary solidarity. The boycott continued for 381 days. The commitment required to maintain these habits was extraordinary.[78] In the end, the U.S. Supreme Court ruled that segregation on public buses was unconstitutional, a turning point in the Civil Rights Movement.[79]

As declarations of shared beliefs, collective habits carry the power to sustain movements against even the staunchest opposition. They can define the future and are the connective tissue between our daily choices and the broader changes we aspire to see in the world. Habits can contribute to something much greater than individual success.

When Habits Outlive Their Purpose

Many habits are not consciously chosen. Instead, they're repetitions of behaviors that help us conserve energy and avoid discomfort, especially during times of high stress.[80] Examples include eating high-sugar food, getting lost in an infinite scroll, binge-watching screens, or drinking too much alcohol.

These habits often emerge as quick solutions to immediate problems and may keep us from being overwhelmed in the moment, but their utility is questionable once the crisis passes. Because of their familiarity, they might become default responses even when the challenging context changes. What once helped us endure can also keep us stuck.

Before jumping into habit change, it's important to acknowledge that old habits carried us through difficult times. They reflect our capacity to adapt and protect ourselves under pressure. Moving forward, however, occurs when we intentionally recognize habits that no longer serve us so that we can create space for more adaptive choices. When we view our habits as strategies that once helped us but no longer do, we can release them with compassion instead of shame.

Like many young people, I started drinking alcohol as a teenager to feel closer to others and to be less afraid. Over time, it became part of my identity. I even got a tattoo of a wine bottle on my arm as a not-so-subtle declaration that alcohol and all its cultural associations were an important part of my life.

For years, I told myself that I was a social drinker who drank to have fun. I was productive and disciplined, so it couldn't be a problem. But I was ignoring important signs, like counting down the days from Sundays until Thursdays when I allowed myself to drink again. Alcohol helped me escape the relentless hum of my thoughts, softened my anxiety, soothed the ever-present drive to achieve, and gave me a sense of connection when I felt most alone.

I didn't realize then that I was drinking to regulate my nervous system. It was an off switch. Alcohol provided a temporary escape by easing tension in my body. Only the relief never lasted.

In December 2021, this belief was profoundly challenged when family from overseas had come to visit as COVID-19 restrictions began to lift. After months of isolation, it felt like a reason to celebrate. One night, the drinks flowed with less restraint than normal, and I enjoyed the laughter and connection. But the next morning, my wife told me that seeing me drunk had left one of my kids confused and scared. He had asked her, "Is Papa ever going to be himself again?"

I had never considered that alcohol might make me unrecognizable to the people who mattered most. I felt an immediate and visceral shame, and I decided that something had to change.

Change is rarely simple. Alcohol was a ritual, a permission slip to unwind, a bridge to belonging, and a way to silence the noise in my mind. It had been a companion in joy and a refuge in stress. The hardest part of letting go was facing what alcohol had been doing for me and wondering if I could meet those needs any other way.

My deepening interest in thriving eventually led me to explore the potential of psychedelic-assisted therapy. For my master's research,

I focused on how altered states of consciousness might help people heal psychological wounds. My investigation led me to a practice that, for many, can be a powerful tool for personal change: psychedelic-assisted therapy using psilocybin, a natural compound found in certain mushrooms. Research shows that psilocybin can enhance the brain's flexibility and openness to new perspectives and changes in beliefs.[81]

Before the experience with psilocybin, if someone had told me I would regularly stroll through a cemetery as a mindfulness practice, I would have dismissed it immediately. My fear of death was paralyzing. Now, quiet walks among gravestones have become a source of grounding that reminds me of life's impermanence.

For some people, psychedelics can interrupt automatic loops and allow them to see their experiences and behaviors from a distance. In therapeutic settings, this has led to insights and belief changes that have helped many individuals break free from deeply ingrained habits.[82]

Psilocybin is not for everyone. Psychedelics can bring up intense emotional material, and without the right guidance, the experience can be distressing or even overwhelming. There are risks, particularly for those with a history of certain mental health or physical conditions, and it's essential to approach this kind of work with care and professional support.[83]

The work I did in therapy with psilocybin did much more than help me drink less. It gave me an opportunity to understand why I had held onto alcohol so tightly for so long. It allowed me to distance myself from the situation and step outside the usual justifications. I was able to see alcohol as a personal tool that had served a purpose, but now it had run its course. My relationship with alcohol was fundamentally changed.

Changing Habits Using AIR

I used the AIR approach to interrupt the automatic impulse to drink.

Awareness: I asked myself, "What am I feeling right now? Where do I notice it in my body? Where does the urge to drink come from? Is this about the drink, or is there something else going on?" Reflecting on these questions, I saw alcohol as a kind of medicine because it helped me through difficult times and gave me a way to unwind when nothing else did.

Inquiry: Then I asked myself, "What is drinking really doing for me? What beliefs do I hold about alcohol and my ability to relax? What other effects is it having on my life?" I got curious about other ways to soothe the drive to achieve and allow myself to stay within my window of tolerance without numbing.

Reframing: After I explored the need that alcohol was meeting for me, I was able to ask, "If alcohol is no longer the medicine I need, what could take its place?" I told myself, "I've found other ways to find peace, to connect, to feel at ease in my own skin, including deep breathing, going for long walks, talking with friends, or simply sitting with the discomfort. I don't need alcohol to unwind anymore."

I replaced alcohol with sparkling water in a wine glass, removed triggers like the bottle positioned just-so on the sideboard, and avoided the liquor aisle when shopping. Over time, these small choices retrained my nervous system so that I could find ease without alcohol. What once felt essential gradually became optional.

As for the tattoo of the wine bottle, I'm now in the slow, painful process of removing it. Change often requires much more than just breaking an old habit. It requires rewriting the story we tell ourselves about who we are.

Physician and author Gabor Maté suggests that *addiction* often takes root in the habits we crave, that are hard to let go of, that offer temporary relief or pleasure, and that carry long-term negative consequences.[84] While addiction was once seen as a personal failing, research now reveals that it emerges from the interplay of neurobiology, psychology, physiology, environment, and much more. According to this perspective, many addictive behaviors develop as coping mechanisms to ease stress.[85] Recognizing this dynamic invites a more compassionate approach to breaking these patterns, like asking ourselves, "What is this habit doing for me?"

Reducing my drinking has been a long road with ups and downs, but the rewards are incredibly meaningful. I feel closer to my sons and more present in my own life. I'm grounded in my relationships and more attuned with my clients. Today, drinking alcohol feels like a personal choice rather than an unconscious habit. The clarity and agency I've gained by working on this habit feels like a pro-found victory.

The Tension Between Acceptance and Change

Growth requires holding the paradox of two essential forces: *acceptance* and *change*. Using this lens, psychologist Marsha Linehan, founder of Dialectical Behavior Therapy, teaches that transformation begins when we can fully accept ourselves as we are while also committing to change.[86]

While acceptance means honoring the habits that have carried us this far, seeing them not as mistakes but as signs of our resourceful-ness and adaptability, change invites us to create something new.[87] Without acceptance, the desire for change can become self-punishment. Without change, acceptance can settle into compla-cency. Moving forward begins with recognizing where we are and finding the courage to step beyond it.

"This habit helped me survive, and now I'm ready to let it go" are words that encourage self-compassion instead of self-criticism. Instead of berating ourselves for having the wrong habits, we can recognize that every habit has a purpose. And once that purpose is acknowl-edged, change becomes far more possible.

The relationship between acceptance and change is deeply embod-ied. This means that our nervous system holds onto what has kept us safe, even when those patterns no longer serve us. Letting go of an ingrained habit requires learning to listen to the messages our bodies have been trying to tell us all along.

In my work with Robyn, I learned that what my body had been asking for was not discipline or stricter rules but permission to feel all my emotions. In one of my earliest sessions with her, I told her, "I'm not an angry person," believing it to be true.

She didn't argue. She just invited me to notice.

A few months later, I sat across from her again and said, "I was wrong."

She smiled.

"I think anger has been keeping me alive," I said, recognizing the breakthrough as the words left my mouth.

I saw that my anger had served me as a superpower to walk into difficult situations and hold my ground. It gave me the fire to challenge power and do very hard things. Anger was energizing, and the possibility of letting it go felt like a loss.

Robyn just nodded. "Good. Now you can decide what you want to do with it."

That was the real work: not just noticing patterns but choosing how to engage with them. Not just breaking habits but learning to handle what had been waiting to be acknowledged.

Speaker and writer James Clear argues that small, incremental changes are far more effective than drastic cold-turkey approaches because they compound over time and lead to deeper transformation.[88] When change is gradual, success depends less on willpower and more on redesigning the environment and routines that support behavior. First, we understand the existing system (acceptance), and then we modify it in small but meaningful ways (change).

Clear also suggests that the most enduring habit changes are those rooted in identity. That is, rather than setting a goal like "I want to drink less" or "I want to work out more," he recommends starting with "I'm the kind of person who . . . drinks less" or "I'm the kind of person who . . . works out every day." This subtle shift turns habit change from something we do into something we embody.[89]

Behavior change is often easier when our environment makes good choices easier and bad choices harder. To drink less, keeping alcohol out of the house removes the need to make daily decisions, and laying out workout clothes the night before makes exercise more likely.

Individual habits may seem small, but their cumulative impact is profound. One tiny change, like practicing gratitude each morning, altered my entire outlook. This activity reorganized the neural pathways that govern how I interpret the world, rewiring my brain's default approach from scanning for threats into noticing abundance.

The same was true in my somatic work with Robyn, where change didn't come through grand gestures but through small moments of noticing. Instead of telling me what to do or how to change, she asked simple questions at the right moments. The work I did with her helped me feel safer in my body and question the invisible rules that restricted who I allowed myself to be.

That is the power of sitting across from someone who listens so deeply that you begin to hear yourself. Robyn didn't try to fix or direct me; she simply held up a mirror until I could finally see what had been there all along.

Using AIR to Explore Sensations and Actions

Sensations

You can use the AIR approach to explore how your relationship with your body might be keeping you in survival mode.

Awareness: Noticing the Sensations in My Body

- *Do I tend to ignore the sensations in my body throughout the day?*
- *When I feel strong emotions, do I notice how they manifest in my body?*
- *Are there recurring areas of tension, pain, warmth, tingling, or numbness in my body?*

Inquiry: Exploring the Meaning of My Sensations

- *How do the sensations in my body change depending on my environment, stress levels, or emotional state?*
- *What happens when I pause and focus on a sensation instead of pushing it away?*
- *If this sensation had a message for me, what might it be trying to communicate?*

Reframing: Engaging with Sensations as a Source of Wisdom

- *How can I respond to sensations with curiosity instead of resistance?*
- *What might become possible if I trusted my body's sensations as sources of insight rather than inconvenience?*
- *What's one small practice that could help me reconnect with the sensations in my body today?*

Actions

AIR can also help you understand how your patterns of action and habits might be keeping you in survival mode.

Awareness: Recognizing My Patterns of Action

- *Do my daily actions reflect my deepest values?*
- *Are there automatic behaviors I turn to for comfort, even when they don't truly serve me?*
- *When faced with stress or uncertainty, what are my usual reactions?*

Inquiry: Questioning the Purpose of My Actions

- *What habits have helped me in the past but may no longer align with who I want to become?*
- *What new behaviors can replace my least adaptive habits?*
- *If someone observed my daily actions, what would they assume I prioritize in life?*

Reframing: Aligning My Actions with Growth

- *What small shift could I make today to bring more alignment between my actions and my values?*
- *What new patterns can I reinforce by showing up differently?*
- *How might I experiment with habits that foster thriving?*

6

Transcendence
The Courage to Go Beyond

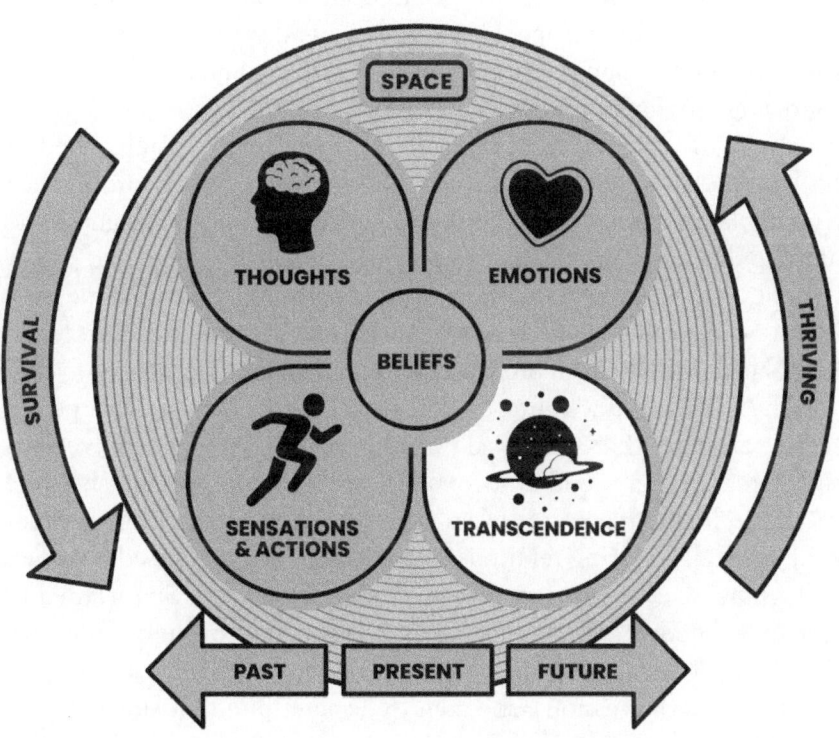

EVENTUALLY, THE PATH inward points us outward. After all the inner work, after the reckoning with beliefs, thoughts, emotions, sensations, and actions, something larger calls us. We begin to feel the pull to connect to something beyond ourselves, something we may not fully grasp with our minds but somehow sense is there.

Transcendence invites us to see our growth as an act of service and a way to contribute meaningfully to the lives we touch and beyond. To understand this, we must step back and see ourselves from a more expansive perspective. In this chapter, we'll pivot from "me" to "we."

How Can I Turn My Pain into Purpose? Meet Maria

Maria reached out for coaching because she found herself trapped in a pattern she couldn't escape. Deadlines for her dissertation submissions kept slipping through her fingers, and each missed milestone added to a growing sense of helplessness.

As a PhD student, her life revolved around her research. She was brilliant and driven, but our coaching conversations often circled back to complaints about supervisors who criticized her, colleagues who didn't pull their weight, friends who never understood her, and a family that, despite caring deeply, kept asking why she wasn't "done yet." Maria saw herself as a victim of circumstances beyond her control, and her relationships had suffered as collateral damage.

She carried the weight of her frustrations everywhere as a persistent resentment that shadowed even her happiest moments. Even sitting across from a friend at a coffee shop, she felt as though she were observing life from behind a glass wall. Her mind was constantly occupied, mentally drafting rebuttals to colleagues who dismissed her ideas and replaying conversations in which she felt unseen. She wanted to feel understood, but at the same time, she had unknowingly built walls that kept people at what she believed to be a safe distance.

In one of our sessions, she admitted something that startled even her. "I don't think I know how to let people in," she said faintly. "It's easier to point out what they've done wrong than to admit I might be the one that needs to change."

Not too long after that, a classmate invited her to volunteer at a community shelter, and though Maria initially dismissed the idea, she found herself signing up. That morning, she nearly canceled, feeling overwhelmed by one more thing on her to-do list, but she went anyway.

Maria spent the day in the shelter's kitchen, preparing meals along-side a group of strangers. At first, the chaos of pots clanging and voices shouting orders felt like too much. But gradually, she fell into the rhythm of plating. Later, as she handed out meals, she locked eyes with an elderly woman who whispered, "Thank you, sweetheart," her smile tender and weary. In that moment, Maria felt a connection she hadn't experienced in years. "For the first time," she told me later, "I felt like I was part of something much bigger."

In that brief exchange, something shifted. The woman's gratitude was so simple, so authentic, that it cut through Maria's mental noise. The need to be validated, which had dominated so much of her thinking, suddenly felt secondary to the power of simply being present for someone else.

That day didn't end Maria's struggles, but it transformed something fundamental. She reframed her challenges as invitations to contribute to the world. Instead of focusing solely on what she needed to accomplish, she wondered, "How can I turn this pain into purpose?" With that perspective, she found herself engaging with life's hardships in ways that allowed her to rise above survival mode and step into thriving.

Transcendence, a Connection to Vastness

Maria was experiencing transcendence, a word that comes from the Latin *transcendere*, meaning "to climb beyond" or "to rise above." Transcendence is the ability to expand our perception beyond the self and to recognize that we're part of something far greater.[1]

In spiritual traditions, transcendence is often associated with the divine as it comes in moments of deep connection that lift us beyond our individual concerns into something sacred. It's the thread that runs through acts of profound love, and it's the same drive that led our ancestors to look up at the stars and wonder.[2]

Zooming out to see the big picture, our sun is just one among an estimated 100–400 billion stars in the Milky Way galaxy. Widening the lens even more, the Milky Way is just one of up to 2 trillion galaxies in the observable universe, each containing billions of stars and countless planets. Somewhere, right this minute, galaxies are colliding, stars are igniting, black holes are pulling entire worlds into their mysterious depths, and new planets are forming from clouds of dust and gas.[3] Against this backdrop, the concerns that so often consume us, like a missed deadline or a disappointing meeting, shrink to insignificance.

Paradoxically, this perspective doesn't diminish us. In *Pale Blue Dot*, a book by the famous astronomer Carl Sagan inspired by a photograph of our planet taken by the Voyager 1 spacecraft from 6 billion kilometers away, the author broadens our perspective:[4]

> *"Look again at that dot. That's here. That's home. That's us. On it everyone you love, everyone you know, everyone you ever heard of, every human being who ever was, lived out their lives. The aggregate of our joy and suffering, thousands of confident religions, ideologies, and economic doctrines, every hunter and forager, every hero and coward, every creator and destroyer of civilization, ever king and peasant, every young couple in love, every mother and father, hopeful child, inventor and explorer, every teacher of morals, every corrupt politician, every 'superstar,' every 'supreme leader,' every saint and sinner in the history of our species lived there—on a mote of dust suspended in a sunbeam."*

Our perceived smallness isn't a limitation but a testament to the wonder of being. To put it simply, the sheer improbability of our lives makes our existence extraordinary. In recognizing the power of our journey through life, we step beyond the fleeting concerns of the moment into something far greater. To survive, to thrive, to think, to feel, and to love are not mundane acts. They're cosmic privileges.

Experiencing Transcendence

Our ancestors painted cave walls with handprints, pictures of animals, humans, celestial patterns, and abstract symbols. It's possible that this ancient artistic expression was an early attempt to communicate with forces beyond their physical world. Some people believe they were stories meant to be passed down, a way of reaching across generations. Others suggest they were efforts to connect with the spiritual realm, or to honor the mysteries of life and death.

As humanity evolved, this yearning for transcendence became more sophisticated. The pyramids of Egypt are monumental expressions of humanity's desire to touch the divine. Thousands of miles away, the builders of Cambodia's Angkor Wat mirrored the cosmos in stone to bring together earthly and celestial realms.[5] Light streaming through stained glass in Europe's cathedrals reminded worshipers of the infinite divine.

This yearning for the infinite plays out in everyday life. A teacher sparking curiosity in a reluctant student or a plumber cleaning out a kitchen's blocked pipes can also be expressions of a purpose greater than the self. Transcendence invites us to reach beyond our own needs to build a world that will endure long after we're gone.

Across cultures and throughout history, people have reached for the ineffable in countless ways. Some describe brief glimpses into a greater reality through moments of awe, like standing before a mountain range or hearing music that stirs something. Psychologist Dacher Keltner at the University of California, Berkeley, describes *awe* as an emotion that shifts our focus outward and makes us feel connected to something vast beyond ourselves. Studies suggest that awe can improve well-being and even reduce inflammation in the body.[6]

Maria's day at the shelter was a brief but meaningful encounter with awe. The woman's smile and the gratitude in her voice touched something in Maria. "It was the first time in a long time I wasn't thinking about myself," she told me. The moment prompted her to reconsider how she was moving through the world and why.

Transcendence also finds us in other ways. While some speak of *synchronicity* as unexpected alignments that feel too meaningful to ignore,[7] others experience transcendence as sudden moments of clarity or wisdom that arrive from somewhere beyond the self.[8] There are also people who sense an unseen presence that feels real, even if it can't be explained. Mystics from various cultures have described moments when the boundaries between the self and the universe appear to dissolve, giving way to a profound sense of unity and peace.[9]

Although transcendental experiences may unfold spontaneously, they're also accessible through intentional practices like meditation,[10] breathwork,[11] or the guided use of psychedelics,[12] which can open a different kind of doorway into altered states of consciousness.

Even stories of sensing a loved one after death or awakening from a near-death experience suggest that the longing to connect with something more continues beyond loss.[13]

I've brushed against that mystery many times, but one moment stands out. When I turned 27, the lower back and sciatic pain from an old rugby injury became almost unbearable. I went to see a doctor, and three weeks later, I found myself face down in the operating room of a hospital in Caracas.

While I was under anesthesia, something went wrong, and my lungs collapsed. My mother and my wife, who had been sitting in the waiting room, were summoned into the hospital boardroom, where they found themselves sitting across from a row of surgeons dressed in pale green gowns and suited lawyers. They were told I was unresponsive in the ICU. No one could say whether I would wake up or if my brain had been damaged.

I don't remember anything after the anesthetist's countdown. The next thing I heard was my mother's voice cutting through the darkness. "Jona," she said in a resolute tone, "Adri and I are here, waiting for you as soon as you're ready to wake up." I immediately began coughing and tried to pull the breathing tube from my throat. Alarms blared, and nurses rushed in. I had no idea where I was.

That night, the sterile silence of the hospital was anything but peaceful. Machines hummed and the hallways were filled with hushed voices. Sometime after midnight, I asked one of the nurses if she could help me to the bathroom. As we made our way slowly through the ICU, she walked me past a long row of cubicles where I saw middle-aged men lying unconscious in hospital beds. "You see them?" she said, pointing at the patients. "Most of them suffered heart attacks. They spent the first half of their lives chasing success. Now they'll spend the second half trying to buy their health back."

Coming that close to the edge of life revealed to me that there's far more to this existence than being successful, even if it took 20 years for that lesson to sink in.

Suffering and Groundlessness

Transcendence can help us face whatever we're experiencing, whether we're celebrating or suffering.

During his time in Nazi concentration camps, Viktor Frankl noticed that survival was not guaranteed by toughness alone. He saw that some of the physically fittest didn't make it, while others with less physical strength found ways to endure. Frankl believed the difference lay in meaning. "Man is not destroyed by suffering," he wrote. "He is destroyed by suffering without meaning."[14]

The suffering that breaks us in survival mode can become a source of meaning in thriving. Many religious and spiritual traditions emphasize that suffering, while painful, can also be transformative. In Buddhism, suffering teaches us where we cling too tightly and where we might grow. Suffering can also lead people to become more compassionate and attuned to the pain of others.[15]

Reframing suffering under the lens of transcendence invites us to move from asking, "Why is this happening to me?" to "What is this doing for me?" This reframing certainly doesn't erase pain, but it can transform it into something we can bear.

According to psychologist Michael Steger at Colorado State University, people who find meaning in their struggles tend to experience greater resilience and emotional well-being. Transcendence integrates even our most difficult moments into meaningful stories that help us move forward.[16]

Similarly, philosopher Albert Camus used the Greek myth of Sisyphus to explain transcendence. Sisyphus was condemned by the gods to roll a boulder uphill repeatedly, only to have it tumble back down each time. Camus argues that transcendence happens when we embrace the challenge and find meaning in our difficulties and struggles, just as Sisyphus might have.[17]

Buddhist teacher Pema Chodron popularized the term *groundlessness* for the unsettling and liberating state in which familiar certainties slip away, leaving us to face the raw nature of existence. Groundlessness is the moment after a job loss when identity and purpose suddenly feel uncertain. It's the end of a relationship that once seemed unshakable. It's sitting with grief and realizing that the world keeps moving forward even while we're frozen in loss. It's the panic of looking in the mirror and questioning whether the path you're on truly points in the direction you want to go.[18]

Groundlessness also invites us to trust in what we can't fully explain and to allow balance to emerge in its own time. Clarity comes not by force but by staying open until understanding emerges, even when it feels uncertain or incomplete.[19]

Maria talked a lot about disconnection and the sense that no one around her truly understood her, and as we slowed down together, something began to surface. "It's not just that things are hard," she said. "It's that I've been holding everything together so I don't have to feel how lost I actually am." For the first time, she faced the uncertainty she had been trying to outrun, and it was uncomfortable.

In the openness of groundlessness, existential questions arise:

Who am I?

What determines my life? Is it my decisions or unseen forces that guide me?

What does it mean to live a good life?

What connects me to something greater than myself?

What will remain of me when I'm gone?

Humanity has wrestled with questions like these for thousands of years, finding them both a burden and a gift. These inquiries pull us out of our comfort zone and into the unknown. They compel us to look beyond the immediate. As we ask, we transcend.

The Courage to Transcend

Fifteen-year-old Malala Yousafzai was targeted by the Taliban because she advocated for educating girls in her native Pakistan. Recovering from being shot and left for dead, Malala could have chosen a path of self-preservation, but instead she chose to dedicate Instead, she chose to dedicate herself to a cause far greater than her own survival.

Reflecting on her experience, Malala said, "The terrorists thought they would change my aims and stop my ambitions. But nothing changed in my life except this: weakness, fear, and hopelessness died."[20]

Malala's recovery was an inspiring triumph. She used her suffering as a rallying cry for millions of girls worldwide who are denied the right to learn. By creating the Malala Fund, she amplified their voice and fought to ensure that education is a universal right.

Transcendence doesn't just occur in monumental moments, but also in the daily acts of care and compassion. Mother Teresa saw her work with the poor and dying in Kolkata as a spiritual calling. James Harrison, the Australian called the Man with the Golden Arm, donated blood every few weeks for 60 years. By some calculations, his small acts saved more than two million lives.

My wife Adriana's aunt, Lizzie Lee, lost her son, Officer Diego Moreno, in the line of duty. Diego was the type of person who lifted others up, a kind and devoted father, son, brother, husband, friend, and public servant who believed in selfless acts, such as volunteering to help those in need. In the wake of Diego's death, Lizzie found herself drawn to the Pan Am Flight 217 tragedy in which my family lost my maternal grandmother. The official reports suggested that city lights on the horizon may have disoriented the pilots and caused a miscalculated descent, but the exact cause of the crash was never fully determined. Aunt Lizzie decided to piece together the fragments of this story.

Her investigation and writing started as a way to deal with her own loss but became a tribute to those who perished in the accident and the loved ones they left behind. She gave voice to a grief that had never been fully articulated. On December 12, 2018, she and my mother hosted a reunion for the bereaved families on the 50th anniversary of the crash. Aunt Lizzie's book *The Lost Lives of the Clipper Malay* transformed her pain into healing for dozens of others.

As these stories illustrate, transcendence often emerges in adversity. When life presents us with challenges, we can either retreat into survival mode or rise above them by stepping into thriving. This change doesn't erase suffering, but it allows us to find meaning within it. A single act of kindness can inspire a ripple of generosity, and a moment of courage can ignite a movement. The more we give of ourselves, the more expansive our lives become.

Maria wouldn't have called her shift spiritual. For most of our work together, she met anything that sounded abstract with a skeptical smile or an eye roll. Then, one afternoon, she told me she had been slicing bread in the shelter's kitchen when something inside her stilled. "I felt . . . not alone," she said. "Like I was part of something bigger that I didn't really have to understand." Instead of trying to explain it, as she usually would, she just let the experience be what it was. A simple gesture, repeated without fanfare, revealed that even small offerings could open the door to connection.

Finding Transcendence

I was born into a secular Jewish home. My grandparents escaped the Holocaust and the pogroms of Lithuania, so by the time they rebuilt their lives in Venezuela, practicing Judaism was secondary to survival.

When I was 12 and preparing for my bar mitzvah, I made my first deep spiritual connection to my religion. My teacher was a kind man who carried the weight of Jewish wisdom with humility. He taught me about philosophy and traditions that were never fully explained at home or school.

That year, I began walking to synagogue alone on Friday nights to welcome the Shabbat, captivated by the melodies of its prayers. At the time, I even considered joining a yeshiva, a school dedicated to the study of Jewish texts and traditions. As I got older, my connection to Judaism slowly faded, but I still couldn't bring myself to skip the Yom Kippur fast, and certain holidays felt sacred. Even when I drifted from religion, my Jewish identity stayed in the background.

Since my wife Adriana was born into a Catholic family, we were forced to confront the struggles of loving across a religious boundary. My father didn't approve, and the conflict between us became so sharp that we stopped speaking entirely. When he died, the silence between us hadn't been broken. Still, I wish he could see the life Adriana and I have built together. I wish he could meet his two grandsons, one of whom we named Charles, after him.

After my father's passing, I found myself returning to synagogue to recite kaddish, the mourning prayer to honor the departed. As I sat at temple for what seemed like endless days, I was shocked to see the suffering and fear in the Old Testament stories. I felt that if I kept pushing forward, I might never set foot in a synagogue again. After a few months, I stopped going.

In a way I hadn't expected, Adriana led me back to my roots. Wanting to understand my background more deeply, she chose to embrace Jewish traditions. In doing so, I felt that I converted to

Judaism with her. That shared journey brought me closer to my heritage than I had ever been before.

Then came October 7, 2023, a terrorist attack that served as a stark reminder of the long history of violent persecution faced by Jewish people. These events stirred profound pain from the darkest chapters of our history, reopening wounds from the Holocaust, when six million Jews were systematically murdered and refugees were turned away with no place to go. War and violence have scarred many communities across the world, and perhaps shared healing is the clearest path toward a future where thriving together becomes possible.

Amid that backdrop of fear, I helped our son Charles prepare for his bar mitzvah ceremony. In the process, I found myself reconnecting with Judaism once again, this time not out of obligation to meet social expectations, but as a human searching for something transcendental.

Today, my connection with Judaism feels intentional. Through my work with clients, I prioritize Tikkun Olam, the Jewish principle of repairing the world, a call to action where every act of compassion contributes to collective healing. I believe that transcendence is found in how we show up for others.

Transcendence and Faith

Faith is a companion to transcendence. It amplifies its reach by giving us the courage to move forward even when the outcome remains uncertain. Faith helps us transform lofty ideals into lived reality and gives us the audacity to act.

In survival mode, faith becomes transactional, like a shield against unpredictability. A person navigating a painful breakup might pray for reconciliation. Someone awaiting medical test results may bargain with the universe, making promises to change if the outcome is favorable.

In contrast, faith in thriving mode becomes a willingness to act despite uncertainty. It serves as a way to surrender control because we believe something larger is at work. This is the faith that fueled explorers setting sail into the unknown. It's the faith of scientists like Marie Curie, who spent years studying radiation despite skepticism and uncertainty.[21]

Imagine standing by the edge of a pool, watching a swimming instructor show others how to float. Based on what you see, you might believe that the water will hold you. *Belief* is the understanding that floating is possible. *Faith* is stepping into the pool yourself and trusting the water to support you.

Faith became deeply personal for me when Adriana was diagnosed with MS. It all began at a conference in Denver, where she mentioned problems with her vision. At first, we brushed it off, blaming the altitude or the stress. But by the time we returned to Toronto, her symptoms had worsened, and we rushed to the emergency room. Even as we tried to stay calm for each other, there was panic. When the appointment with the neuro-ophthalmologist finally came a couple of days later, we found ourselves sitting in a tiny office inside a very large hospital. The room smelled faintly of antiseptic, and the fluorescent lights buzzed overhead. As Adriana sat in the ophthalmologist's chair, the doctor entered briskly and delivered the news without any warning: "You have multiple sclerosis."

It felt like the air had been sucked out of the room. My mind spiraled into chaos as Adriana sat in shock. I had heard of MS before, but I didn't know what it really meant. Was she going to die? Was she going to lose her ability to care for herself? How fast would this progress?

Multiple sclerosis is a chronic illness in which the immune system mistakenly attacks the myelin sheath that protects nerves, making it harder for the brain and body to communicate. It can cause exhaustion, numbness, trouble walking, and problems with speech, balance, or vision.[22]

Adriana's doctors prescribed a biologic, a new class of medication that some experts hail as a miracle cure. Unlike traditional treatments that merely slowed the disease, this one had the potential to halt its progression entirely. But it was still new and had only been approved by Health Canada in 2021, so we had no way of knowing if it would work for her. The uncertainty of waiting for the scan results after treatment was almost unbearable.

To live with this new reality, we've leaned into faith. Every day, we choose to trust that even when the path isn't clear, there's meaning in this journey. Adriana has tapped into her strength and courage, and she has shown a remarkable agency to confront the challenges with hope and optimism.

Adriana's diagnosis taught me that compassion isn't always about finding solutions. Sometimes, it's about staying present when answers don't come. It transformed how I meet my clients in their deepest struggles and how I sit with the things that may feel too heavy to say out loud, like loss, shame, fear, and regret. I've learned that healing begins when suffering is witnessed, not explained away.

As of today, Adriana's treatment is working successfully, and yet, there's an undercurrent of uncertainty, a constant awareness that the stability we hold onto isn't guaranteed. Above all, this experience strengthened our faith by reminding us not to postpone joy.

Faith reveals itself in everyday activities. I sit down to write this book with faith that my words can reach and uplift readers like you. A nurse starts a long shift with trust that she will provide comfort and healing to her patients. An artist picks up a brush with faith that the result can touch someone's soul. Parents send their children into the world, trusting that they have equipped them with the tools to thrive.

Faith means trusting the process of life. The weather changes without warning, relationships evolve in unexpected ways, politicians come and go, and our own bodies surprise us. Faith steps in where control fails, so we can embrace the unexpected.

Faith in others is an act of vulnerability that leads us to recognize that imperfect people are also capable of extraordinary transformations. Forgiveness doesn't necessarily erase hurt or guarantee reconciliation, but it leaves room to grow from mistakes and for relationships to be renewed.

Faith helps us balance the dualities of life: certainty and doubt, suffering and joy, love and loss, fear and hope, control and surrender, individuality and interconnectedness. Faith can mean honoring the mystery of existence while remaining grounded in reason.

Spirituality and Religion

While faith invites us to trust in the unseen, spirituality invites us to experience it. Put differently, if faith is the bridge between the known and the unknown, spirituality is the journey across it. As we move from faith to spirituality, we transition from trusting the mysteries of existence to embracing them.

For some, spirituality and religion are inseparable because religion structured paths to spirituality through rituals and doctrines. For others, spirituality and religion feel worlds apart. Perhaps they were raised in religious traditions that provided guidance and community but later found themselves disillusioned by rigid dogma or institutional failures. Some may have never belonged to a religious community and still feel a deep yearning for spirituality. Others, including secular thinkers and atheists, find spirituality in moments of awe or connection.

This divide between religion and spirituality is often framed as a choice between doctrine and personal exploration. But the reality is much more complex. Religion, at its best, offers a sense of belonging and a shared moral compass, while spirituality provides a direct, personal relationship with the sacred. Religion can provide rituals that anchor us in community, while spirituality allows for a more fluid experience of the divine.[23]

Neuroscientific research suggests that religious and spiritual experiences activate similar brain regions associated with awe and moral reasoning. These experiences transcend any single tradition, and they're part of what makes us human.[24]

Rather than opposing forces, religion and spirituality can be seen as complementary. Some find comfort in both, while others resonate more with one than the other. What matters isn't the label but the transcendent experience of moving beyond the self and into something greater, like being attuned to the beauty and complexity of existence.

Picture farmers in centuries past stepping into small country temples, where the murmur of prayers fills the space. As they listen, the weight of the plow and the uncertainty of harvests are lifted. They're no longer solitary figures battling the elements. They feel connected to their community, their cultural heritage, their ancestors, and the divine. This experience anchors them in a story that stretches across generations and into eternity.

Feeling attuned to religion or spirituality can be difficult in the midst of so much digital noise. Never before have we had so many tools to connect, from text messages to video calls. Except for many of us, these technologies fail to fulfill our longing for a meaningful existence and the social media promise of bringing people together has instead led us to comparing our unfiltered realities to the curated highlights of others, creating a deep sense of inadequacy and invisibility for many.[25]

Shared spirituality can bring us together in community experiences that enrich our lives and combat the silent epidemic of loneliness. U.S. Surgeon General Dr. Vivek Murthy warned in 2023 that approximately half of American adults are lonely. Research links prolonged loneliness to increased risks of heart disease, depression, and even premature death. Given that the health risks of loneliness are comparable to smoking 15 cigarettes a day, spirituality can offer a powerful way to foster connection among people.[26] When we see ourselves as part of a community, we step out of isolation and into belonging.

In Western cultures, the pull toward self-reliance and hyper-individualism runs deep. My mother captured it bluntly: "You're born alone, and you die alone." She meant it as a lesson in resilience and a reminder that life's challenges were mine to face on my own. I carried that belief like armor until I came to see that we're ushered into this world through connection, that connection can sustain us through every stage of life, and that if we're very lucky, we're held by connection as we leave it, too. Isolation may feel like strength, but growth is found in relationship with others.

Connecting with Something Greater Using AIR

In our work together, Maria explored what might change if she moved her attention from the tunnel vision trap of her daily tasks toward meaning.

Awareness: One afternoon, I asked her, "Have you ever thought about how your research might touch others' lives beyond the lab?" She paused. "Not really. I guess I've always seen it as my job . . . important, but kind of removed from the real world."

We illuminated how her methodical work created ripple effects far beyond what she could see. As she reflected, she recognized that the sense of meaning she felt volunteering at the soup kitchen was also available in her research, and that her contributions helped build the foundation for discoveries that could ease suffering and improve lives. With that realization, the feeling of being trapped in a narrow pattern gave way to a broader sense of purpose.

Inquiry: I then asked, "How does your work connect with the rest of your team's efforts?" Maria admitted she hadn't thought much about that either. "Honestly, I usually just focus on my part. I don't always see how it fits into the bigger picture."

Together, we examined how her work contributed to a shared meaning. As she began asking questions and engaging in conversations with colleagues she had previously avoided, she noticed a growing sense of belonging.

Reframing: With that new lens, I asked, "How could you make someone else's work easier or support your team beyond your role?"

Maria let out a sigh and raised an eyebrow. "As if I don't have enough to do already," she said, half-joking but clearly frustrated. The question touched a nerve. Then she continued, "I guess I could help one of the newer researchers," she added, her voice softening. "I remember how overwhelming it felt when I first joined."

As Maria offered guidance and support, her experience at the lab began to transform, and while the pressure of her workload remained, and on most days she still felt stretched thin, a new way of working that included others began to emerge. Her frustration and resentment gradually eased when she realized she didn't have to carry everything alone, and more supportive relationships began to grow.

Separateness Is an Illusion

Many of us believe that our worth is measured by what we produce, achieve, acquire, and accumulate. This relentless focus on personal success leaves us stranded on islands of self-sufficiency, hesitant to ask for help, and wary of investing in relationships that don't offer immediate returns. As a result, we may find ourselves surrounded by contacts but lacking true companionship.

Meaningful connections among people rarely thrive under survival mode conditions, like scarcity, which can turn relationships into another resource to be optimized. This dynamic was evident in Maria's research lab, where limited promotions and a lack of job security led colleagues to see each other primarily as competitors instead of collaborators. This scarcity-driven way of seeing the world is both emotionally costly and also fundamentally incomplete.

No organism exists in isolation. Bees depend on flowers for sustenance and pollinate them in return.[27] Trees share nutrients and information through vast underground fungal networks that form cooperative communities beneath the forest floor.[28] Entire ecosystems thrive through mutual dependence, where each organism contributes to and relies on the larger whole.[29]

Even our own bodies are not separate from the bigger picture. With every breath, microorganisms from the air enter our respiratory system. Every meal introduces new microbes into our digestive tract, and we interchange microbes with every surface we touch.[30] Far from being an isolated system, the human body is a *microbiome* hosting trillions of living organisms, including fungi, viruses, and bacteria.[31]

Recent estimates suggest that the human body contains approximately 38 trillion bacterial cells, closely matching the number of human cells.[32] Simply put, we each have a community of microorganisms as essential as the cells in our bodies, and these microscopic companions play an essential role in our physical and mental health.[33]

This constant exchange between body and world dissolves the idea that we exist in isolation. The air filling your lungs has passed through forests, animals, and generations of people. The water you drink has moved through oceans, rivers, clouds, and countless living bodies. The carbon in your cells was born in ancient stars and scattered across the cosmos when those stars died. This carbon has lived in countless forms long before becoming part of you. As astrophysicist Neil deGrasse Tyson suggests, we're literally stardust.[34]

At a cellular level, our bodies are in constant renewal. The lining of our intestines, for example, regenerates every five days,[35] red blood cells are replaced every 120 days,[36] and bone tissue, once thought to be unchanging, renews itself every 10 years.[37] The body exists in a dynamic state of flux, continuously shedding the old and rebuilding the new. We're not the same physical selves we were a few years ago.[38]

Teachings from spiritual traditions across the world invite us to step beyond illusions of separateness to connect with a deeper existence. In Hinduism, the concept of *Brahman* describes an ultimate reality where all things are one. Buddhism speaks of *interbeing*, the idea that all phenomena depend on one another and are deeply connected.[39] Indigenous traditions emphasize the seamless relationship between humans, nature, and the cosmos. The Lakota concept of *Mitákuye Oyás'iŋ*, or All My Relations, teaches that all living beings, from the smallest insect to the sky, are interconnected and that harmony comes from honoring these relationships.[40] Christianity and Judaism teach us to love our neighbor as ourselves, and Islam describes the *Ummah* as a global community united by faith and mutual care.[41]

Challenging the belief of separateness became an important part of Maria's coaching journey. When we first started working together, she struggled to let people in and often focused on what others did wrong. As she opened herself to connection and noticed the impact of her research, her support for colleagues, and her volunteering, a sense of transcendence slowly began to permeate her life. She reframed it as the realization that by changing herself, she also changed the world around her.

In one of our conversations, a calling toward spirituality stirred within her. "Maybe there's more to all this than I thought," she said once. It was a small moment, but it opened her to a kind of meaning that couldn't be measured or tested in a lab.

Maria's experience points to a powerful idea: spirituality offers a way out of isolation and into a deeper awareness of connection. Our lives are entangled with the world around us, and we don't have to stand apart.

Ripples in the Pond

Although every person who has ever lived has known loss and grief, people have different ways of reacting to their suffering. In survival mode, suffering can isolate us and make us feel as if we're alone in our pain and cut off from others. Paradoxically, the more we resist connection and withdraw, the heavier our own suffering becomes. This withdrawal narrows our perspective and limits our ability to find comfort or healing through meaningful relationships.

In thriving mode, suffering dismantles the illusion of separateness and tells us that we belong to one another. It connects us to our ancestors, our peers, and the people who will follow after us. We begin to see our hardships as part of a story still unfolding.

When viewed through a spiritual lens, suffering becomes a powerful connector. Neuroscience shows that our brains can naturally respond to others' pain with compassion, and rather than isolating us, emotional suffering can shine a light on our interconnectedness.

When Adriana was originally diagnosed, there were moments when her suffering felt unbearable, and all I could do was sit beside her. Transcendence transformed our relationship by helping us see fear and uncertainty as one piece of something much larger.

Transcendence helps us trust that our lives have meaning beyond immediate struggles, that our pain can be alchemized into wisdom, and that even the smallest acts of compassion can ripple outward and create waves of kindness.

Our time on this planet is brief, but our presence can have a profound impact on those who come after us. We leave a mark not only through monumental acts, but through the ways we choose to show up for one another every day.

Using AIR to Explore Transcendence

The AIR approach can help you explore how your relationship with transcendence might be keeping you in survival mode, and it can offer ways to lean into thriving instead.

Awareness: Recognizing My Connections to Something Greater

- *Does my life generally feel like a series of tasks to complete?*
- *Am I open to feeling connected to something beyond myself?*
- *When was the last time I felt deeply moved by nature, art, a shared experience, or an act of kindness?*

Inquiry: Exploring My Relationship with Transcendence

- *How do I define transcendence in my own life?*
- *What experiences have expanded my sense of self and connected me to something larger?*
- *Knowing that my life's impact can ripple far beyond my time on earth, what do I want my impact to be?*

Reframing: Integrating Transcendence into Daily Life

- *How might I shift my perspective to see suffering as part of a bigger story rather than isolated struggles?*
- *What simple practice could I adopt to cultivate a greater sense of connection to others?*
- *What is one way I can contribute to the world today?*

PART

III

Integration

7

Past
The Stories We Carry

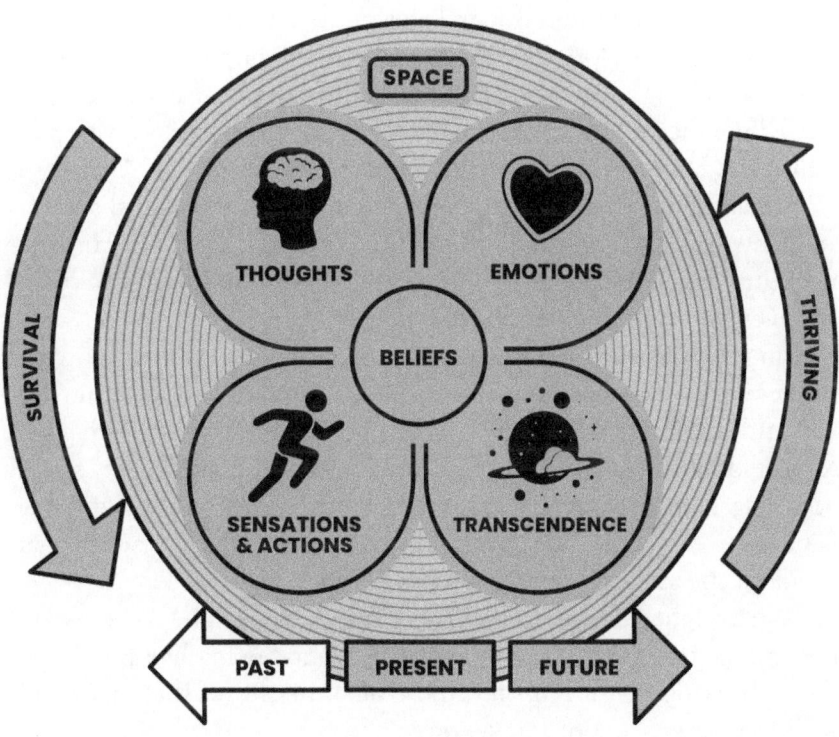

Imagine walking into a room with three doors. Behind the first door lies the past, a space filled with every setback and triumph in our story. The second door opens into the present, where life pulses in real time and agency becomes possible. The third door reveals the future as a blank canvas ready to be painted or a piece of jade waiting to be carved.

The past remains with us both in the stories we tell about our earlier lives and in the ways our bodies store joys and traumas. The past colors our beliefs, thoughts, emotions, sensations, and the actions that make us who we are today. By understanding the way the past shows up now, we can turn its influence toward helping us thrive.

How Is My Past Affecting Me Today? Meet Ronan

It was mid-morning when Ronan logged into our Zoom session. At the encouragement of a longtime client he deeply respected, Ronan agreed to give coaching a try, although part of him doubted it would make much difference. His body seemed relaxed, but I saw a heavy weariness in his gaze. He was wrestling with big questions.

Ronan had an amazing résumé. He had built his financial services company from the ground up and poured everything into it. His partner, Nina, had once been his biggest cheerleader and had believed in him even when he doubted himself.

But lately, everything was unraveling. A major client terminated their contract, two key investors had pulled out, layoffs were inevitable, and his leadership was being openly questioned. Nina was exhausted by the late work nights and the way Ronan always seemed more engaged in company matters than in conversations with her. Fights between them had given way to silence, which made Ronan wonder if she still cared enough to push back.

Ronan sighed deeply. "I feel like I'm living the same day over and over. No matter what I accomplish, I wake up feeling like I've failed. I keep thinking that if I just reach the next milestone, then maybe I'll finally feel at peace. But I never do."

We started addressing Ronan's discomfort by looking at his past. He initially felt that acknowledging old wounds would give them new power, but I reminded him that the past lingers in the patterns we repeat and in the emotions that surface unexpectedly.

"I'm going through tough times, but my life's not bad," he said apologetically. "I've got a company, a beautiful home, money in the bank, and people who care. I built all of this thinking it would fix me, but it hasn't."

Like many of us, Ronan believed that happiness results from external circumstances going well.

"Tell me more about the part of you that you want to fix," I prompted.

"It's not like there's one big thing. I had a happy childhood. My parents weren't abusive. They loved me in their own way, but they were just . . . busy. My dad worked a lot, and my mom had her own stuff going on. It was hard to connect with them. Sometimes, I wonder how our relationship would've been if I had just been easier or maybe more impressive . . . I just learned not to bother them unless it was really important."

"What about the part of you that learned to stay quiet to keep the peace? What do you think that part of you might say if it could speak now?" I asked.

Ronan's eyes widened as he thought. Finally, he spoke in a low voice, "It would say that it feels small . . . like it's still waiting to be noticed." His past was peppered by a series of subtle moments of feeling unseen. Over time, these cumulative experiences defined many of the beliefs he carried about himself and the world.

"I don't think I ever realized how much of my life I've spent trying to take up less space," he admitted. "Not because I wanted to disappear, but because I thought that if I didn't ask for much, I'd finally be loved."

This realization wasn't immediate or easy for Ronan. It took time for us to connect the dots and see the ways that small moments in his past had left a large imprint on his sense of self. Naming the perceptions that had lived unnamed for so long was the start.

Ronan's experience reflects what research increasingly shows: even subtle forms of disconnection in childhood can leave lasting marks on how we navigate adulthood. A 2024 study found that children exposed to greater adversity showed changes in parts of the brain that affect motivation and regulation. These changes were connected to higher levels of anxiety, depression, and struggles with substance use later in life.[1]

Many people feel uncomfortable looking back. "The past is the past," we tell ourselves, or "I've already dealt with that." But whether we examine it or not, the past influences us. The question is whether we let it guide us from the shadows or bring it into the light of awareness.

Defining the Past

The past is not a static record of events filed in chronological order, unchanging, and objective. Instead, the past is personal and profoundly subjective, an ever-evolving narrative stored in our bodies, affecting thoughts, coloring feelings, and reflected in the beliefs we carry about ourselves and others.[2]

Positive memories are important and powerful sources of thriving. When my family and I visited the Douro Valley in Portugal, we pulled off the road and found a small hotel nestled between terraced hills and winding vines. The kids were still buzzing from the drive, and we stepped into our room just as the afternoon light began to shift. Below us, the river glowed amber, lit by the sun and painted by the slow drift of boats as they moved up and down the water. The four of us sat there together, suspended in a golden hour.

That moment lives in my memory like a warm ember. *Savoring*, an important aspect of thriving, includes lingering in positive moments and letting them nourish us long after they have passed. Positive emotions leave an imprint and help us balance the negative memories that often pop up in our internal narratives.[3]

Recent research suggests that memories are reconstructions instead of fixed recordings. Each time we recall a memory, it's subtly rewritten in response to our current emotional state.[4] This fluidity is why the same memory can feel sharp and painful one day but distant and soft on another.

This chapter focuses primarily on the impact of negative memories because they are the ones most likely to keep us in survival mode. We'll explore the relationship between survival mode, memory, beliefs, and the brain's negativity bias, a protective mechanism that keeps us alert to potential threats but also makes us more prone to recall criticism and failure than praise and success. When this bias is active, the mind becomes a spotlight searching for danger.[5]

Ronan once shared the way a client's offhanded comment about his company's branding unleashed a cascade of memories laden with self-doubt. Interpreting the comment as a sign his business was at risk, he immediately plunged into researching branding consultants, a behavior driven by fear instead of strategy.

Had Ronan been in thriving mode, his mind might have accessed a fuller spectrum of memory, including moments that affirmed his competence. He could have remembered the praise he received for his logo design when he first unveiled it, the time he navigated a cash flow crisis with grace, the standing ovation from his team after a town hall meeting, or the product launch he spearheaded that exceeded projections and put them ahead of competitors. When we're thriving, the brain has access to a more balanced set of narratives, including positive and neutral ones. That broader range enables us to respond rather than react. When we're stuck in survival mode, the mind often filters out positive memories entirely.[6]

The Past Influences Us but Doesn't Define Us

Even when the past influences who we are, it doesn't have to be a burden that we drag behind us. Healing old wounds begins when we revisit our history to reframe its lessons so that they move us forward rather than hold us back.

Silent anger, defensive withdrawal, relentless striving, or the impulse to please others at all costs can all be visible expressions of invisible pain born of past experiences. Understanding the distinction between the wounds we carry and the beliefs, thoughts, emotions, sensations, and behaviors they produce is crucial for growth. This understanding requires us to revise past survival strategies while extending compassion, both to ourselves and others, because much of what we struggle with today started as earnest attempts to survive what once hurt us.[7]

Many people assume that healing emotional wounds requires retrieving every painful detail from the past. Healing, however, often comes not from reliving old experiences, but from learning to relate to them differently.[8]

While in coaching we don't diagnose or dwell on the past, we do explore it to understand its influence on the present and the choices we make. Shifting from survival mode to thriving mode often requires us to look at our memories through the lens of our current beliefs to modify their impact on our mood and behavior. Since memory isn't a static recording, we can use its reconstructive nature to turn old patterns into paths to resilience.[9]

Explicit and Implicit Memory

Explicit memory involves what we consciously recall, including specific events, like a birthday party, or facts, like the capital of France. These memories feel accessible, like pages in a mental scrapbook.[10]

Implicit memory operates beneath our awareness. Since it doesn't come with a clear narrative, it reveals itself through automatic responses and habitual reactions. It guides instinctive behaviors like tying a shoe or feeling uneasy about an aggressive tone of voice.[11]

Together, explicit and implicit memory influence the way we navigate the world by blending conscious recollection with instinctive responses in ways we often don't fully recognize. Some memories speak to us in images or facts, while others whisper through instinct or intuition.

Ronan didn't remember specific moments of rejection from his childhood, but he did recall waiting for attention and feeling that his small triumphs went unnoticed. Over time, these scattered memory fragments formed a perception of invisibility.

In our coaching sessions, Ronan reflected and pieced together fragments of memory, like the ache of wanting his father's attention after a long day at work or the guilt of needing help when his mother seemed overwhelmed.

Carl Jung, the founder of analytical psychology, suggested that much of what determines our identity lives beneath the surface of our awareness. These unconscious narratives are often influenced by memory, even when those memories remain out of reach. Sometimes we need support to bring them into view, and once we begin to recognize these patterns, even in small ways, we open the door to change and gain the agency to rewrite the story.[12]

I was 20 when my best friend and I set off on a backpacking trip through Europe, including a stop in Munich, Germany, where we wandered through the cobblestone streets.

Fast-forward 25 years, and I found myself in conversation with a German friend who had grown up in Dachau. She spoke of her experience visiting the Nazi concentration camp, first as a kid with her parents and later on a school trip. As I listened, something unsettled me. "I've never visited a concentration camp. I want to see Dachau one day," I told her.

A couple of weeks after that conversation, I was having dinner with the friend I had traveled with through Europe all those years ago. As we reminisced about our time abroad, I mentioned my desire to go to Dachau.

He turned to me in surprise, "You know we went to that concentration camp, right?"

I laughed nervously, "No, we didn't."

"Yes, we did," he insisted. "We rented a car in Munich so we could spend the day at the camp."

I was stunned. The certainty in his voice clashed with the absolute blankness in my mind. I had no recollection of it, but as he continued describing the experience, something moved inside me. Details that had been locked away for decades began to surface. I could picture the cold, stark corridors and the gravel crunching beneath our feet. Then, like a wave crashing through a broken dam, the memory of standing inside one of the gas chambers came rushing back.

I sat there in disbelief. How could I've completely erased such a profound experience from my conscious memory? Apparently, my mind had deemed the event too overwhelming to keep. Now, many years later, my friend helped me bring fragments back to consciousness at a time when I was able to deal with them.

From Reaction to Reflection

After a board member sent Ronan a curt late-night email, Ronan's body reacted as if he was facing imminent danger, his pulse accelerating and his chest tightening. Trying to make sense of his physical reaction, he started to catastrophize, jumping to worst-case scenarios: "What if I've messed up? What if this is the beginning of the end? What if I'm about to get fired from the company I founded?"

Our nervous system doesn't always distinguish between past and present. Even when we understand something intellectually, our bodies may still react as though we're unsafe.

"My body feels stuck in the past," said Ronan once. "I know there are many steps between here and losing my job or my company, but my emotions don't seem to care."

Ronan's needs had been inconsistently met by his father, who, though not unloving, was emotionally distant and unable to provide reliable reassurance and validation. His father's long hours and detachment reflected the broader cultural narrative that providing material security was more important than being emotionally available, especially for male caregivers.

During our conversations, Ronan realized that having unpredictable caregivers had influenced his need for certainty in other areas of life. Striving for excellence became his way of securing approval, and the fear of rejection kept him in a constant state of vigilance.

Patterns of this kind are described by what psychologists call *attachment theory*, which explores how we learn to connect and protect ourselves through our earliest relationships.[13] When caregivers are consistently warm and responsive, *secure attachment* tends to develop. We come to believe that closeness to others is safe, that our needs will be met, and that relationships can hold both joy and strain without falling apart.[14]

When care feels inconsistent, sometimes present and sometimes not, *anxious attachment* may emerge. We often become uncertain about our place in relationships, scanning for signs of social disconnection and working hard to prove our worth.[15]

If care is mostly distant or dismissive, *avoidant attachment* can take hold. In these environments, we learn to quiet our needs and rely only on ourselves because we believe that closeness to others might come at too high a cost.[16]

Last, when caregivers are both comforting and frightening, often in chaotic or unpredictable environments, *disorganized attachment* can develop. Interpersonal connection becomes confusing, and while we yearn for closeness, we also prepare for potential harm.[17]

Attachment theory isn't a diagnosis but one of many tools for understanding the past. It serves as a framework to explore patterns as adaptive responses to what once felt necessary for safety. In practice, most of us carry a blend of attachment styles that can evolve using AIR.

Understanding Past Attachments Using AIR

Using AIR, Ronan was able to understand more about his attachment styles and found ways to change how he responded to events in the present.

Awareness: At first, Ronan could only identify physical sensations, such as the tension in his chest during a stressful day at work or the panic that followed a missed call. He recognized these sensations were protective, like bracing for rejection before it ever arrived. The more he noticed the patterns, the more he understood the cycle.

Inquiry: From there, Ronan started to ask questions he had never thought to ask. "What did I believe about myself when I was eight, sitting alone at the kitchen table? What did I learn when my parents didn't come to my school performance?" As these questions led him to shift from judgment and blame to curiosity, he used agency to explore how his early experiences had molded his nervous system. In tracing his conditionings, Ronan began to understand why he often felt like he was living the same day over and over, trapped in past patterns.

Reframing: What began as self-judgment turned into self-compassion, leading Ronan to change his narrative of unworthiness. He stopped asking what he had done wrong and began to wonder why his parents had never learned how to give. This reframing was not meant to minimize the impact of his early experiences but to make new choices possible and to live differently in the present

By looking at old patterns in his past, Ronan discovered that the very strategies that once protected him were now keeping him stuck. The relentless drive to prove his worth left him unable to enjoy his success. His need for validation made him hyper-aware of other people's moods and caused him to overanalyze social interactions. Even in moments of praise, he felt as if approval could be revoked at any time.

Ronan also acknowledged he had to work on the painful distance that had formed between him and his wife, Nina. Even though she had been steady and supportive, his focus on work had slowly pushed her to the side. Letting go of the belief that love had to be earned through achievement was perhaps the bravest work of all.

When the Past Feels Present

Wounds from the past can ripple through our lives. *Trauma*, derived from the Greek word for wound, is not just about a specific event but also about the impact it has on our beliefs, identity, sense of safety, the way we respond, and the roles we take in relationships.[18] Two people can live through the same experience and walk away carrying very different stories.[19]

Trauma isn't limited to responses to major events, such as war, sexual violence, illness, major accidents, or natural disasters. These are often called *Big T* Traumas, experiences that overwhelm our capacity to cope and leave a visible mark. Trauma can also arise from more subtle experiences, sometimes referred to as *small t* traumas, such as chronic invalidation or feeling unsafe in a relationship that was supposed to offer care.[20] Some traumatic experiences may seem small from the outside, but they can leave lasting marks, especially when they're repeated or kept in the dark.[21]

When we face something traumatic, our internal alarm system gets triggered. Stress hormones flood the body, activating the fight, flight, or freeze response. In the midst of true danger, this reaction can be lifesaving by sharpening our senses and preparing us for action.[22]

Although this emergency response is meant to be temporary and the body typically returns to balance once the danger has passed, sometimes that return doesn't happen. The system stays on high alert, and the alarm keeps ringing, even when there's no clear threat. In this way, reminders of the past can feel as if they're happening in the present.[23]

Triggers are stimuli that reawaken difficult past experiences. A certain sound, a comment, a nonverbal cue, or even a particular smell can consciously or unconsciously transport us back to a painful moment, unleashing fear, sadness, anger, or shame.[24]

Although triggers can be distressing, they can also point us toward wounds that need our care. As my colleague, psychiatrist Reid Robison, often says, "triggers are friends to follow."[25]

Ronan once admitted, "I get triggered by the smallest things. I see someone not paying attention to what I'm saying in a meeting or even a slight sighing, and I'm suddenly a kid again, trying to prove myself to my dad."

What Ronan described is more common than we tend to admit. A moment that seems minor to others can stir up something deep and familiar within us. For some, these moments pass quickly because, as the nervous system settles, the story fades. But for others, the reaction lingers and loops. The difference often depends on how resourced we feel in the present and how resourced we were when the original wound was inflicted.

Coping mechanisms play an important role in developing *resilience*, our ability to adapt and recover after hardship. Resilience is influenced by what we lived through, who stood beside us, how we made sense of the pain, what we learned to expect from others, and the internal and external resources we had available.[26] Although some of us were taught to self-soothe, while others had to figure it out alone, none of this is fixed. Our minds and bodies can learn to find calm, and present relationships can repair what past disconnection once damaged. Even if we didn't have the tools early on, we can still find them now.[27]

Shared Trauma and Recovery

In September 2022, my family flew to Vienna to unveil a *Steine der Erinnerung*, a Stone of Remembrance, for my great-grandparents and grand-aunt, murdered in the Holocaust. As we stood on the street, reading their names etched into the pavement, I felt the weight of the inherited grief that lingers across generations and influences us in ways we don't always recognize.

My maternal grandfather was the only survivor of the Holocaust in his family. His sense of loss became part of our family's undeclared inheritance. It emerged in the silence that followed certain questions and in the constant fear that we might have to emigrate again.

Gathering in remembrance in Vienna, we named the grief that had been carried in silence for so long, and in doing so, we loosened trauma's grip and created space for healing.

Some wounds are passed down through generations and imprinted into family dynamics, while others ripple outward and leave their mark on entire communities and nations. After Vienna, I began to reflect more deeply on how grief that's never fully named can continue to reverberate through time.

When the terrorist attacks of September 11, 2001, happened, I was studying in New York City. Just before 9 a.m., our professor rushed into the classroom, turned the TV on, and announced that a plane had crashed into the World Trade Center. We watched in shock as the second plane struck the South Tower just minutes later.

My roommate and I decided to leave our building at 27th Street and 7th Avenue and walk downtown, thinking we might be able to help in some way. The city, usually vibrant and noisy, had fallen into an eerie silence, broken only by the desperate wail of sirens rushing through the streets. As we walked down Broadway, we witnessed from a distance the collapse of the first and then the second tower. Cars sped past us, covered in ash, their drivers' faces frozen in dismay and disbelief.

In the days that followed, we braced for more attacks. New York, one of the most alive cities on Earth, was enveloped in a death-like silence for weeks. Street corners became memorials adorned with pictures, flowers, tributes, and handwritten notes, and while the city's resilience showed up as collective unity, the trauma lingered and affected collective mental and physical health for years to come.

The entire city changed as a sense of survival clung to the air. Even after life resumed, many of us remained on edge. Sirens startled us. Sleep became harder to come by, and for some, even the simplest tasks felt charged with tension.

Collective healing takes time and often begins with shared acknowledgment of pain. My experiences in Vienna and New York taught me that when communities gather testimonies, create memorials, offer support, fund research, and honor loss, they help loosen the tight bonds of trauma.

Updating Our Coping Strategies

When life throws us challenges, we develop ways to protect ourselves. These *coping strategies* can help us survive difficult times, but as we grow, the very strategies that once kept us safe can begin to hold us back, affecting our relationships and even the way we see ourselves. Becoming aware of these patterns is an important step toward thriving.

Hyper-independence comes from the belief that we can only count on ourselves.[28] Maybe we were disappointed too many times, our needs were met with indifference, or accepting help was risky, so we stopped asking. As adults, this might show up as refusing help even when we need it or pushing people away when they try to get close. Healing begins with allowing ourselves to be supported by others. Each time we let someone in, we replace the belief that we need to be hyper-independent to survive with the belief that connection is a source of strength rather than weakness.[29]

People-pleasing is based on the belief that the safest way to belong is to put other people's needs first.[30] If love or approval felt conditional when we were young, we may have learned to avoid conflict by saying yes when we wanted to say no. Healing starts with small acts, such as setting boundaries to honor our own needs or pausing before automatically agreeing to something we're not sure about.

Perfectionism is a strategy based on the belief that our worth is defined by what we achieve.[31] If praise only came after performing well or mistakes were not met with kindness, we may have learned to push ourselves harder, convinced that anything less than perfect would lead to rejection. While perfectionism might bring external success, it often leaves us feeling as if we're never enough. Healing starts when we separate achievement from worth, give ourselves permission to make mistakes, and learn to seek approval not just from others but from within.[32]

Caretaking is a strategy based on the belief that we must be strong and helpful to earn love.[33] If emotional support was scarce, we might have taken on the role of the fixer, believing that our value came from taking care of others. This can lead to feeling responsible for everyone else's well-being while neglecting our own. Healing starts when we recognize that we, too, deserve care. Allowing others to show up for us and resisting the urge to fix everything can help us modify this pattern.[34]

Using humor as a shield is a strategy we often learn early, especially in environments where authentic emotional expression felt unsafe or was discouraged.[35] Jokes and sarcasm offer a quick escape hatch because they allow us to shift the focus and move on without directly addressing what aches. Humor can be a powerful tool for connection, but it can also become a mask. Healing starts with noticing the impulse to deflect and choosing honesty instead.

Micromanaging and *control-seeking* are strategies for creating safety in an unpredictable world.[36] Maybe we learned that if we planned every detail, we could prevent bad things from happening. As adults, this can make it hard to delegate or to accept help when things are not going exactly as planned. Healing starts when we learn to tolerate uncertainty by embracing small moments of letting go of control.

Expressing self-criticism is a strategy that involves turning harsh judgment inward. If we grew up in environments where high expectations or negative feedback were constant, we might have developed an inner critic that keeps us stuck in cycles of shame.[37] This voice tells us we're not good enough, no matter how much we do. Healing starts with noticing negative self-talk, challenging its messages, and replacing self-judgment with self-compassion.

Becoming inconspicuous is a strategy of staying quiet and fading into the background.[38] As a child, Ronan figured out that minimizing his presence and downplaying his needs were the safest ways to navigate a home where emotional support was scarce. This strategy helped him survive the gaps in family support, but it left him feeling invisible. For him, healing started by reconnecting with his sense of safety and allowing himself to be seen.[39]

It's very common to use one or a combination of these strategies to adapt to difficult circumstances. Trauma pushes us to endure, but often, the tools we developed to cope come at the cost of feeling stuck. The good news is that these patterns don't have to define us forever. By reflecting on the past and understanding how it has influenced us, we can take small steps to let go of the habits that no longer serve us.[40]

The Other Side of Pain

While the concepts of *post-traumatic stress* (PTS) and *post-traumatic stress disorder* (PTSD) are widely known, they're not the only responses to trauma. Some people experience *post-traumatic growth* (PTG), a term coined by psychologists Lawrence Calhoun and Richard Tedeschi to describe how adversity can become a catalyst for growth and positive transformation.[41]

PTG often emerges from the agentic choice to engage with pain differently. It invites us to recognize that although trauma left a mark on us, we can use it to deepen our understanding of ourselves and the world.[42]

The Japanese art of *kintsugi* emerged in the fifteenth century from the practical need to repair broken pottery, but it evolved into an aesthetic philosophy rooted in *wabi sabi*, the appreciation of imperfection and impermanence. In kintsugi, broken pottery is repaired using powdered gold, silver, or platinum to highlight the cracks instead of hiding them. Kintsugi pieces are unique works of art in which the metallic veins make the objects whole again and more beautiful after having been broken.[43]

Maya Angelou, the acclaimed poet, author, and civil rights activist, had a childhood marked by racial violence and sexual abuse. Angelou spent years in silence, believing that her voice had caused harm. Through this period of pain, she began to develop her love for literature and storytelling. When she emerged as a writer, she reclaimed her voice and transformed her suffering into a source of power and beauty.[44]

One key element of PTG is *meaning-making*, the ability to reframe painful experiences in ways that connect to a larger story and draw out wisdom. By finding meaning in suffering, adversity can transform us in empowering and healing ways.[45]

Many who face adversity find unexpected ways to transform their suffering into service. As the initial shock of my wife's MS diagnosis receded, Adriana began to search for ways to move forward. She found resources to help manage her symptoms and tools to navigate the emotional weight of her condition, but the most profound transformation came when she chose to study and practice social work.

Her first internship was working at an infant and child center, where she helped children who faced significant developmental and physical challenges. Many of them required specialized support to communicate and engage with the world. In these children, Adriana saw that the act of supporting others softened the edges of her own pain. She discovered joy despite hardship.

Later, at *Chai Lifeline*, an organization dedicated to helping children and families affected by serious and terminal illnesses, Adriana became part of a community bound by love and resilience. She met parents carrying the unbearable weight of a child's end-stage diagnosis, siblings navigating emotions too complex for their ages, and young patients with remarkable courage. Witnessing their struggles, she discovered strength within herself she hadn't seen before.

PTG doesn't mean gratitude for suffering, nor does it erase grief of loss. It simply represents the possibility that, in time, the weight of pain may give rise to meaning.[46] A parent who loses a child might channel grief into creating art or working with an organization to support other families facing unimaginable heartache. A veteran returning from war may find a renewed sense of purpose by mentoring others struggling through combat trauma.

Since trauma often isolates us, PTG is more likely to occur when there's *social support* from friends, family, colleagues, or communal networks. Survivors of natural disasters often report that their sense of community increased by sharing loss and offering mutual support. In connecting with others, they discovered strength that felt impossible in isolation.[47]

PTG also draws on *curiosity*. Questions such as "What now?" or "How can I rebuild?" can open new paths. Shifting from "Why is this happening to me?" to "What is this doing for me?" can transform pain into possibility, allowing growth to emerge from even the hardest experiences.

While PTG offers hope, it's important to note that it's not guaranteed. Trauma's impact is deeply individual and influenced by numerous factors, especially the nature of the experience itself, the existing support, and the resources available.[48] PTG isn't a measure of worth, simply one possible outcome among many.

Converting the Past into a Bridge Using AIR

One day, with the faintest trace of a smile, Ronan said to me, "I used to feel I was carrying my past like a heavy shadow, but now I see it more like a road. It's not perfect or straight, but it's what got me here."

These words hold a powerful idea that can resonate with many of us. The past, no matter how painful, doesn't have to be an anchor pulling us down. It can become a bridge connecting us to a thriving future.

At the beginning of our work together, Ronan and I used AIR to explore his attachment styles. Ronan also applied AIR again to turn his past into a bridge between old patterns and new ones.

Awareness: Ronan started to notice how quickly he shut down in moments that called for vulnerability. A question from Nina or a misstep at work could trigger a heaviness in his stomach, a sinking weight that seemed to pull him downward. At first, he assumed it was stress, but with time and practice, he learned to name it more precisely: shame. Naming the emotion helped him separate the feeling from his beliefs and identity. Shame was something he was experiencing, not something he was.

Inquiry: When Ronan felt the urge to withdraw or defend himself, he began to ask, "Is this reaction about the present, or is it touching something in my past?" and "What am I protecting myself from right now?" These questions helped him recognize that moments of tension often activated old beliefs about failure and rejection. With each question, the story became less fixed, and he began to imagine alternative, kinder interpretations.

Reframing: Rather than seeing his emotional reactions as signs of weakness, Ronan began to view them as old survival strategies that were once protective but no longer aligned with the person he was becoming. This shift softened his self-criticism and opened the door to greater self-compassion

Ripples in the Pond

The impact of Ronan's transformation rippled outward. As his leadership changed, so did his company. He re-engaged his team with curiosity and trust, inviting them to have more open conversations. At the same time, the culture started to soften and strengthen, marked by greater honesty and resilience. A year later, the business was stable and thriving in ways Ronan once believed were only possible through relentless pressure.

After months of tension and silence, Ronan and Nina decided to separate. They both acknowledged that an important part of what had existed between them had faded. The ways they had learned to relate, driven by performance and perfection, distance and avoidance, were no longer enough. They both needed space to heal and rediscover who they were outside the patterns they had unknowingly reinforced together.

"I thought separating would feel like failure," Ronan told me. "But it's strange. There's grief, of course. But there's also unexpected clarity. I'm just learning to show up for myself."

Ronan learned that the stories he told himself about the past were not set in stone. Now, he could see old events from other angles that offered different and more expansive perspectives. The way he had moved through his relationship with Nina had been molded by old patterns he learned in childhood. With the newfound clarity, he could begin to choose differently.

Like Ronan, many of us carry old narratives that silently determine our choices. The AIR approach can illuminate these hidden influences and help us transform our relationship with the past so that we can move intentionally toward thriving.

Using AIR to Explore the Past

You can use the AIR approach to help you explore how your relationship with your past might be keeping you in survival mode.

Awareness: Recognizing the Stories I Carry

- *Are there patterns in my life that keep repeating, even after I try to change them?*
- *When I think about the past, are there memories that evoke strong emotional reactions?*
- *Am I reliving old narratives that no longer serve me?*

Inquiry: Questioning the Influence of My Past

- *What beliefs about myself have I carried for years? When did they begin?*
- *What would my younger self tell me I need the most?*
- *How have the experiences of my past influenced the way I see myself and others?*

Reframing: Integrating the Past into My Growth

- *How can hold compassion for the parts of myself that learned to adapt for survival?*
- *How might I reinterpret a painful experience to empower rather than limit me?*
- *How could I use my past as a bridge to move forward?*

8

Present
The Moment We Come Alive

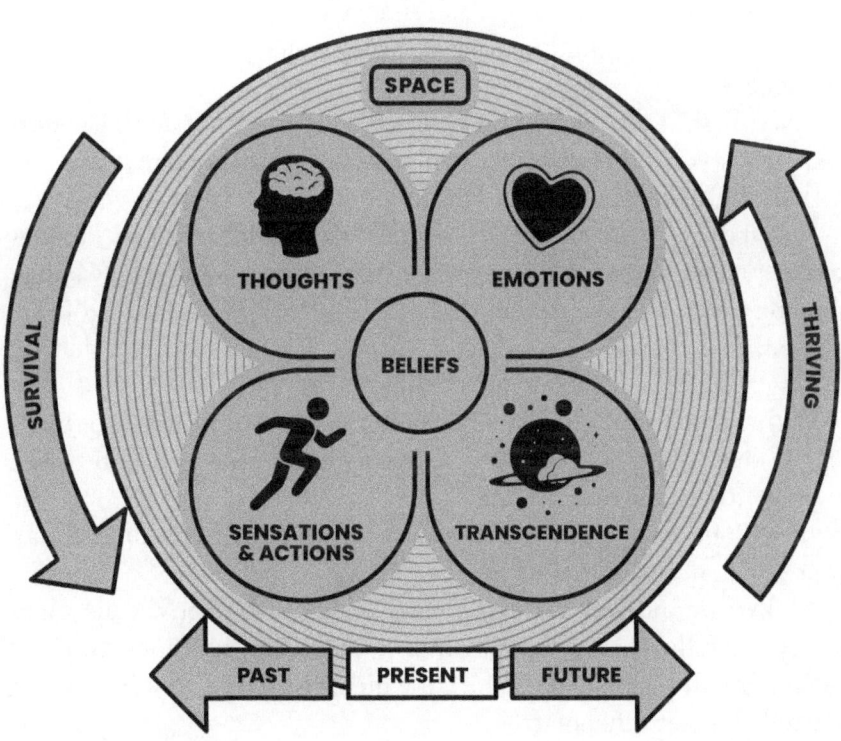

THE PAST INFORMS us, and the present transforms us. In this chapter, we'll explore ways to embrace the present fully and use the power of now as a tool for clarity and meaningful action. The present is where we find our agency.

Pausing

Before diving in further, I invite you to pause just for a few moments.

Wherever you are, let everything else fade into the background. It doesn't matter what came before this moment or what might come after.

Feel the weight of your body being held by the surface supporting you. Notice how this support requires no effort on your part. It's simply there, steady and grounding, carrying your weight without conditions or demands.

Gently shift your attention to your breath. Feel the air as it enters and leaves your body. Your breath has its own natural rhythm, and with each inhale, you can say *I am here*.

Maybe you feel a subtle tension in your shoulders or jaw. Perhaps you feel an urge to check your phone. Your mind may start to wander, slipping into a memory or a to-do list. These feelings and thoughts are normal, and there's no need to stop them. Let them come, and let them go, like waves rolling onto a shore.

Whatever arises, it's completely natural. The mind's job is to think, and it loves to travel. Simply notice where it goes and return to the breath without judgment.

Take one deep breath and feel the sensation of the air entering your nose, chest, and belly.

Take a second deep breath and loudly exhale through the mouth as slowly and fully as you can, releasing any tension or heaviness you may be carrying. If your shoulders feel like dropping even just a bit or your jaw relaxing, let it happen.

For the third breath, there's nothing to change. Notice the feeling of presence, a natural sense of being alive and aware.

Let this moment be enough.

■   ■   ■

Connecting to the breath may seem small, but it carries a lot of power. A single breath can begin to change the way we show up for ourselves and for the people we care about.

This practice has many names, shapes, and forms. In my work with clients, we call it *grounding*. Our world is constantly pulling us in different directions, so noticing the breath offers a surprisingly simple and effective way to return to ourselves. With time, these small moments of mindfulness accumulate and create a foundation of presence that supports us through life's challenges. The simple act of pausing and resting attention on the present moment strengthens our agency.

How Can I Be More Present? Meet Layla

Layla, a tech industry leader and a single mother of two, is a breast cancer survivor. While her battle with cancer left her with a heightened awareness of how precious life could be, she was also caught in a fast-paced routine that seemed relentless and often unrewarding.

While Layla and her ex-husband shared custody, she often had to reschedule meetings to pick up the kids when he failed to show up. As her teenage daughter, Olivia, retreated behind closed doors and eye-rolls, her son, Theodore, started acting out in school. Layla wondered if it was all her fault.

"My days are packed with meetings and deadlines, and my evenings aren't any better. Even when I'm home, my mind is somewhere else. I might be rehashing a mistake I made or preparing for tomorrow's meetings. I feel like I'm in a constant fog."

Layla rarely felt that she deserved what she had. As the daughter of immigrants who made many sacrifices to build a better life for her in a new country, she felt she owed it to her parents to prove that their struggles hadn't been in vain.

At our initial session, Layla came armed with an app that tracked her activities down to the minute. "I need to be more productive. I don't have enough hours in the day."

I paused. "What would having more hours give you?"

She blinked. "More time to get things done."

"What happens once you get everything done?"

She sighed. "I don't know. I guess . . . I could finally breathe."

I suggested that maybe Layla needed permission from herself to slow down rather than improve her time management.

She let out a sharp laugh. "You don't get it. I don't get to slow down. If I do, everything will fall apart."

In her mind, she wasn't being dramatic. Her team relied on her, her kids needed her, she had a mortgage to pay, and her parents had sacrificed so much for her. Despite all her efforts to hold everything together, she felt that the most important things in her life were slipping through her fingers.

"I miss my kids. I miss the way I used to play with Theo and the long talks I had with Olivia about her dreams."

One Saturday, Layla had promised Theo she'd be at his soccer game, but the morning got away from her. One last email turned into five and by the time she arrived, the game was over, and the field was nearly empty. Theo stood by the goal, kicking a ball at the net in frustration. When he saw her, he just shrugged and said, "It's fine, Mom." Her heart sank. She had missed another memory, and no rescheduled meeting could give it back.

That same night, she stood outside Olivia's door, hesitating before knocking. "Hey," she said, pushing it open. "How was your day?"

Olivia looked up from her phone, "Fine."

"Anything new?"

Olivia shrugged indifferently, clearly waiting for her mother to finish the small talk and leave. Layla wondered when Olivia had stopped confiding in her and whether this was fixable.

Layla's story is familiar to many of us. We sit at the dinner table, but instead of savoring the food or enjoying the company, our minds drift somewhere else, perhaps to an unresolved problem. We walk through the park on our way to work but barely register the surroundings, too busy thinking about a strained friendship or an issue at work. We move through our days surrounded by life but disconnected from it.

Time Travel

Mental time travel is very common. We may visit the past for the wisdom of lessons learned, but it can also bring rumination about events we can't change. On the other hand, thinking of the future may spark anticipation and hope, but it can also bring fear of the unknown.

Unlike the past and future, the present is the only place where we can be agentic by making choices and acting on them. If life unfolds in the now, why are we so often mentally in the past or future instead?

The present doesn't exist in isolation. It's often influenced by what came before and points toward what comes next. What we experience in the now is informed by previous learning and influenced by perceptions about future consequences.

In a 2010 study, Harvard psychologists Daniel Gilbert and Matthew Killingsworth found that people, on average, spend nearly 47% of their waking hours thinking about something other than what they're doing in the moment. The researchers titled their paper "A Wandering Mind Is an Unhappy Mind" after discovering that people were less happy when their thoughts drifted. Their findings reflect how being mentally elsewhere often traps us in cycles of comparison and problem-solving that disconnect us from what's actually going on in the current moment.[1]

Layla was an expert time traveler, especially during evenings at home with her kids. "I hear them playing in the next room," she said, "but I'm always at the kitchen table, unable to enjoy any of it because I'm thinking about work." Her voice wavered, "I hate that." At work, it was no different. She often found herself replaying conversations from earlier meetings or worrying about deadlines weeks away, barely registering the person speaking in front of her. "It's like I'm always somewhere else," she admitted.

Like many of us, Layla's mind often looped through past mistakes or jumped ahead to everything that could go wrong. This mental treadmill left her feeling exhausted and detached from experiences she wanted to enjoy. It affected her well-being, her relationships, her creativity, and her ability to make decisions. She had spent years chasing a future where everything would finally settle into place, but the more she achieved, the further that future seemed to slip away. She was stuck in survival mode.

Mindfulness

Mindfulness is the practice of bringing full attention to the present moment, intentionally and without judgment, over and over again.[2] In the short term, mindfulness shifts the brain from a narrow and hypervigilant focus to a calm and expansive awareness. Over time, it can lead to detectable biological changes in the brain's structure and function.[3]

Research by psychiatrist and neuroscientist Judson Brewer at Brown University has shown that mindfulness practices quiet the part of the brain responsible for mind wandering, dialing down the mental chatter that pulls us out of the present.[4] There's also ample evidence that mindfulness strengthens the area of the brain responsible for emotional regulation and decision-making.[5] In other words, a regular mindfulness practice gives us more control over our reactions, making it easier to practice awareness, inquiry, and reframing, the AIR tool used throughout this book.

Mindfulness affects the entire body by decreasing stress hormones, slowing down heartbeat, reducing blood pressure, and supporting immune function. It also helps the nervous system shift from fight-or-flight to rest-and-repair.[6] Mindfulness contributes to thriving because the calmer and more centered we feel, the more effectively we can engage with the world.

In 2017, I was in the middle of one the most demanding periods of my career, expanding a multi-million-dollar distribution center for a major retailer. It was a task that would normally take more than a year to complete, but I was given less than six months. My days were consumed by a relentless whirlwind of meetings, arguments, decisions, and high-stakes problems to solve. Even when I wasn't at my desk or meeting with the team, my mind raced through potential risks and braced for possible disasters.

After one particularly intense meeting, my boss pulled me aside and suggested I join a mindfulness-based stress reduction (MBSR) course. "You're carrying a lot," he said, "and this might help."

I was very skeptical because, at the time, I thought mindfulness was for people with more time on their hands and fewer responsibilities than I had. I couldn't picture myself sitting still with so much to do, but I chose to sign up anyway.

The sessions were held in an old downtown Toronto church, where the wooden floors creaked with every step, and sunlight poured through colorful stained-glass windows. Walking through the heavy doors felt like entering a sanctuary removed from the relentless pace of impending targets and key performance indicators.

Our teacher was an older woman with a serene presence that I found both intriguing and unnerving. She also wore modest dresses that seemed chosen more for comfort than appearance, as if the trappings of the material world held little interest for her. Her voice was gentle, and she radiated a calm authority. On the first day, she handed each of us a single raisin.

"We're going to eat this," she said, "and it's going to take us twenty minutes."

I nearly laughed out loud. Twenty minutes for a raisin? I had dozens of people waiting for me at work, and here I was, being asked to commune with dried fruit. But curiosity beat skepticism, so I stayed and followed her lead.

"Look at it," she began. "Really look. Notice its texture, the tiny ridges, and the creases where it folds in on itself. Pay attention to how the light touches its surface, creating highlights and shadows. Take in every detail."

She paused, giving us time to examine the small, unassuming raisin as if it held something important. Then, she continued, "Picture its journey. Imagine how it started as a grape on a vine, ripening in the sun. Think about the hands that picked it, the process that dried and packaged it, the journey that transported it to a store, and how it eventually came to be here, in your hands."

"Now bring it to your nose. Smell it slowly and fully. Let the scent settle. Does it bring anything to mind? Maybe a memory or a feeling? Let whatever comes up just be there."

I began to see that raisin in a way I never had before. It was a marvel of texture and scent. When she finally instructed us to place it in our mouths, I felt that I was experiencing raisin flavor for the first time. I was amazed by its weight on my tongue and the burst of sweetness as I bit into it.

That exercise wasn't about raisins, of course. It was about slowing down and being present in a way that felt entirely foreign to me. This small act of mindfulness felt like pulling the emergency brake on the speeding train of my existence.

Week by week, the course unfolded with practices that seemed simple but held profound lessons. We learned to observe our thoughts without judgment, to accept whatever arises, to tune into the sensations in our bodies, and to breathe through moments of stress. The chaos around me was still there, but I was learning to navigate it with a grace I didn't know was possible.

Mindfulness gives us tools to face difficulties in a grounded and calm state. Whether we're leaders making high-stakes decisions or parents juggling countless responsibilities, mindfulness can open up space to engage more thoughtfully with the present moment.[7]

The Paradox of Control

One key reason we resist the present is our relentless desire for control. Either we cling to the past, replaying it like a scratched record, with the hope of changing the ending, or we fixate on the future as if it were a puzzle we could solve. Instead, the present asks something far harder: *surrender*. This doesn't mean surrender as in giving up, but surrender as in trusting life as it is, letting go of the need to control it.

Many of us grow up being told that control is the key to a successful life. Control your grades, your career, your relationships, your image, your future. Choose the right path, the right partner, the right investments. Control your inbox. Control your emotions. If you just grip tightly enough, you'll have it all. But what can we actually control?

"The ability to voluntarily bring back a wandering attention, over and over again, is the very root of judgment, character, and will," wrote the father of American psychology, William James, more than a century ago. True power, he argued, is much less about controlling circumstances than it's about controlling our attention. For him, strength was found in the simple act of deciding, moment by moment, where to direct the beam of our awareness.[8]

During the 2008 Beijing Olympics, Michael Phelps was swimming the 200-meter butterfly final when his goggles filled with water, leaving him with no visibility halfway through the race. Phelps had trained for this exact scenario, so instead of letting panic derail him, he trusted his body and his preparation. Counting his strokes, he let muscle memory guide him to the wall. Swimming blindly, he finished the race.

In fact, he won it and set a world record. He couldn't stop the water from flooding his goggles, but he could ground his presence in the moment. He took charge by letting go of what he couldn't control.[9]

Anyone who has driven on black ice is familiar with this principle. Our instinct is to grip the wheel tighter and fight the skid. But stability rarely comes from resistance. Instead, it comes from easing our grip, turning into the skid, and letting the car find its balance again. Similarly, surrender is moving along with the uncertainty instead of bracing against it.

If the idea of surrendering feels inaccessible to you, think of its cousin *flow* instead. First described by psychologist Mihaly Csikszent-mihalyi, flow is a state that many of us have experienced without even realizing it. It happens when we're so immersed in what we're doing that awareness of time passing and concern about control all fade into the background. Many of the world's highest performers, from athletes and artists to innovators and entrepreneurs, describe some of their greatest moments as being in flow rather than being in control.[10]

While few can enter flow at will, we can take steps to make it more likely. Flow tends to arise when we carve out uninterrupted time and immerse ourselves in something that feels meaningful and important. The task must stretch us just enough because if it's too simple, our attention drifts, and if it's too complex, we tense up. Having clear goals with immediate feedback in rich environments that offer autonomy, novelty, and a touch of unpredictability tend to invite the kind of presence that draws us into flow.[11]

Jazz musicians often describe flow as the moment the music seems to play itself. In a legendary performance at the 1991 Montreux Jazz Festival, Miles Davis seemed to vanish into his music, closing his eyes and letting his trumpet guide him.[12] In those moments, it's likely that he wasn't trying to control every note or anticipate what would come next. He trusted the years of practice behind him and the connection with the other musicians on stage. Miles Davis let the unfolding music flow in the moment.

Like many of us, Layla had many reasons to want to be in control. Controlling her career mattered because success represented security. Then came the breast cancer diagnosis that stripped away any illusion of control, exposing how fragile that sense of safety really was.

Determined to prove nothing could slow her down, she kept on working from home. She was afraid of the questions that emerged when she slowed down: "Who am I without constant activity? Am I only valuable when I'm useful? What will people say?"

In a culture where worth is tied to productivity, slowing down can feel almost subversive. What if our value is defined by our very presence? Whether we're facing flooded goggles, navigating icy roads, playing music, or facing life-altering diagnoses, the path to thriving begins when we trade the illusion of control for faith.

A close friend once reminded me that we're called human *beings*, not human *doings*. You don't have to earn the right to exist. You only need to give yourself permission to be.

Living with Intention

Philosopher Søren Kierkegaard proposed that the modern obsession with external accomplishments often pulls us away from ourselves and scatters our energy across endless pursuits. In his journals, he lamented that "the busier a man is, the more quickly he forgets himself." For Kierkegaard, true fulfillment comes from inward reflection and a willingness to sit with life's questions, not from external achievements.[13]

Bringing presence into our lives aligns with the idea of living with intention. In turn, intentionality is grounded in agency and invites us to embrace the paradox that sometimes, the most meaningful choice isn't to push forward but to pause and be in the moment. In this stillness, we discover meaning and navigate life with more clarity.

Many traditions view the act of being present as sacred. In Zen Buddhism, the concept of *shoshin* or beginner's mind invites us to experience each moment as if for the first time, free of judgment.[14] The Jewish concept of *kavannah* (intention) teaches that presence can transform mundane acts into spiritual practice.[15] Likewise, the Sufi poet Rumi wrote that presence requires letting go of control and embracing the flow of life with openness and mindfulness: "You have been stony for too many years. Try something different. Surrender."[16]

Vietnamese Buddhist monk Thich Nhat Hanh described being present as an act of love because it allows us to build meaningful connections with ourselves and others. Bringing presence to our social interactions through the intentional act of focusing on another person, engaging with curiosity and compassion, opens space for others to feel seen and heard. This dynamic can have a profound impact on both the individual being acknowledged and the one offering attention.[17]

Presence Brings Us Closer

We can strengthen our connections to others through small acts of presence, such as listening without an agenda or simply asking, "How are you, really?" and waiting for an authentic response. These moments, though deceptively simple, can dissolve barriers and promote intimacy. Authentic relationships often begin when we're willing to meet another person where they are.

Confucius, the great Chinese philosopher, taught that attentiveness to others was an ethical obligation and the foundation of a harmonious society. He introduced a term he called *ren*, which refers to a profound sense of humanity and kindness in relationships. For Confucius, ren can be practiced through small, deliberate acts of care in daily interactions, like greeting someone with sincerity or listening fully.[18]

Studies show that people who feel seen and understood in their relationships report higher levels of well-being.[19] Neuroscience research by Paul Zak at Claremont Graduate University and Jorge Barraza at the University of Southern California supports this idea by revealing that empathetic listening produces the release of oxytocin, the bonding hormone. This process strengthens our sense of safety and connection with others and demonstrates how presence in conversations can foster thriving.[20]

Recognizing the importance of presence is one thing, but putting it into practice is another, especially in modern times when many of us struggle with the pull of screens and the many habits that keep us half-present. Learning to bring presence into our lives requires leaning into our agency, again and again, so we can gently guide our attention back when it has drifted.

Listening with Intention Using AIR

Awareness: Layla decided to keep track of her presence by paying attention to her interactions with others. After observing herself for a week, she admitted that she often found herself as if moving through a fog, disconnected and distracted, nodding along while scrolling on her phone or thinking about the next thing on her to-do list.

Inquiry: When I asked Layla what happened when her attention drifted from the present, she realized that those moments of mindless inattention represented missed opportunities to create genuine connection. We then talked about what would be different if she were fully present and listening actively. To find out, she committed to creating more space for authentic conversations by focusing on fully being with the person in front of her and ignoring the many distractions that pulled at her attention.

At first, she found it uncomfortable and difficult. For example, one evening, she forced herself to sit on the couch next to Olivia, determined to be fully present. In less than five minutes, her hand twitched toward her phone for just a quick glance, and Olivia noticed.

"So inspiring, Mom." The sarcasm landed like a punch, and Layla swallowed hard and set the phone face down on the table. She thought that maybe this change was impossible for her.

Reframing: An insight from our sessions resonated with Layla: "I don't have to do it perfectly. I just have to notice when I'm not paying attention and try again." And so, she kept practicing, noticing her mind wandering, and trying again.

One night, something unexpected happened. She left her phone in another room during dinner, hoping to resist the itch to check her Slack channels.

"You actually listened to me today," Olivia said as she cleared her plate.

Layla blinked. "What do you mean?"

"I don't know. Normally, you say 'uh-huh' a lot and look at your phone. But tonight, you were here." Olivia gave her mother a genuine smile.

Layla sat in stunned silence as her daughter walked away. It was a brief but powerful moment that reminded her of the joy of being with her family.

"I used to blast through conversations, always half-listening," she confessed. "Now, I try to really listen to people, and they notice it. It's like I'm existing in a way I wasn't before."

Increasing Mindfulness Using AIR

Layla and I used AIR to build her overall mindfulness.

Awareness: I asked her, "What cues tell you that you're getting caught in mental time travel?" By watching herself closely, she observed that feeling detached from her surroundings often indicated that her mind had wandered away from the present moment. She also noticed that a string of "what if" questions frequently signaled that she had drifted into the future.

Inquiry: When her mind traveled into imagined catastrophes or past regrets, Layla learned to pause and ask herself, "What do I need right now to feel grounded?" That small shift helped her view her thoughts as stories rather than predictions, creating enough space for her to lean into her agency and make more intentional choices.

Reframing: I asked Layla, "What is one small practice you can adopt to become more mindful?" She decided to introduce breath-based meditation into her daily routine. Every morning, she paused for a few minutes to focus on her breath and center herself, a simple and quick daily check-in.

"At first, it felt strange," she admitted. "But the more I did it, the more I noticed my mind wandering, and it became easier to bring it back." Over time, that moment of stillness became a way to begin the day with presence instead of pressure.

Ripples in the Pond

Layla realized that presence was about tiny, everyday instants. She had believed that connection to others required more time, more effort, more doing. But maybe it required less distraction and doing fewer things at once.

Layla's transformation took time. She learned slowly, breath by breath, to lean into her agency to make courageous decisions that aligned her values with her actions, such as reorienting her attention to the present moment. Layla realized that real change often begins with small breakthroughs.

Layla's growth improved her interactions with others and inspired change in those around her. Her colleagues began copying her attentiveness, which created a more collaborative and supportive work environment. When we bring presence into our relationships, we inspire others to do the same.

Social attunement can happen when we pause to set our own agendas aside and step out of the transactional mode that dominates so much of modern life. By embracing presence, we move toward a thriving life, choosing depth over breadth, listening over rushing, and relationships over results. The rewards of authentic social connection are immense: stronger communities with richer agency and humanity.

When Layla began reclaiming her presence, the relentless fog of never-ending tasks lifted. In its place came a clarity she hadn't felt in years and a renewed understanding of her priorities. Although she still found herself overly busy at times, she developed the ability to recognize when to take breaks to reconnect with herself and come back to the present. Ironically, by doing less at once, she got more of what mattered done, and her team became more efficient and engaged as they followed her lead.

She described how one Saturday, she shut her laptop, ignoring the unread emails and Slack notifications blinking in the corner of her screen. For the first time in years, she chose not to feel guilty about it.

She found Theo's soccer ball and walked into the living room, where Theo and Olivia were sprawled on the couch, half watching TV and half scrolling their phones.

"Want to go to the park?" Layla suggested.

Olivia looked up, skeptical. "Who are you?"

Layla smiled. "I don't know yet," she admitted. "But I'd like to find out."

Olivia stared at her, not saying anything. Then, she put her phone in her pocket. "Okay," she said. "Let's go."

Theo's face lit up. "For real?" He launched off the couch before she could answer, already lacing up his cleats.

For the first time in years, Layla stopped seeing stillness as a threat and started to trust it. In that moment of calm, she was finally able to face the thoughts she had been outrunning: "Who am I without constant activity? Am I only valuable when I'm useful?" The questions felt heavy, and she didn't have all the answers yet but asking them made space for the possibility of being enough by just being.

Honoring the Present

The past and future are not inherently good or bad. They hold valuable lessons and dreams, but they're places to visit, not to live. Our lives are constructed in the now, with each moment holding its own value and serving as a building block for what comes next. By choosing to live in the moment, we honor life as it unfolds.

As Layla discovered, presence is a way to meet others more fully and respond to life from a place that feels authentic. Sometimes being here means sitting with discomfort or uncertainty. Other times, it opens the door to moments of joy and genuine connection.

We reclaim power over our lives when we decide to focus on being present, right here, right now. Presence is an act of defiance against a world that places too much value on productivity. Instead of focusing on the constant rush to do more, we can return our attention intentionally with a single breath and embrace the current moment as it is. We don't need a perfect practice or a silent retreat, just a willingness to align our actions with our values in a way that feels meaningful. In returning to the present, we remember what really matters.

Using AIR to Explore the Present

You can use the AIR approach to help you explore how mental time travel may be keeping you in survival mode.

Awareness: Recognizing My Relationship with the Present

- *Where am I right now? Am I here, or am I lost in the past or future?*
- *Are there signals that tell me when "for" Can I recognize when my attention is wandering from the present moment?*
- *Do certain situations, thoughts, emotions, sensations, or actions consistently pull me away from the present moment?*

Inquiry: Questioning the Barriers to Presence

- *How do I feel when I slow down? Does stillness bring ease or discomfort?*
- *What do I need in this moment to feel more present?*
- *How would things change if I noticed what's present rather than what's missing?*

Reframing: Cultivating Presence as a Way of Living

- *If this moment was the only one that mattered, what would I do differently?*
- *How might being more present deepen my relationship with myself and others?*
- *What is one small ritual I can practice daily to anchor myself in the present?*

9

Future
The Possibility Ahead

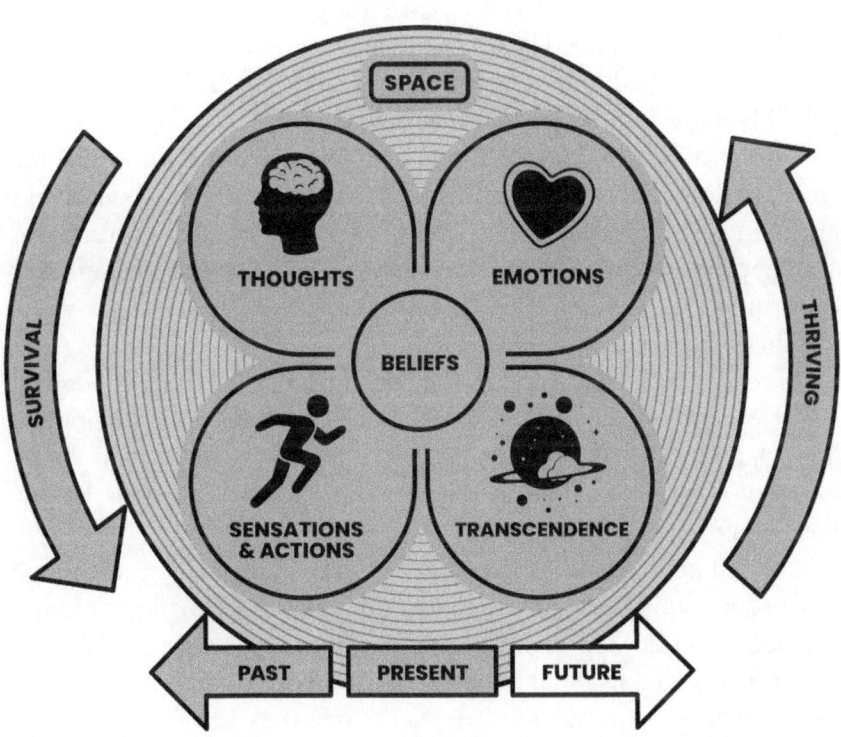

We've explored the weight of the past and the power of the present. Now, we turn to the future as a dimension of possibility. What happens when we shift from fearing the unknown to actively constructing it? How do we step into a thriving future that aligns with our values and highest aspirations? If imagining the future is one of the defining abilities of our species, how might we use it in service of thriving?

A Midlife Breakthrough

It was early 2021, and the world was still shaking from the pandemic. I had just turned 42 and, although I had spent years climbing the corporate ladder, reaching for what I thought was stability and success, I wanted more. When I was invited to join a fast-growing startup, I pounced.

The company was led by brilliant, ambitious founders in their mid-twenties. They had built something extraordinary and were ready to scale. My job was to help make that happen.

The pace was relentless. Within months, we had secured nine figures in debt and equity funding. We rebranded, doubled our workforce, moved to a much bigger office space, and signed new customers at a dizzying speed. Every day was high stakes, and I told myself that I was thriving.

Then, one afternoon, I hit a wall.

I had just returned from Los Angeles after negotiating the acquisition of assets to sustain our expansion. Sleep-deprived, over-caffeinated, drained, and wired all at once, I jumped on an important call. When the conversation escalated into a heated argument, it finally hit me that I was burned out.

I closed my laptop, turned off my phone, took a deep breath, and walked downstairs, drawn by the laughter of my children playing in the basement. I sat down with them, with my mind still racing.

At first, I couldn't shake the endless loop of to-dos, but after a few minutes, the noise inside quieted. For the first time in months, I wasn't thinking about the next deal or the next move. I was just there, building Legos with my kids. I felt the plastic pieces click into place, and as I watched their small hands move, I realized how much I missed them.

That night, after they went to bed, I sat in my favorite chair, staring at the ceiling. Adriana walked in and sat beside me. "Are you okay?" she asked.

I took a breath. "I think I'm done."

As I untangled myself from the company, I realized that I had spent too much time constructing a future without knowing if I really wanted to live in that version of it. Walking away meant surrendering control over what would come next. It felt like free falling.

Slowly, I began to rebuild. I started a business that aligns with my values. I went back to school, and I wrote this book. In that process, I learned that we can visualize a future that helps us thrive in the present.

Creatures of Imagination

We're all creatures of imagination. Over the course of history, humans have traveled all over the globe, envisioned new ways of living to adapt to unfamiliar environments, and gathered resources to prepare in advance for challenges to come. We plan ahead for futures that don't yet exist.

Today, the spark of imagination drives us to engineer microscopic robots, cure diseases, create meat without animals, explore distant planets, and stretch the boundaries of what was once thought possible. This capacity to imagine what lies beyond today's reality fuels human creativity and turns abstract possibilities into tangible realities.

In their book *Homo Prospectus*, psychologists Marty Seligman, Peter Railton, Roy Baumeister, and Chandra Sripada call this human trait *prospection*. Their work suggests that we're perpetual time travelers, wired to look into the future.[1]

As we explored in the previous chapter, being in the present moment is essential to thriving. However, there's a natural tension between staying fully here and imagining what comes next. Too much focus on the future can pull us out of life, while too much presence can limit our capacity for creativity and innovation. Thriving invites us to look ahead when needed and return to the present.

Mental time travel is a central feature of how humans learn and evolve. Every time we imagine the future, we pull from a well of beliefs, thoughts, emotions, and sensations to control a mental simulation of what might happen. These simulations allow us to experiment with possibility before we decide whether to step into a particular path.[2]

The ability to imagine possible futures also has a shadow side. Sometimes, we respond to imagined outcomes as if they're already happening, leaving us vulnerable to paralyzing fears.[3] An entrepreneur might dream of the success of the business they will build or be haunted by worries of bankruptcy. When our minds leap ahead, we can envision opportunities and growth, but we can also picture catastrophe and loss. Using prospection to thrive requires skill.

Negative prospection, the tendency to look for threats and rehearse worst-case scenarios, is an essential part of human planning. While it allows us to design lifesaving vaccines and buildings that can withstand earthquakes, negative prospection can also trap us in cycles of unnecessary anxiety that keep us in survival mode.[4]

Alternatively, *positive prospection* enables us to imagine opportunities rather than dangers. Instead of fixating on what might go wrong, prospecting positively helps us visualize success and move toward the future with optimism and hope. Thriving requires balancing negative and positive prospection to prepare for future challenges and opportunities.[5]

Japan's reaction after the devastating Fukushima nuclear disaster of 2011 is a communal example of moving from survival mode into thriving mode using balanced prospection. In the immediate aftermath, the country was focused on survival. More than 15,000 lives were lost, and entire towns were obliterated. All efforts centered on rescuing people and providing temporary shelter for those displaced.[6]

As the shock subsided, Japan began its transition to thriving mode. Communities in the hardest-hit regions undertook ambitious rebuilding projects. Architects and engineers collaborated to design homes and infrastructure capable of withstanding future disasters. Green energy initiatives, such as the construction of wind and solar farms, emerged to reduce reliance on nuclear power. The town of Minamisanriku used the tragedy as an opportunity to invest in infrastructure, including the relocation of public buildings and community centers to higher ground. Disaster preparedness became a cornerstone of education in local schools, and residents planted thousands of cherry trees along evacuation routes as a symbol of hope.[7]

From Scarcity to Abundance

The way we think about the future colors how we live in the present.

Positive prospection leads to an *abundance mindset*, the belief that there's enough to go around and that opportunities and resources are expandable. When we view the world through the lens of abundance, we're more willing to take risks and invest in long-term goals that align with our aspirations.[8]

On the other hand, too much negative prospection leads to a *scarcity mindset*, a mentality in which time, money, energy, and opportunities are limited, and every gain comes at someone else's loss. Instead of fostering exploration and growth, a scarcity mindset traps us in a fragile sense of security and makes us reluctant to share resources or power.[9]

When we reorient from scarcity to abundance, we trade survival for thriving. We stop seeing life as a competition and choose instead to help each other grow. As historian Yuval Noah Harari writes in *Sapiens*, our species thrives not through brute strength or intelligence alone, but through our unique ability to cooperate in large groups around shared beliefs. Our capacity for collective prospection helped us transform the world for the better.[10] Moving from isolation to collaboration unlocks a potential far greater than anything we could achieve alone. Simply put, we thrive most when we thrive together.

Contrary to popular belief, an abundance mindset isn't blind optimism. First introduced by educator Stephen Covey, the term invites a way of thinking grounded in the understanding that we're wired for connection and that opportunities tend to expand when we stay open to engaging with others.[11] Research shows that acts of generosity can improve our well-being, not because they promise a return but because they affirm that we're part of something larger than ourselves. When we give, even in small ways, we feel more whole.[12]

In 2022, Yvon Chouinard, founder of the outdoor clothing and gear brand Patagonia, made a decision that surprised the business world. Rather than sell his company or pass it down to his descendants, he gave it away to the planet. Ownership was transferred to a specially created trust and nonprofit with the single mission of protecting the Earth.[13]

The act reflected Chouinard's long-held belief that business could serve something greater than itself. Some called it naïve, others visionary. Either way, it challenged the idea that profit and purpose must be at odds.

Patagonia is far from perfect, but its evolution was supported by the powerful idea of aligning traditional success metrics with the well-being of others. By giving away a $3 billion company, Chouinard transformed private wealth into a public commitment and demonstrated how thriving can ripple out when we choose to transcend self-interest. That kind of thinking requires tremendous courage.[14]

Resilience

As we learned in Chapter 7, resilience is often described as bouncing back from hardship, but it can also mean bouncing forward and using adversity as a springboard for positive transformation.[15] Bethany Hamilton is a professional surfer who lost her arm in a shark attack when she was 13 years old. Trusting in the future, she pictured herself riding waves again, and within months she returned to the ocean and rose to global prominence as a world-class athlete.[16]

Psychologist Ann Masten at the University of Minnesota refers to resilience as "ordinary magic" arguing that the ability to adapt is built into us. Her research shows that resilience depends much more on everyday habits and support systems, like believing in our own capacity to grow and having stable relationships, than on rare traits or heroic strength. In essence, resilience is something we can nurture and develop.[17]

Difficulties can show us the path to thriving when we trust our capacity to learn from our failures and mistakes. Thomas Edison famously faced thousands of unsuccessful attempts while inventing the lightbulb. Rather than viewing these missteps as failures, Edison pictured them as bringing him closer to success: "I have not failed. I've just found 10,000 ways that won't work."[18]

People who see skills or talents as something that can be developed are more likely to persist through setbacks and learn from mistakes. When we understand failure as part of the process and adjust our approach, we choose to move forward in a new way. This growth mindset fuels the belief that progress is still possible, even when we're facing strong headwinds.[19]

We humans are not particularly good at predicting how future events will make us feel. We often overestimate the joy of good outcomes and the pain of bad ones.[20] Take buying the dream home we believe will bring us endless happiness. At first, it feels like the pinnacle of success, but before long, the initial excitement settles into the reality of daily expenditures and responsibilities. On the pain side, think of a breakup that initially feels like the end of the world. In those first days, joy seems impossible, and then, as time passes, we adapt and often find gratitude for the chance to start fresh.

Psychologists Daniel Gilbert at Harvard and Timothy Wilson at the University of Virginia asked college students to predict how they would feel if they were assigned to a less desirable dormitory. Most believed they would be significantly less happy than students placed in more popular dorms, but when researchers checked in later that year, their happiness levels were nearly the same as those living in preferred housing. The study suggests that what we think will sink us or elevate us often turns out to be less powerful than we imagined.[21]

We are far more resilient than we think, and our future selves are often better at adjusting than we give them credit for.

Psychological Flexibility

If resilience helps us endure, *psychological flexibility* helps us evolve. Imagine you're driving, navigating a hectic city after carefully planning the route. Suddenly, you encounter a series of streets unexpectedly blocked by heavy traffic. You have a choice: to stick to the original plan, growing frustrated as you wait for traffic to clear, or adjust course by finding alternative paths. With psychological flexibility, unexpected events turn into opportunities to move forward in new directions.[22]

Psychological flexibility is one of the strongest predictors of wellbeing. It helps us stay grounded in the present while responding skillfully to what's unfolding around us. Researchers have found that people who cultivate psychological flexibility are better at recovering from setbacks and making decisions, especially in times when great change presents unexpected turns.[23]

To describe the unpredictability of modern warfare, military leaders introduced the acronym VUCA, which stands for *volatile, uncertain, complex,* and *ambiguous.* Volatility refers to the speed and magnitude of change, uncertainty highlights the lack of clarity about what lies

ahead, complexity acknowledges the interconnected nature of problems, and ambiguity conveys the difficulty of interpreting events and
predicting outcomes. VUCA captures the intensity of modern times,
and why adapting quickly matters more than ever.[24]

In the late 1990s, Blockbuster was an unstoppable force. With
thousands of stores worldwide, it dominated the video rental market.
At its peak, Blockbuster earned billions in revenue by relying on a
tried-and-true business model of physical rentals and late fees. This
system worked until digital streaming emerged as the future of
entertainment.

Despite multiple warning signs, Blockbuster's leadership remained
anchored to the methods that had once brought them success. They
dismissed digital streaming as a passing trend and doubled down
on brick-and-mortar operations. In 2000, Netflix co-founder Reed
Hastings pitched a partnership to Blockbuster, proposing that Netflix
handle Blockbuster's online presence and Blockbuster promote Netflix
in stores. Blockbuster leadership famously laughed him out of the
room, a refusal that marked the beginning of Blockbuster's decline.[25]

Meanwhile, Netflix embodied learning agility at every stage of its
evolution. It began as a DVD-by-mail service but quickly recognized
that streaming would redefine entertainment. Instead of resisting
change, Netflix leaned in, invested in infrastructure, secured licenses,
and eventually created its own content with hits like the successful
show *Stranger Things*. Today, Netflix is a global leader in both technology and entertainment, while Blockbuster has one remaining store in
Bend, Oregon, or at least it does at the time of this writing.[26]

Thriving is most accessible to those who remember that what got
us to where we are today won't necessarily get us to where we want to
go next. To successfully adapt to a VUCA world, we need resilience
and psychological flexibility. These skills contribute to prospection,
both the negative kind that prepares us for obstacles and the positive
kind that creates new alternatives.[27]

Hope and Optimism

Hope and *optimism* are future-oriented strengths that frame the way
we perceive what hasn't yet happened. Hope is often described as the

bridge between possibility and action because it invites us to visualize a life beyond our current limitations and motivates us to take purposeful steps toward that vision.[28]

Contrary to popular belief, hope isn't innate but a choice against letting adversity dictate the course of our lives. Research suggests that individuals with high levels of hope tend to set more ambitious goals and persist through life's challenges with greater tenacity. With hope, we believe that obstacles are conquerable.[29]

According to psychologist Rick Snyder at the University of Kansas, hope is built on three essential elements. First, we need *goals* or visions of the future we want. Second, we need *agency*, which he defines as the internal belief that we can take action toward goals and sustain momentum over time. Third, we need *pathways*, the ability to generate multiple strategies so we can adapt when obstacles arise. When these three elements align, hope can transform effort into growth.[30]

While hope envisions the future, optimism gives us the confidence to make it real.[31] According to Marty Seligman at the University of Pennsylvania, whose research popularized the field of positive psychology, optimism is a skill that can be cultivated and applied across most areas of life. He suggests that our *explanatory style*, the way we interpret life's events, deeply influences our position on the range between optimism and pessimism.[32]

People who mostly rely on a *pessimistic explanatory style* see obstacles as permanent ("this will never change"), pervasive ("this affects everything"), and personal ("it's all my fault"). For instance, imagine someone who doesn't do well in a job interview and thinks, "I'm never getting a job" (permanent), "Nothing ever works out for me" (pervasive), and "No one likes me" (personal).[33]

In contrast, people who learn and apply an *optimistic explanatory style* see setbacks as temporary, specific, and external. They acknowledge failure but see it as fleeting, confined to a particular context, and often influenced by external circumstances rather than intrinsic flaws. For example, the same failed job interview might be framed as "I didn't prepare enough, but I can next time" (temporary), "That wasn't the right job for me" (specific), or "The interviewer was having a bad day" (external).[34]

Research shows that optimism, like hope, is a powerful predictor of well-being. Optimistic individuals are more likely to push through challenges, maintain stronger relationships, and enjoy better heart health and immune function.[35] In one study, children who were taught to reframe their thinking in more optimistic ways showed a lasting drop in depressive symptoms, even years later. The same holds true for adults, as research suggests professionals with an optimistic explanatory style tend to perform better under pressure and bounce back faster from setbacks.[36]

Haben Girma, the first deafblind graduate of Harvard Law School in 2013, embodies the transformative power of hope and optimism. Born with visual and hearing impairments, she grew up navigating a world not designed for her needs. Taking an unusual pathway to learning, she mastered braille and other assistive technologies to access lectures and participate in class discussions. Rather than internalize exclusion or frustration as signs to give up, it's likely that she reframed them as signals to adapt and persist. This is an example of the everyday practice of an optimistic explanatory style.[37]

Today, Girma is a tireless advocate for accessibility, collaborating with leading tech companies to create better tools for people with disabilities. As she often emphasizes, "Disability is not a barrier, but accessibility can be."[38]

Hope and optimism can also be found in the dark corners of life. Anne Frank, a Jewish teenager hiding with her family in a secret annex during the Holocaust, spent more than two years in constant fear of being discovered by the Nazis. From her small window, Anne found solace in the beauty of a chestnut tree with branches that reached toward the sky. She wrote in her diary, "I don't think of all the misery, but of the beauty that still remains."[39]

For Anne, the tree became a symbol of possibility, standing strong in a world consumed by chaos. In its enduring presence, she defied despair and saw evidence that life could still be beautiful. Anne's hope anchored her, and her story demonstrates that hope isn't a naive denial of reality but a courageous choice. Her diary, published in more than 70 languages, invites us to find light in our darkest moments.

Balancing Hedonia and Eudaimonia

Every day, we make choices toward the life we dream of, even when we're still discovering what that dream might be.

Present action and future planning can both be evaluated in terms of two pathways to well-being: *hedonia*, the pursuit of pleasure and comfort, and *eudaimonia*, the pursuit of meaning and purpose.[40] When we focus too narrowly on one and neglect the other, life can feel either hollow or burdensome. When we learn to balance both, we can thrive.

Hedonia, from the ancient Greek *hēdonē* (pleasure), is the practice of enjoying life's pleasures, such as the warmth of sunlight streaming through a window, laughter shared over a meal, or the thrill of a well-timed joke. These pleasures, though fleeting at times, anchor us in the present and prompt us to cherish the beauty of now. When planning for the future, hedonia invites us to choose actions today that will bring joyful moments tomorrow.[41]

Eudaimonia combines *eu* (good or well) and *daimōn* (spirit or inner guide). Eudaimonia is the state of being in harmony with one's highest self, living in alignment with our values. It usually emerges when our daily efforts feel meaningful and transcendental, contributing to something beyond personal gain.[42]

The question isn't whether to prioritize hedonia or eudaimonia but how to integrate both into our vision of the future. By embracing hedonia, we bring vitality to our days, and by grounding ourselves in eudaimonia, we anchor our aspirations to what truly matters to us. This balance creates a future that's both enjoyable and deeply meaningful.

These dimensions are captured in the Japanese concept of *ikigai*, often described as "the reason for being." Ikigai illustrates the intersection of four elements: what you love, what you're good at, what the world needs, and what you can be paid for. The concept offers a path to a life that's both satisfying and meaningful.[43]

Personally, a lightbulb went on when I learned about ikigai, and the balance between hedonia and eudaimonia. I realized I didn't need to search for enjoyment all the time if my actions were in service to a greater purpose, and that meaning can also be found in moments of pleasure.

What Kind of Future Do I Want to Create? Meet Marco

When Marco first came to me, he was searching for a way out of the rut he had fallen into. He was referred by a former client who recognized in him the same dissatisfaction she had once felt. Marco had spent years mastering techniques under the leadership of Michelin-starred chefs. He had climbed the ranks in some of the world's most prestigious kitchens, but the higher he climbed, the more disillusioned he became.

"I should be happy," Marco confessed during one of our sessions. "I worked my ass off to get here but I feel so empty."

At first, he thought his emptiness came from burnout, the long hours, high stress, and unrelenting perfectionism of working in fine dining. Marco had spent his career in places where the culture was ruthless and where mistakes were severely punished: plates were thrown, tempers exploded, people were fired for the slightest misstep, and chefs wielded power through intimidation.

"Let your guard down, and someone will take advantage of you," he admitted. "I don't trust anyone. Not my bosses, not my coworkers, not our suppliers, not even the guests we serve. I've spent years waiting for the other shoe to drop." He believed that, given the chance, those who worked with him would exploit, humiliate, or discard him. His success had been built on survival, on staying sharp enough and tough enough to never be on the receiving end of that cruelty. But the cost was loneliness and exhaustion.

Changing the Future Using AIR

Awareness: When I asked Marco, "Why did you become a chef in the first place?" He told me about his grandmother's tiny kitchen in Naples, where meals stretched to feed anyone who showed up. The scent of simmering tomatoes and garlic filled the air. From an old radio on the counter, romantic Italian classics played softly in the background.

"My nonna cooked with so much love," he said. "Making food was never about ego but about taking care of people."

"She made this ragù Napoletano." He smiled, remembering, "You could smell it from the street. Slow-cooked for hours until the sauce was deep and rich. When she put a plate in front of you, the world felt steady again."

Inquiry: Recalling that particular memory ignited something positive in Marco, so I invited him to consider what actions could bring those feelings back. "How could that memory inform the future you want to create?"

For the first time in years, Marco imagined a place where food was a way to show generosity. The idea terrified him because leaving fine dining felt like throwing away everything he had achieved. He feared regret, losing people's respect, and, more than anything, the possibility that he wouldn't be able to support himself. His identity was so entangled with his career that tugging at a single thread felt like it could cause everything to come undone.

Reframing: Ultimately, Marco reached the tipping point at which the fear of staying the same became greater than the fear of change. He left his job and partnered with a small neighborhood restaurant, where he had the freedom to cook in a way that felt true to him. He sourced ingredients from nearby farmers and introduced a pay-what-you-can initiative for community members in need. For the first time in years, he was crafting his own vision.

Ripples in the Pond

It wasn't an easy journey for Marco. "I don't know how to cook without constantly looking over my shoulder," he once confided. Sometimes, his old patterns crept in, taking him into survival mode and assuming the worst in people. At the same time, he had many moments of thriving, like when guests lingered after meals to extend their gratitude for the moments of comfort he provided. One evening, he plated his grandmother's ragù for a regular customer, who took a bite and closed her eyes in delight.

Marco's hedonic pleasures of cooking were infused with the eudaimonic dreams that had led him to cook in the first place. Planning for a future in which hedonia and eudaimonia aligned transformed the way he saw others. He started to relearn trust as a choice that could create something beautiful. The emptiness that once reverberated inside him began to fade, replaced with a sense of meaning in the life he was now choosing to live.

For most of my corporate career, when I envisioned the future, I desperately chased titles or a raise, believing they could somehow keep me safe. That cycle left me depleted and made many of my relationships feel transactional. I measured my worth by comparison, always looking to see who was succeeding more than I was.

Looking back, I can see how quickly joy can disappear when our worth is tied to someone else's highlight reel. Social comparison is the thief of joy.

I began to experience more frequent moments of thriving when I realized that no title or raise could offer no title or raise could offer the sense of security I was searching for. Letting go of the need to prove myself through status felt both freeing and grounding, and it allowed me to focus on connection and meaningful work.

Warren Buffett, the famous investor, suggested in a talk at the University of Georgia that at some point we want to pursue work that aligns with who we are and brings genuine fulfillment, rather than taking jobs simply because they look good on our resumes. Buffett argues that choosing passion over prestige makes life richer and more meaningful. Life, he suggests, is too short to spend climbing someone else's ladder.[44]

I acknowledge that this transformation is a privilege not everyone can afford. For many, the ability to choose work that aligns with beliefs and values is constrained by circumstances, systemic barriers, financial pressures, or a lack of opportunity. This makes it even more essential to advocate for a world where more people have the freedom to pursue meaningful work for themselves and for the collective flourishing of society.

I've also come to realize that thriving requires us to engage with risk instead of avoiding it. Growth rarely happens in comfort zones but rather in spaces where we stretch and stumble. Avoidance may protect us from pain, but it also keeps us from possibility. Over and over again, we have a choice: will we shrink into survival mode, holding onto what we believe feels safe, even if it no longer serves us? Or will we dare to embrace uncertainty as a space where both hedonia (pleasure) and eudaimonia (meaning) can coexist and guide us toward a more fulfilling future?

Using AIR to Explore the Future

You can use the AIR approach to help you explore how your relationship with your future might be keeping you in survival mode.

Awareness: Recognizing Our Relationship with the Future

- When I think about the future, am I more focused on obstacles, opportunities, or a mix of both?
- Are my future expectations truly mine, or have I picked them up from others?
- When I think about the future I want, do I believe I'm capable of pursuing it?

Inquiry: Questioning Our Vision of What's Ahead

- What kind of future am I currently planning for? Do I want to live in it?
- If I could tolerate uncertainty better, what would I pursue?
- Who would I need to become to live the future I long for?

Reframing: Creating a Future that Aligns with Our Personal Values

- What new story do I want to tell myself about my future?
- What would change if I trusted myself to figure things out along the way?
- What's one small step I could take today that would bring me closer to the future I want to create?

10

Space
The Power of Our Surroundings

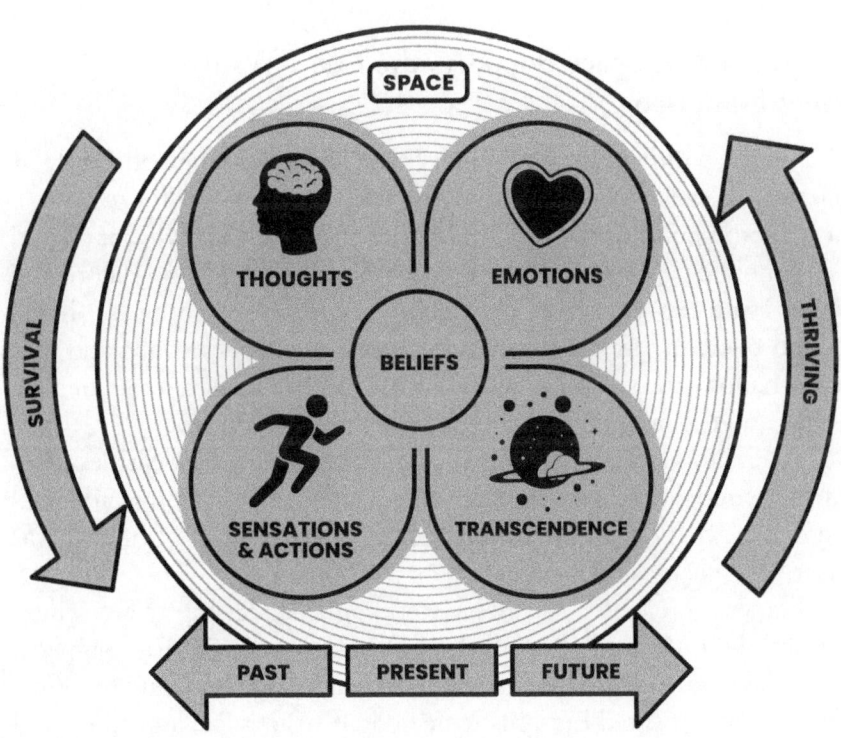

WHILE WE HOLD immense power to influence our inner world, life unfolds within the complexity of systems and circumstances that surround us. The spaces in which we live exert a powerful influence and often determine the opportunities available to us or the challenges we face. The external world is a co-creator in our pursuit of what lies ahead.

How often are our best-laid plans altered by forces beyond our control? A sudden economic downturn may delay a long-anticipated goal, or a natural disaster may transform entire communities in a single moment. Even in the face of such unpredictability, we're not powerless. Much like a river finding its way around stones, bending and carving, we can adapt to the flow of circumstances and use every twist and turn to find space for thriving.

What Kind of Space Supports the Life I Want?
Meet Francisco

One sunny winter afternoon, I met Francisco in his cramped, dimly lit office at the edge of an industrial district. The room was tucked into a nondescript building, its exterior as unremarkable as the view it offered of a concrete parking lot. A few sparse trees struggled to grow along the curbs against a backdrop of warehouses. Inside, fluorescent lights buzzed overhead as the harsh glare bounced off beige walls and cast long shadows into every corner. The air was heavy with a mix of stale coffee and the faint chemical tang of nearby machinery.

As Francisco sat at his desk, his posture revealed a weariness that went beyond physical exhaustion. His eyes flicked briefly toward me as I entered, then quickly returned to the papers in front of him. It was clear his focus was elsewhere.

Francisco reached out after attending a leadership event where I spoke about thriving. He was the CEO of a manufacturing company, someone who had climbed the ranks through hard work and sacrifice. His clients respected him, his team sought his advice, and the board and shareholders valued his reliability. Despite this, it became evident as we talked that there was a gap between the life he was living and the one he longed for.

"Last week, I missed my son's rugby game. Instead of being there, I was here," he said, gesturing at the chaotic spread of binders, reports, post-it notes, and half-finished tasks competing for space. "I want to be the kind of father who shows up. But what if I've already missed my chance?" His voice carried a mix of guilt and resignation.

"I don't think anything I do makes a difference," he admitted. "It's like I'm treading water and the current keeps pulling me back." As he spoke, I couldn't help but notice how much the office seemed to mirror his words. The suffocating atmosphere felt like an extension of his current state.

I asked him about a framed photo of his family on his desk. "That's from our vacation two years ago," he said wistfully. "We were in the mountains. No deadlines, no emails. I didn't even check my phone because there was no signal. Sometimes, I imagine packing a bag and disappearing back into that mountain. The thought tempts me as much as it terrifies me."

We generally perceive the space around us as uninvolved in our lives, but our surroundings, including objects, places, people, and all living beings, are active participants in our stories. Elements in our environment influence our beliefs, thoughts, emotions, sensations, actions, and ability to transcend, yet each of us responds in unique ways. A busy city street might energize one person while leaving another overwhelmed with anxiety. The stillness of a mountain trail can instill a profound sense of peace for some and distress for others.[1]

As Francisco looked around his office, he admitted how draining the space felt. Studies in environmental psychology confirm that cluttered spaces increase stress hormone levels.[2] Similarly, exposure to natural light boosts serotonin, which improves mood and energy. Our bodies and minds are deeply affected by the spaces we inhabit.[3]

"I know I'm burning out," Francisco said, "I've always been the guy who gets it done. I've spent my whole career fighting fires, only for new ones to keep starting. I push and push, but it never ends."

Francisco was trapped by the demands of his role and by a space that offered no invitation to thrive. Without intervention, it's all too easy to remain caught in an environment that perpetuates survival mode. However, research and experience show us that small modifications to our surroundings can influence both individual and collective well-being.[4]

The Power of Objects

When I was eight or nine, I went on an excavation of my dad's closet, filled with an adventurous collection of artifacts from his life before I existed. Among the old jackets and forgotten keepsakes, I found a soccer ball signed by soccer star Pelé.

"Can we play with it?" I asked my dad excitedly. He shook his head. "Can I take it to school just to show my friends?" Another no. The ball was off-limits, so it went back into the depths of the closet.

Fifteen years later, I found myself in that same closet, this time cleaning up after my father's unexpected passing. As I neatly folded his shirts into donation boxes, my hands found the soccer ball. I picked it up, and it crumbled. The years of humidity had rotted it from the inside out, and Pelé's signature was nothing more than dust in my hands.

The ball had been cloistered for years, and in the end, it was lost anyway. As I held the decaying leather, I wondered how many things we guard so carefully that we never truly experience them. Meaning often resides in the objects, places, people, and living beings we choose to engage with actively and intentionally.

The objects around us reveal details about our lives. The stack of books on the nightstand, the coffee mugs in the sink, the exercise equipment in the corner, and the clothes in the back of the closet, all tell stories. Some may speak of meaning, like the framed photo of a loved one or the journal filled with dreams. Others may reveal obligation or impulse, like the never-used fine china, the exercise equipment under the bed, or the art supplies still waiting to be opened.

When we're in survival mode, our narrowed focus is on *instant gratification*, the impulse to seek quick relief or pleasure in the moment, sometimes at the expense of future well-being. This evolutionary mechanism, originally developed to ensure we see the next sunrise, favors immediate rewards over thinking long-term.[5]

In moments of discomfort, the act of purchasing can feel like a quick fix. A flash sale grabs our attention, and we pounce, convinced we're miss out if we don't act immediately. Acquiring a new item might offer a brief sense of satisfaction or control in a restless moment, but the relief fades quickly and we find ourselves scanning for the next purchase.[6] Advertisements take advantage of this belief by blurring the line between *need* and *want* and feeding the illusion that our fleeting desires are urgent.

Thriving invites us to approach material possessions in a different way by prompting us to ask, "Is this something I need or something I want?" Needs sustain us and provide the foundation for well-being, like food, shelter, tools, and cherished items that remind us of who we are. Wants, on the other hand, are optional. They can enrich our lives when chosen wisely, but when accumulated indiscriminately, they can weigh us down. Recognizing the difference between needs and wants is subtle, but it can significantly impact how we approach life's choices.

Our relationship with objects is tied to our sense of security. Research suggests that we often project emotions onto possessions, seeing them as extensions of ourselves or as anchors in an uncertain world, like my father's soccer ball, which might have reminded him of a peak moment when he met a legendary figure.[7] Similarly, people who experience *hoarding disorder* often describe their possessions as safe or comforting, even when those items have no practical use.[8] While most of us may not struggle with this disorder, we still feel the tug of attachment to the emotions carried by particular objects.[9]

In the TV show *Alone*, contestants are dropped into the wilderness with only 10 items of their choice. As participants are stripped of everything they own, each carefully chosen object takes on profound significance as a tool for survival. A fishing line becomes the difference between hunger and sustenance. A simple photograph of family becomes a lifeline in moments of isolation. Watching the participants navigate these choices tells us that objects are rarely just things because they have the power to keep us grounded and safe when life feels uncertain.[10]

As we step away from survival mode, our relationships with objects can change considerably. Thriving isn't necessarily about having less or depriving ourselves but about making sure the things we own add value to our lives.

The goal of what to keep and what to release is to intentionally surround ourselves with objects that reflect our values and aspirations.

That way, we can transform our spaces from repositories of impulse into sanctuaries of meaning.

The Power of Place

The spaces we create, from office cubicles to entire cities, can either keep us in survival mode or invite us into thriving. For people like Francisco, a chaotic environment can reinforce stress and deepen negative patterns. Small adjustments in the environment hold the potential to create big change.

Modern workplaces reveal the tremendous impact that carefully designed spaces can have on human potential. For instance, Google's headquarters in Mountain View, California, is a shining example of intentional design. The Googleplex feels more like a university campus than a traditional office, as sunlight filters through wide windows, the outdoor spaces encourage movement and connection with winding paths and shaded seating. Inside, features like meditation rooms and fitness centers reflect a growing awareness that well-being and performance are intricately connected. These design choices draw from research suggesting that physical environments can influence mental states.[11] At the same time, it's important to acknowledge that such environments are not purely altruistic, as they are often carefully engineered to advance corporate goals.

Likewise, the Japanese practice of *shinrin-yoku*, or forest bathing, is a deliberate immersion in nature. The practice lowers stress and enhances physical health. Trees release volatile compounds called phytoncides that, when inhaled, boost immune activity and nudge us toward thriving.[12] On the other hand, the chaos of a crowded subway train during rush hour radiates an unrelenting sense of urgency that can easily put our bodies on high alert. Even without an immediate threat, our brains can perceive overstimulation as a potential danger, making it harder to focus or to think expansively.

Fostering spaces where form and function align can be a strategic business advantage. Studies suggest that workspaces that support well-being lead to higher job satisfaction and greater innovation. In these environments, employees are more likely to feel valued and approach challenges with more resilience.[13]

Compare Google's headquarters to the stark spaces of many warehouses and industrial complexes designed with efficiency as the only priority. In these environments, workers often endure long hours in dimly lit, noisy, overcrowded spaces with minimal ventilation because their health is secondary to production goals. These spaces force workers to focus solely on productivity, making it much harder for them to thrive.[14]

The Power of Culture

Culture surrounds us and influences how we see the world, including how we define safety, success, worth, beauty, and so much more. It includes the beliefs we inherit, often without question.[15] For instance, in cultures where achievement is equated with value, slowing down can feel unsafe. Similarly, in places where vulnerability is seen as weakness, expressing emotion may come with shame. Whether we choose to accept these cultural narratives or to challenge them, they play a powerful role in our ability to thrive.[16]

My father taught me that more money meant more security. Exiled from Cuba and stripped of home and safety at 16, he spent his life working 12-hour days, six days a week, because as he often said, "If there's enough in the bank, I don't need favors from anyone." His example taught me to see money as a shield against an unpredictable world, a belief that seems to have taken hold of much of our modern world.

That belief stayed with me, mostly unquestioned, until one Friday night, at our usual family dinner, when we regularly play a game we call "high points and low points of the week." My youngest son's high point was that we're all together eating a delicious meal. His low point? "Dad's been working too much, and we barely get to spend any time with him."

I laughed and felt a strange rush. I first mistook it for pride, but then I wondered. After dinner, I sat alone at the table, staring at my glowing phone. For years, I'd told myself I worked hard for my family, but I wasn't working just to provide, I was working to convince myself that I was safe, that I was worthy, and that I belonged. My values said family came first, but my choices told another story.

This is how culture works invisibly. It tells us what success looks like and what happens if we fall short. But even cultural narratives are constantly changing across time and space.

During much of the modern era, progress was measured by expansion, and economic development came at the planet's expense, with many cultures prioritizing more production, more consumption, and more growth. That cultural mindset started to change in the 1960s as environmental degradation became impossible to ignore.

In 1962, Rachel Carson's book *Silent Spring* revealed the devastation caused by pesticides, leading to the banning of DDT or dichlorodiphenyltrichloroethane, a synthetic chemical compound widely used on crops, in mosquito spraying, and even shaken onto the heads of children to prevent lice infestations. The first Earth Day in 1970 sparked global conversations about sustainability and challenged the idea that progress was only about profit. Since then, our cultural awareness has deepened as the realities of climate change have become more visible.[17]

What began as a fringe movement is now a global reckoning. In recent years, climate activism has amplified public pressure on governments and corporations to act with urgency. New ideas about renewable energy, circular economics, regenerative design, and ecological responsibility have transformed cultural perceptions about what it means to thrive, prioritizing sustaining the planet so that life can flourish long after we're gone.[18]

The Power of Systems

Culture includes systemic factors that structure our lives, including demographics, religion, governance, tradition, and language.

Demographic factors like gender, race, sexual orientation, ability, and socioeconomic status determine our access to opportunity in profound ways.[19] The privilege of belonging to certain groups can open doors, but it doesn't guarantee thriving in every part of life. In countries like Iceland, where gender equality is supported through policies such as parental leave, the gender pay gap still persists.[20] In contrast, in places like Afghanistan, where education and work are largely restricted to men, women continue to resist, learn, and earn.[21] Oppression can limit access, but it doesn't make thriving impossible.

Religions play a similar dual role in determining culture. At their best, religious traditions can create connection and shared meaning. The Hindu festival of Diwali, for example, invites gratitude through communal rituals that help strengthen bonds across families and communities. At the same time, religious institutions can also restrict belonging and self-expression, like some conservative faith communities where LGBTQ+ individuals are often left with the painful choice between concealment and exclusion.[22]

Institutional structures can either support or suppress the conditions people need to thrive. Some faith communities are working to change this, like the United Church's Open and Affirming initiative, where spiritual belonging promotes inclusion.[23]

Likewise, governments play an essential role in designing and sustaining cultures. After the devastating genocide of the 1990s, Rwanda invested in public restoration through efforts like the National Unity and Reconciliation Commission and increased representation of women in government. Still, Rwanda has faced ongoing criticism for suppressing dissent and limiting political freedoms. While collective healing is possible, the conditions for thriving remain an ongoing process that requires continuous commitment.[24]

In other contexts, governments marked by high levels of corruption or authoritarian control often create environments of chronic instability. In Venezuela, persistent constraints on autonomy and expression make it harder for many to move beyond survival. Political systems, like cultural ones, have a profound influence on the conditions in which people thrive.[25]

Despite challenges, thriving may still be possible through solidarity networks. In some of the most marginalized spaces, people have built communal aid groups that provide support, food, housing, and legal help where government institutions fail. For example, intergenerational knowledge within immigrant families helps younger members preserve a sense of identity that bridges their heritage with new opportunities.[26] Similarly, mentoring programs in corporate settings help people from underrepresented backgrounds navigate unfamiliar structures. In this way, thriving becomes a collective achievement nurtured through the mutual exchange of support.

Some traditions offer belonging and serve as a bridge across generations. In Mexico, Día de los Muertos invites people to honor their ancestors through food, altars, music, and storytelling. The holiday offers a culturally grounded way to navigate grief and fosters continuity between the living and their ancestors.[27]

In contrast, there are practices described as traditional that cause harm when passed down without reflection, such as child marriage, which persists in some cultures due to the intersecting forces of poverty, limited access to education, systemic inequality, and social expectations. These obsolete practices often restrict autonomy and opportunity, particularly for girls, and raise critical questions about which inherited norms we choose to preserve and which we must outgrow.[28]

Traditions are determined by the choices we make over time. When carried forward with awareness, they support healing and connection, and when left unquestioned, they have the potential to inflict tremendous harm.

Finally, language guides the way we move through the world by influencing our stories and beliefs. The Bantu word *ubuntu*, loosely translated as "I am because we are," reflects a cultural emphasis on interconnectedness and communal thriving. It reinforces shared humanity and influences the way people approach communication, from conflict resolution to community-building.[29]

Other words reflect emotional states that help us make sense of our lived experience. In Czech, *litost* describes the sudden, often painful recognition of our suffering, sometimes sparked by another person's success.[30] It captures a blend of envy and self-awareness that rarely gets named. These linguistic nuances show us what different cultures notice and nurture while reminding us that words do a lot more than express our thoughts. They help define them.

Evolving Culture and Systems to Support Thriving

What cultural changes would support widespread thriving? What actions can we intentionally take, both personally and together, to make these changes happen?

Possibilities include investing more time and energy in our loved ones and mentoring others. We can also promote the preservation of cultural institutions such as schools, city parks, museums, and libraries.

We can help our communities evolve to meet the needs of modern life, just as many libraries now offer online access and streaming video for those who might otherwise be left out. In describing the role of public libraries, the U.S. Center for an Urban Future notes, "No other institution, public or private, does a better job of reaching people who have been left behind in today's economy, have failed to reach their potential in the city's public school system or who simply need help navigating an increasingly complex world."[31]

We can also work to evolve away from cultural norms that undermine well-being, such as the widespread glorification of overwork and hustle culture. In many spaces, constant busyness is worn as a badge of honor that reinforces the idea that our worth is tied to productivity.[32] We live in a time of rising global burnout, fueled in part by a lack of rest and connection with family or community. Choosing not to feed into this harmful cultural pattern is a powerful act of resistance. Setting boundaries around work time and encouraging others to do the same can help us carve a more sustainable path to collective thriving.[33]

Cultural transformation begins with questions that reframe how we live and invite us to reflect on what we most value.

What does a meaningful life look like?

Which parts of my culture keep me stuck in survival mode, and which ones lead me toward thriving?

What unspoken rules have I been following, and are they still serving me?

How can I honor both my roots and my growth?

These questions encourage us to examine the beliefs we've inherited and help us discern what is worth carrying forward and what we can gently set down. Culture is not fixed or inevitable, and we have the agency to question and transform it.

Who Gets to Thrive?

The spaces we inhabit tell a story about who is most likely to thrive. The difference between a neighborhood surrounded by nature and an industrial complex isn't accidental. Systemic decisions give some people easy access to thriving while leaving others to struggle.

We know that poverty isn't just about low income but also about exposure to overcrowding, noise, pollution, and environmental inequality.[34] For instance, for many people living in densely populated urban spaces, the closest thing to nature is a patch of grass in a highway median. Although access to large green spaces isn't available to everyone, thriving can occur without abundance when we find small spaces of renewal. In the midst of hardship, it may still be possible to tap into resources like taking a mindful breath or briefly connecting with nature in whatever ways our circumstances allow.[35]

For much of my life, I believed I had to earn safety. Living in Venezuela in the early 2000s, survival meant staying alert, staying busy, and staying ahead. After Hugo Chávez came to power in 1999, the country's growing sociopolitical unrest, institutional erosion, rising violence, and economic collapse worsened.[36] Violence surged, and by the mid-2000s, some reports estimated that Caracas had reached a murder rate of 130 per 100,000 inhabitants, a staggering contrast to the average of 6 per 100,000 in a typical U.S. city.[37]

Daily life became a matter of constant vigilance. We memorized which streets to avoid and which conversations demanded silence. We stood in hours-long lines for basic supplies like rice and toilet paper, knowing they might be gone the next day. As the rule of law faded and institutions crumbled, survival required moment-by-moment calculation. Like many others, my family learned to improvise and adapt to the fear that we could lose what kept us safe in a moment.

When Adriana and I started a new life in Canada, I believed that slowing down would leave me vulnerable, so I felt I couldn't afford to rest. I pushed forward with the conviction that one misstep could unravel everything and leave me and my family without a home. I was running from scarcity so fast I didn't realize it had taken hold of me.

A turning point came when my coach asked me to reflect on what it would take for me to end up living on the streets. I slowly listed the steps: losing my job, failing to find another, spending all my savings, wearing out every family member and friend, exhausting every safety net, and using up every last resource. As the list grew, I realized how unlikely that scenario really was.

I organized my life around the unexamined belief that I was one step away from losing everything. I was no longer in Venezuela, but my body and nervous system hadn't gotten the message. To thrive, I had to revisit and update the stories I had learned in my past environment and recognize that I was now in a different space.

Looking at Spaces Using AIR

Using the AIR framework, Francisco chose to take deliberate steps toward thriving.

Awareness: Looking around his office, I asked, "What is it like for you to work in this space?"

He shrugged it off. "It's just an office," he said. But as we sat in the silence that followed, he began to describe the low-level tension he felt every time he walked in. The stacks of paper reminded him of unfinished tasks. The buzzing lights gave him headaches. The lack of natural light made him feel disconnected from the world outside. He noticed that his workspace was impacting both his mood and his approach to work.

Inquiry: I then asked, "If your office reflected the energy you want to feel, what might it look like?"

Francisco chuckled, a dry, self-deprecating laugh. "Well, for starters, I'd actually be able to find a pen when I need one," he said, holding up a cup full of mismatched markers and dried-out ballpoints. "Maybe I'd have a chair that doesn't feel like it's conspiring against my back."

He took that insight and began with the tangible. He stood for a moment, holding a forgotten coffee mug from a shelf, its rim stained and chipped at the edge. "I've had this cup since my first promotion," he said with a faint smile. "I told myself I'd replace it when I had time. Funny how that time never comes."

Reframing: Finally, I asked, "What could you do before our next session to give you a greater sense of agency?"

Francisco answered this question with action. When I returned for our next session, he had cleared away the clutter, swapped out the fluorescent lights for softer, warmer bulbs, and added a couple of live plants and art on the walls. He commented, "I guess I deserve a space that supports my well-being. Now when I come into the office, it doesn't feel heavy. Even breathing feels easier."

Deconstructing Being Busy Using AIR

Next, we explored how Francisco responded to a culture of overwork.

Awareness: "What drives you to work so hard? How do you know when you've done enough?"

At first, he talked about his upbringing, where being busy was celebrated, and rest was seen as laziness. In his company's culture, long hours were the norm.

"Even when I hit big milestones," Francisco admitted, "it never feels like enough. My mom used to say, 'Don't stop until the work is done.' But when is the work ever done? That's why I feel nothing I do makes a difference." He realized he kept pushing the finish line further and further. Like treading water, he was always moving and always striving, just to avoid going under. He came to see that an important source of his burnout was mistaking his worth for how much he could carry.

Inquiry: I asked, "What happens if success isn't about working harder but about working with more intention?" Although his first response was silence, over time, Francisco began to explore setting intentions as a compass to guide his daily work and life. Each morning, he chose a single word, like "patience" on Monday and "listening" on Tuesday.

Reframing brought one of the most powerful shifts. "If we turn away from what's not working, what's one thing that you're grateful for today?" At first, he dismissed the idea of gratitude as overly simplistic. Then, he agreed to keep a notebook on his desk and write down three things each day that brought him a sense of gratitude. Later, I asked him how it felt to stay attentive to those moments when things went right.

"I didn't realize how much I was ignoring," he admitted. "There's more to appreciate than I thought."

Curiosity Enhances Thriving

Cultural transformation is fueled by the curiosity to ask how our surroundings influence us and what could be different. The answers are not in some distant ideal future but already in the present, waiting for us to notice if we only pay attention.

What kind of spaces are we creating for ourselves, for our loved ones, and for our communities? When we examine our surroundings with curiosity, we take a step toward creating spaces that support thriving.

Thriving is a shared practice that's more likely to occur in some environments than others. A child with access to inspiring teachers has a different trajectory than one who lacks educational support. A mentor can help a worker see paths that might otherwise be invisible. A neighborhood with libraries and gathering places supports well-being in ways that a neglected, resource-starved environment can't. No one thrives in isolation.

Because thriving is harder for some people than others, it's important to maintain compassion for those who are carrying heavier loads or lack the resources that are plentiful for some of us. Perhaps offering our support could make it easier for them to thrive.

In the end, Francisco did much more than redesign his office. In our last session, he shared that he had reclaimed a practice that for a long time felt out of reach: rest. As part of that, he was planning a return to the mountain with his son. "I want to be there for him," he said, his voice catching like it might give way to a tear. "It's never too late to show up for the ones we love most."

Using AIR to Explore Spaces

Now use the AIR approach to explore the impact of different spaces on your life.

Awareness: Recognizing the Influence of My Surroundings

- *Do I feel energized or drained by the spaces I spend the most time in?*
- *Do I experience my spaces as fixed, or do I believe I can change them?*
- *In what ways do my surroundings support or limit my well-being?*

Inquiry: Questioning the Role of Space in My Life

- *What beliefs or habits determine the way I interact with my space?*
- *How much of my space is the result of personal choices versus others' expectations?*
- *If my space could speak, what would it be telling me?*

Reframing: Creating a Space That Supports My Thriving

- *If my space reflected the life I want to lead, what might it look or feel like?*
- *What is one small, intentional change I could make to align my space with the life I want to live?*
- *What's one way I can engage with my surroundings to make thriving more likely for me and for others?*

Conclusion

BEFORE YOU TURN the final page, I invite you to pause and reflect. What parts of this book feel especially relevant to you right now? Where do you notice resistance? How does this experience shift what you believe is possible for you and those around you?

Survival mode and thriving mode are both daily life experiences available to all of us. While some people find moments of thriving even during hardship, others may feel stuck in survival mode, even when surrounded by comfort and opportunity. What makes the biggest difference is how we use our agency to meet what's happening around us.

You've already started doing this work. Every time you face a challenge and decide to learn from it rather than be defined by it, you open the door to go beyond survival and into thriving.

In the work of thriving, like in most important practices, we stumble, we forget, we fall short, and we slip back into old patterns we thought we had already outgrown. The key is to notice when we've drifted away, get curious about our experience, and then gently find our way back to the thriving path.

A Map to Thriving

Each of the nine elements presented in this book offers a unique entry point into thriving. By bringing awareness to them, you may begin to sense what parts of your life already support your well-being and what adjustments might open new possibilities. Remember that each element is connected to the others, and together, they form a living system where a small breakthrough in one area can unlock growth in another. As you become attuned to the challenges and opportunities within each element, you'll naturally act with greater agency and navigate your life more intentionally.

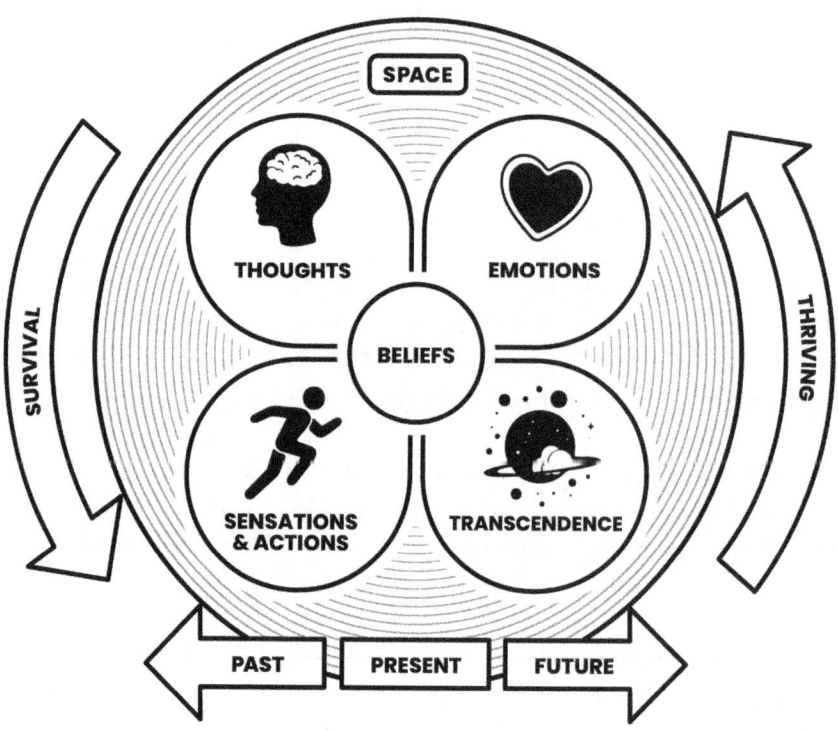

We started with *Beliefs*, the conscious and unconscious ideas that define what we consider true and what we imagine is possible. What we believe influences what we think, how we feel, and what we do. Beliefs live beneath our choices, and when we bring them into the light, they often surprise us. Beliefs can be questioned and rewritten. Emily showed us how even a single shift in our beliefs can positively rearrange our life experience, rippling outward and affecting those around us.

Next came *Thoughts*, the stream of mental narratives that influence our moment-by-moment experience. Simon showed us how easy it is to fall into thinking traps such as catastrophizing and mind reading. We also learned that our thoughts don't define us, so we can assess their accuracy and choose whether to follow where they lead.

From there, we moved into the *Emotions* that many of us were taught to ignore or tightly manage. Deanne helped us recognize how emotions frequently point to what we care about the most. They often arrive in the body before the mind catches up, asking for our attention and helping us connect with ourselves and others. Our emotions can bridge the gap between our internal experience and outward action.

Sensations and *Actions* are how the body speaks. The nervous system carries the imprint of what we've endured, but it also carries the capacity to regulate and change. Many of the patterns we repeat without thinking originate from what our bodies learned to protect us. We all have the capacity to use our agency to form new habits that will serve us better and improve our well-being. Through my work with Robyn, I discovered that listening to my body's messages was a way to reclaim my agency and consciously choose new responses to old patterns.

We then turned toward *Transcendence*, the experience of connecting with something greater than ourselves. This is where we encounter the feeling of being both small and wondrous in a vast universe. Maria's story reminded us that transcendence often begins with service to others. Transcendence may be experienced through meditation, faith, spirituality, religion, mystical experiences, the awareness that all things are interconnected, and countless other ways.

In the *Past*, Ronan helped us notice how unresolved experiences can influence our present choices. By using our agency, we can revisit and reframe memories once colored by feelings of powerlessness and victimhood, opening space for the present and future to become something new.

In the *Present*, we watched Layla reconnect with herself, her children, her friends, and her colleagues through mindfulness. By cultivating awareness, we soften the impulse to judge ourselves and others, signaling safety and creating space for connection. The present moment is a meeting point where all elements of the map converge, where we can integrate our beliefs, thoughts, emotions, sensations, actions, and sense of transcendence into a unified experience of thriving.

In the *Future*, Marco's story helped us explore prospection, the ability to imagine futures that align with our values and to take steps to make them possible.

Finally, we arrived at *Space*, the physical objects, places, living beings, and systems around us. Francisco showed us how our environment can impact our mood. Space has the power to nourish or constrain us and to liberate or diminish our lives. Through agentic choices, we can influence culture to create environments that support both our own thriving and that of others. Ultimately, thriving is a collective endeavor.

Each of the nine elements offers its own kind of wisdom. Together, they form an interconnected map to know yourself better, again and again. Whether you begin by exploring your beliefs or understanding the spaces around you, each element supports and amplifies the others.

Along the way, you've been practicing agency by coming up for AIR: Awareness, Inquiry, and Reframing. Awareness enables you to become the observer and gain perspective on your experience. Inquiry invites you to question the patterns you carry and their origins. Reframing opens the door to possibilities by helping you choose responses more aligned with who you are and who you want to be.

You've done something courageous. By practicing AIR, you've returned to old narratives with new eyes. You've disrupted patterns and opened yourself to new ways of being. That's the brave work of transformation.

The Edges of the Map

The ideas in this book are invitations, not conclusions. They come from a particular place and time, influenced by the questions I've asked, the research I've studied, the cultures I've moved through, the work I've done, the experiences that have formed me, and the stories other people have told me.

The most valuable frameworks are flexible. The one in this book is meant to support you, not define you. If something helped, keep it. If something didn't land well with you, trust yourself to let it go. What feels accessible and helpful for one person might be less so for another, and what doesn't work for you today might work for you tomorrow.

Science plays a vital role by giving us a container to test hypotheses and understand patterns. Although the ideas in this book are grounded in research, science has its limits. It can quantify outcomes and reveal trends, but it can't fully hold the richness of the human experience. It can only measure what is measurable. Above all, trust that your story, in all its specificity, matters more than any study, no matter how rigorous. The most meaningful breakthroughs often emerge in the space where science and experience meet. Data may point the way, but only you can know what thriving feels like for you.

At the heart of transformation lies your ability to choose and to respond using your agency. Even in constrained circumstances, when choices feel narrow, there's still a space, however small, where thriving can emerge.

It's important to acknowledge that the shift from survival to thriving can feel especially complex for individuals in the neurodivergent community or those carrying the lingering effects of trauma, whose brains may process the world differently and experience these modes in uniquely personal ways.

While the ideas in this book may be broadly applicable, thriving sometimes calls for additional support. This book does not replace medical care, and I offer these ideas as an author, coach, entrepreneur, and fellow human. If you find yourself deeply stuck in survival mode or if life feels overwhelming, please consider reaching out for help.

Thriving doesn't happen in isolation. It's heavily influenced by the resources available to us and the barriers that stand in the way. Our unique cultural backgrounds and life circumstances play an important role in how we experience thriving. Our lives are inseparable from the spaces we inhabit, and those spaces can either support or strain our capacity to move beyond survival.

Thriving isn't a matter of personal growth and willpower alone. It's augmented when our communities foster healing and a sense of belonging. Thriving becomes more likely when we're seen, supported, and believed in. Seek out the people who expand your sense of possibility and pay it forward by offering your presence to others who might need it. If you find ways to thrive in a difficult environment, see if you can make it easier for someone else who is walking a similar path.

What Is Thriving? Meet Yourself

You've had glimpses of my journey and the journeys of my clients, but the story that matters most is yours.

Getting to know yourself is a path only you can walk. Whether your next breakthrough comes from these pages, a moment of reflection, a question, a conversation, or an unexpected decision you didn't think you were ready to make, consider this ongoing process an invitation to stay curious and continue defining thriving on your own terms.

What comes next in your life may be a grand metamorphosis or a light shift, like pausing before reacting, choosing a new thought, feeling your feet firmly on the ground, discovering a personal mission, making peace with your past, or dreaming more expansively about your future. These shifts might be subtle, but they're real, and they accumulate.

There will be days when survival mode takes over, because transformation moves like the tide, sometimes pulling you into clarity and creativity, and other times into anxiety and doubt. That back-and-forth rhythm is how growth unfolds, and thriving often emerges from those messy and uncomfortable in-between spaces. Even when progress feels invisible, trust that change is moving beneath the surface.

May you meet each chapter of your journey with grace, curiosity, wisdom, compassion, and the understanding that your moments of survival and thriving both contribute to the masterpiece that is your life.

If something in these words moved you, consider sharing it. It might be a passage, an idea, an insight, a practice, a question, or simply a moment that left a positive mark. When we speak from our own breakthroughs, we invite others into theirs. Perhaps that's the most powerful kind of thriving.

Notes

Preface

1. Ware, B. (2012). *The Top Five Regrets of the Dying: A Life Transformed by the Dearly Departing.* Carlsbad, CA: Hay House.

Chapter 1

1. Shields, G.S. et al. (2019). Mild Acute Stress Improves Response Speed Without Impairing Accuracy or Interference Control in Two Selective Attention Tasks: Implications for Theories of Stress and Cognition. *Psychoneuroendocrinology* 108: 78–86. https://doi.org/10.1016/j.psyneuen.2019.06.001.
2. McEwen, B.S. (2007). Physiology and Neurobiology of Stress and Adaptation: Central Role of the Brain. *Physiological Reviews* 87 (3): 873–904. https://doi.org/10.1152/physrev.00041.2006.
3. Brenner, S.L., Jones, J.P., Rutanen-Whaley, R.H. et al. (2015). Evolutionary Mismatch and Chronic Psychological Stress. *Journal of Evolutionary Medicine* 3: 1–11. https://doi.org/10.4303/jem/235885.
4. Cisler, J.M. and Koster, E.H.W. (2010). Mechanisms of Attentional Biases towards Threat in Anxiety Disorders: An Integrative Review. *Clinical Psychology Review* 30 (2): 203–216. https://doi.org/10.1016.j.cpr.2009.11.003.

5. Hanson, R. (2013). *Hardwiring Happiness: The New Brain Science of Contentment, Calm, and Confidence.* New York: Harmony Books.

6. Godoy, L.D., Rossignoli, M.T., Delfino-Pereira, P. et al. (2018). A Comprehensive Overview on Stress Neurobiology: Basic Concepts and Clinical Implications. *Frontiers in Behavioral Neuroscience* 12: https://doi.org/10.3389/fnbeh.2018.00127.

7. Kim, E.J., Pellman, B., and Kim, J.J. (2015). Stress Effects on the Hippocampus: A Critical Review. *Learning & Memory* 22 (9): 411–416. https://doi.org/10.1101/lm.037291.114.

8. Roberts, B.L. and Karatsoreos, I.N. (2021). Brain–Body Responses to Chronic Stress: A Brief Review. *Faculty Reviews* 10: https://doi.org/10.12703/r/10-83.

9. Brown, B. (2012). *Daring Greatly: How the Courage to Be Vulnerable Transforms the Way We Live, Love, Parent, and Lead.* New York: Gotham Books.

10. Porath, C.L., Gibson, C.B., and Spreitzer, G.M. (2022). To Thrive or Not to Thrive: Pathways for Sustaining Thriving at Work. *Research in Organizational Behavior* 42: 100176. https://doi.org/10.1016/j.riob.2022.10.176.

11. Ibid.

12. Dweck, C.S. (2006). *Mindset: The New Psychology of Success.* New York: Random House.

13. Zaki, J. (2019). *The War for Kindness: Building Empathy in a Fractured World.* New York: Crown Publishing Group.

14. Friedman, N.P. and Robbins, T.W. (2021). The Role of Prefrontal Cortex in Cognitive Control and Executive Function. *Neuropsychopharmacology* 47 (1): 72–89. https://doi.org/10.1038/s41386-021-01132-0.

15. Kong, F., Heller, A.S., van Reekum, C.M., and Sato, W. (2020). Editorial: Positive Neuroscience: The Neuroscience of Human Flourishing. *Frontiers in Human Neuroscience* 14: Article 47. https://doi.org/10.3389/fnhum.2020.00047.

16. Rakic, P. (2009). Evolution of the Neocortex: A Perspective from Developmental Biology. *Nature Reviews Neuroscience* 10 (10): 724–735. https://doi.org/10.1038/nrn2719.

17. González-Burgos, I. (2022). *Psychobiological Principles of the Memory Process,* 1–35. https://doi.org/10.52305/ghet8304.

18. Gaynes, R. (2017). The Discovery of Penicillin—New Insights after More than 75 Years of Clinical Use. *Emerging Infectious Diseases* 23 (5): 849–853. https://doi.org/10.3201/eid2305.161556.

19. "Life Expectancy at Birth, Total (Years)." World Bank Open Data. Accessed March 22, 2025. https://data.worldbank.org/indicator/SP.DYN.LE00.IN.

20. Fredrickson, B.L. (2001). The Role of Positive Emotions in Positive Psychology: The Broaden-and-Build Theory of Positive Emotions. *American Psychologist* 56 (3): 218–226. https://doi.org/10.1037/0003-066X.56.3.218.

21. Senge, P.M. (1990). *The Fifth Discipline: The Art & Practice of the Learning Organization*. New York: Doubleday.

22. Doidge, N. (2007). *The Brain That Changes Itself: Stories of Personal Triumph from the Frontiers of Brain Science*. New York: Viking Press.

23. Pittenger, C. and Duman, R.S. (2007). Stress, Depression, and Neuroplasticity: A Convergence of Mechanisms. *Neuropsychopharmacology* 33 (1): 88–109. https://doi.org/10.1038/sj.1038/sj.npp.1301574.

24. Code, J. (2020). Agency for Learning: Intention, Motivation, Self-Efficacy and Self-Regulation. *Frontiers in Education* 5: https://doi.org/10.3389/feduc.2020.00019.

25. Piazza, V.H. and McEwen, B.S. (2011). Development of Maladaptive Coping: A Functional Adaptation to Chronic Stress. *Neuroscience and Biobehavioral Reviews* 35 (7): 1562–1573. https://doi.org/10.1016/j.neubiorev.2010.11.008.

26. Thompson, R.J., Mata, J., Jaeggi, S.M. et al. (2010). Maladaptive Coping, Adaptive Coping, and Depressive Symptoms: Variations across Age and Depressive State. *Behaviour Research and Therapy* 48 (6): 459–466. https://doi.org/10.1016/j.brat.2010.01.007.

27. Bandura, A. (2006). Toward a Psychology of Human Agency. *Perspectives on Psychological Science* 1 (2): 164–180. https://doi.org/10.1111/j.1745-6916.2006.00011.x.

28. Thomson, M. and Hartley-Margolin, D. (2020). *Syria's Secret Library: Reading and Redemption in a Town Under Siege*. Washington, D.C.: CNIB/CELA.

29. Cavanna, A.E., Purpura, G., Riva, A. et al. (2023). The Western Origins of Mindfulness Therapy in Ancient Rome. *Neurological Sciences* 44 (6): 1861–1869. https://doi.org/10.1007/s10072-023-06651-w.

30. Porges, S.W. (2011). *The Polyvagal Theory: Neurophysiological Foundations of Emotions, Attachment, Communication, and Self-regulation*. New York: W. W. Norton & Company.

31. Fredrickson, B.L. (2001). The Role of Positive Emotions in Positive Psychology: The Broaden-and-Build Theory of Positive Emotions. *American Psychologist* 56 (3): 218–226. https://doi.org/10.1037/0003-066X.56.3.218.

Chapter 2

1. Dweck, C.S. (2006). *Mindset: The New Psychology of Success*. New York: Random House.
2. Clifton, J. "When Demographics Aren't Destiny." Psychology Today. Accessed March 23, 2025. https://www.psychologytoday.com/ca/blog/primal-world-beliefs-unpacked/202312/when-demographics-arent-destiny.
3. Crum, A.J., Corbin, W.R., Brownell, K.D., and Salovey, P. (2011). Mind over milkshakes: mindsets, not just nutrients, determine Ghrelin response. *Health Psychology* 30 (4): 424–429. https://doi.org/10.1037/a0023467.
4. Zubieta, J.-K., Bueller, J.A., Jackson, L.R. et al. (2005). Placebo effects mediated by endogenous opioid activity on μ-opioid receptors. *The Journal of Neuroscience* 25 (34): 7754–7762. https://doi.org/10.1523/jneurosci.0439-05.2005.
5. Ludwig, D.S. and Willett, W.C., (2014). Vile fats versus sugar—facing the facts. JAMA 312 (9): 887–888. https://doi.org/10.1001/jama.2014.6963.
6. Kris-Etherton, P.M., Hu, F.B., Ros, E., and Sabaté, J. (2008). The role of tree nuts and peanuts in the prevention of coronary heart disease: multiple potential mechanisms. *The Journal of Nutrition* 138 (9): https://doi.org/10.1093/jn/138.9.1746s.
7. Lemay, E.P. and Cutrl, J.N. (2024). Implications of daily world beliefs for relationship satisfaction: the role of positive relationship illusions. *The Journal of Positive Psychology* 20 (3): 1–10. https://doi.org/10.1080/17439760.2024.2387352.
8. Dweck, C.S. (2024). Personal perspectives on mindsets, motivation, and psychology. *Motivation Science* 10 (1): 1–8. https://doi.org/10.1037/mot0000304.
9. Ibid.
10. Qin, X., Wormington, S., Guzman-Alvarez, A., and Wang, M.-T. (2021). Why does a growth mindset intervention impact achievement differently across secondary schools? Unpacking the causal mediation mechanism from a national multisite randomized experiment. *Journal of Research on Educational Effectiveness* 14 (3): 617–644. https://doi.org/10.1080/19345747.2021.1894520.
11. Kegan, R. and Lahey, L.L. (2009). *Immunity to Change: How to Overcome It and Unlock the Potential in Yourself and Your Organization*. Boston: Harvard Business Press.
12. Scheffer, M., Borsboom, D., Nieuwenhuis, S., and Westley, F. (2022). Belief traps: tackling the inertia of harmful beliefs. *Proceedings of the*

National Academy of Sciences 119 (32): https://doi.org/10.1073/pnas .2203149119.

13. Lindquist, K.A. and Barrett, L.F. (2012). A functional architecture of the human brain: emerging insights from the science of emotion. *Trends in Cognitive Sciences* 16 (11): 533–540. https://doi.org/10.1016/j.tics .2012.09.005.

14. Kahneman, D. and Frederick, S. (2002). Representativeness revisited: attribute substitution in intuitive judgment. In: *Heuristics and Biases* (ed. T. Gilovich, D. Griffin, and D. Kahneman), 49–81. Cambridge University Press https://doi.org/10.1017/cbo9780511808098.004.

15. Saroglou, V. (2011). Believing, bonding, behaving, and belonging. *Journal of Cross-Cultural Psychology* 42 (8): 1320–1340. https://doi.org/10 .1177/0022022111412267.

16. Friedman, N.P. and Robbins, T.W. (2021). The role of prefrontal cortex in cognitive control and executive function. *Neuropsychopharmacology* 47 (1): 72–89. https://doi.org/10.1038/s41386-021-01132-0.

17. McGaugh, J.L. (2004). The Amygdala modulates the consolidation of memories of emotionally arousing experiences. *Annual Review of Neuroscience* 27 (1): 1–28. https://doi.org/10.1146/annurev.neuro.27 .070203.144157.

18. Kaplan, J.T., Gimbel, S.I., and Harris, S. (2016). Neural correlates of maintaining one's political beliefs in the face of counterevidence. *Scientific Reports* 6 (39589): https://doi.org/10.1038/srep39589.

19. Anderson, C.A., Lepper, M.R., and Ross, L. (1980). Perseverance of social theories: the role of explanation in the persistence of discredited information. *Journal of Personality and Social Psychology* 39 (6): 1037–1049. https://doi.org/10.1037/h0077720.

20. Kaplan, J.T., Gimbel, S.I., and Harris, S. (2016). Neural correlates of maintaining one's political beliefs in the face of counterevidence. *Scientific Reports* 6 (1): https://doi.org/10.1038/srep39589.

21. Paul, S., Salunkhe, S., Sravanthi, K., and Mane, S.V. (2024). Pioneering hand hygiene: Ignaz Semmelweis and the fight against puerperal fever. *Cureus* 16 (10): e71689. https://doi.org/10.7759/cureus.71689.

22. Ibid.

23. Pittenger, C. and Duman, R.S. (2007). Stress, depression, and neuroplasticity: a convergence of mechanisms. *Neuropsychopharmacology* 33 (1): 88–109. https://doi.org/10.1038/sj.npp.1301574.

24. Kärtner, J. and Köster, M. (2024). Early social-cognitive development as a dynamic developmental system—a lifeworld approach. *Frontiers in Psychology* 15: https://doi.org/10.3389/fpsyg.2024.1399903.

25. Zoe, H., Dominic, A., Ben, D., and Fanny, L. (2024). Supplemental material for social cohesion and volunteering: correlates, causes, and challenges. *Translational Issues in Psychological Science* 10 (1): https://doi.org/10.1037/tps0000387.supp.

26. Klippenstein, K. (2017). Language appropriation and identity construction in new religious movements: peoples temple as test case. *Journal of the American Academy of Religion* 85 (2): 348–380. https://doi.org/10.1093/jaarel/lfw082.

27. Wnuk, M. (2022). The beneficial role of involvement in alcoholics anonymous for existential and subjective well-being of alcohol-dependent individuals? The model verification. *International Journal of Environmental Research and Public Health* 19 (9): 5173. https://doi.org/10.3390/ijerph19095173.

28. Morgan, T.J., Rendell, L.E., Ehn, M. et al. (2011). The evolutionary basis of human social learning. *Proceedings of the Royal Society B: Biological Sciences* 279 (1729): 653–662.

29. Theise, N. (2023). *Notes on Complexity: A Scientific Theory of Connection, Consciousness, and Being.* Spiegel & Grau.

30. Gravholt, C.H., Viuff, M.H., Brun, S. et al. (2018). Sex chromosome aneuploidies: conditions, diagnosis, and management. *Nature Reviews Endocrinology* 14 (4): 207–220. https://doi.org/10.1038/nrendo.2018.58.

31. Ainsworth, C. (2015). Sex redefined. *Nature* 518 (7539): 288–291. https://doi.org/10.1038/518288a.

32. Griffiths, D.A. (2018). Shifting syndromes: sex chromosome variations and intersex classifications. *Social Studies of Science* 48 (1): 125–148. https://doi.org/10.1177/0306312718757081.

33. Baumeister, R.F. and Leary, M.R. (2017). The need to belong: desire for interpersonal attachments as a fundamental human motivation. In: *Interpersonal Development* (ed. R. Zukauskiene), 57–89. Routledge https://doi.org/10.4324/9781351153683-3.

34. Knapper, C.K., Cropley, A.J., and Moore, R.J. (1976). Attitudinal factors in the non-use of seat belts. *Accident Analysis & Prevention* 8 (4): 241–246. https://doi.org/10.1016/0001-4575(76)90009-9.

Chapter 3

1. Mercan, N., Bulut, M., and Yüksel, Ç. (2021). Investigation of the relatedness of cognitive distortions with emotional expression, anxiety, and depression. *Current Psychology* 42 (3): 2176–2185. https://doi.org/10.1007/s12144-021-02251-z.

2. Barrett, L.F. (2020). *Seven and a Half Lessons About the Brain*. Boston: Houghton Mifflin Harcourt.

3. Hall, K. (2022). *Choose Your Story, Change Your Life: Silence Your Inner Critic and Rewrite Your Life from the Inside Out*. Nashville: HarperCollins Leadership.

4. Tseng, J. and Poppenk, J. (2020). Brain meta-state transitions demarcate thoughts across task contexts exposing the mental noise of trait neuroticism. *Nature Communications* 11 (1): https://doi.org/10.1038/s41467-020-17255-9.

5. Ibid.

6. Gilbert, D.T. (2006). *Stumbling on Happiness*. New York: Alfred A. Knopf.

7. You, L. (2023). The impact of social norms of responsibility on corporate social responsibility. *Journal of Business Ethics* 190 (2): 309–326. https://doi.org/10.1007/s10551-023-05417-w.

8. Bockstaele, V., Bram, B.V., Tibboel, H. et al. (2014). A review of current evidence for the causal impact of attentional bias on fear and anxiety. *Psychological Bulletin* 140 (3): 682–721. https://doi.org/10.1037/a0034834.

9. Somer, E.(E.) and Otgaar, H. (2025). Memory Distortions in Maladaptive Daydreaming: A Study on Source Confusion and Fantasy-Driven Confabulations. *The Qualitative Report*. https://doi.org/10.46743/2160-3715/2025.7031.

10. Broughton, J. (2009). *Descartes's Method of Doubt*. Princeton University Press.

11. Kahneman, D. (2011). *Thinking, Fast and Slow*. New York: Farrar, Straus and Giroux.

12. He, W. and Gan, J. (2025). The relationship between self-reflection and mental health: a meta-analysis review. *Current Psychology* 1: https://doi.org/10.1007/s12144-025-07415-9.

13. Harrington, R. and Loffredo, D.A. (2010). Insight, rumination, and self-reflection as predictors of well-being. *The Journal of Psychology* 145 (1): 39–57. https://doi.org/10.1080/00223980.2010.528072.

14. Beck, A.T. (1976). *Cognitive Therapy and the Emotional Disorders*. New York: International Universities Press.

15. Burns, D.D. (1999). *The Feeling Good Handbook*. New York: Plume.

16. Ayele, F.A. and Barchard, K.A. (2024). Positive reappraisal and catastrophizing mediate the relationship between mindfulness and job burnout. *Discover Psychology* 4 (1): https://doi.org/10.1007/s44202-024-00229-z.

17. Kiesel, A., Steinhauser, M., Wendt, M. et al. (2010). Control and interference in task switching—a review. *Psychological Bulletin* 136 (5): 849–874. https://doi.org/10.1037/a0019842.

18. Ibid.
19. Maric, M., Heyne, D.A., van Widenfelt, B.M., and Westenberg, P.M. (2010). Distorted cognitive processing in youth: the structure of negative cognitive errors and their associations with anxiety. *Cognitive Therapy and Research* 35 (1): 11–20. https://doi.org/10.1007/s10608-009-9285-3.
20. Ickes, W. (1993). Empathic accuracy. *Journal of Personality* 61 (4): 587–610. https://doi.org/10.1111/j.1467-6494.1993.tb00783.x.
21. Bursztyn, L. and Yang, D.Y. (2022). Misperceptions about others. *Annual Review of Economics* 14: 425–452.
22. Nickerson, R.S. (1998). Confirmation bias: a ubiquitous phenomenon in many guises. *Review of General Psychology* 2 (2): 175–220. https://doi.org/10.1037/1089-2680.2.2.175.
23. Hayes, S.C., Strosahl, K.D., and Wilson, K.G. (2011). *Acceptance and Commitment Therapy: The Process and Practice of Mindful Change*, 2e. New York: Guilford Press.
24. Masuda, A., Hayes, S.C., Sackett, C.F., and Twohig, M.P. (2004). Cognitive defusion and self-relevant negative thoughts: examining the impact of a ninety year old technique. *Behaviour Research and Therapy* 42 (4): 477–485. https://doi.org/10.1016/j.brat.2003.10.008.
25. Cavanna, A.E., Purpura, G., Riva, A. et al. (2023). The western origins of mindfulness therapy in Ancient Rome. *Neurological Sciences* 44 (6): 1861–1869.
26. Tucker-Drob, E.M., Briley, D.A., and Paige Harden, K. (2013). Genetic and environmental influences on cognition across development and context. *Current Directions in Psychological Science* 22 (5): 349–355. https://doi.org/10.1177/0963721413485087.
27. Frankl, V.E. (2006). *Man's Search for Meaning: An Introduction to Logotherapy*. Translated by Ilse Lasch. Boston: Beacon Press.
28. Frankl, V.E., Winston, C., and Winston, R. (2019). *The Doctor and the Soul: From Psychotherapy to Logotherapy*. New York: Vintage Books, a division of Penguin Random House LLC.

Chapter 4

1. Ekman, P. and Friesen, W.V. (1971). Constants across cultures in the face and emotion. *Journal of Personality and Social Psychology* 17 (2): 124–129. https://doi.org/10.1037/h0030377.
2. Ekman, P. (2009). Darwin's contributions to our understanding of emotional expressions. *Philosophical Transactions of the Royal Society B:*

Biological Sciences 364 (1535): 3449–3451. https://doi.org/10.1098/rstb.2009.0189.

3. Cowen, A.S. and Keltner, D. (2017). Self-report captures 27 distinct categories of emotion bridged by continuous gradients. *Proceedings of the National Academy of Sciences* 114 (38): E7900–E7909. https://doi.org/10.1073/pnas.1702247114.

4. Barrett, L.F. (2016). The theory of constructed emotion: an active inference account of interoception and categorization. *Social Cognitive and Affective Neuroscience* 12 (1): 1–23. https://doi.org/10.1093/scan/nsw154.

5. Berridge, K. and Winkielman, P. (2003). Unconscious emotion. *Cognition and Emotion* 17 (2): 181–211. https://doi.org/10.1080/02699930302289.

6. Barrett, L.F. (2017). The theory of constructed emotion: an active inference account of interoception and categorization. *Social Cognitive and Affective Neuroscience* 12 (1): 1–23. https://doi.org/10.1093/scan/nsw154.

7. Beedie, C., Terry, P., and Lane, A. (2005). Distinctions between emotion and mood. *Cognition and Emotion* 19 (6): 847–878. https://doi.org/10.1080/02699930541000057.

8. Morin, A. (2009). Self-awareness deficits following loss of inner speech: Dr. Jill Bolte Taylor's case study. *Consciousness and Cognition* 18 (2): 524–529. https://doi.org/10.1016/j.concog.2008.09.008.

9. Greenwood, B.M. and Garfinkel, S.N. (2025). Interoceptive mechanisms and emotional processing. *Annual Review of Psychology* 76 (1): 59–86. https://doi.org/10.1146/annurev-psych-020924-125202.

10. der Kolk, V. and Bessel, A. (2014). *The Body Keeps the Score: Brain, Mind, and Body in the Healing of Trauma*. New York: Viking.

11. Gross, J.J. (2015). Emotion regulation: current status and future prospects. *Psychological Inquiry* 26 (1): 1–26. https://doi.org/10.1080/1047840X.2014.940781.

12. Russo-Netzer, P. and Shoshani, A. (2020). Authentic inner compass, well-being, and prioritization of positivity and meaning among adolescents. *Personality and Individual Differences* 167: 110248. https://doi.org/10.1016/j.paid.2020.110248.

13. Matsumoto, D. (2008). Culture and Emotional Expression. In: *Handbook of Emotions*, 3e (ed. M. Lewis, J.M. Haviland-Jones, and L.F. Barrett), 481–503. New York: Guilford Press.

14. Zheng, W., Yu, A., Li, D. et al. (2021). Cultural differences in mixed emotions: the role of dialectical thinking. *Frontiers in Psychology* 11: 538793. https://doi.org/10.3389/fpsyg.2020.538793.

15. Chaplin, T.M. (2014). Gender and emotion expression: a developmental contextual perspective. *Emotion Review* 7 (1): 14–21. https://doi.org/10 .1177/1754073914544408.
16. Rodríguez-Torres, R., Leyens, J.P., Pérez, A.R. et al. (2005). The lay distinction between primary and secondary emotions: a spontaneous categorization? *International Journal of Psychology* 40 (2): 100–107.
17. Netzer, L., Van Kleef, G.A., and Tamir, M. (2015). Interpersonal instrumental emotion regulation. *Journal of Experimental Social Psychology* 58: 124–135. https://doi.org/10.1016/j.jesp.2015.01.006.
18. Mesquita, B. and Frijda, N.H. (2010). Cultural variations in emotions: a review. In: *Handbook of Social Psychology*, 5e (ed. S.T. Fiske, D.T. Gilbert, and G. Lindzey), 871–890. Hoboken, NJ: John Wiley & Sons.
19. de Oliveira, S. and Nisbett, R.E. (2017). Culture changes how we think about thinking: from 'Human Inference' to 'Geography of thought'. *Perspectives on Psychological Science* 12 (5): 782–790. https://doi.org/10 .1177/1745691617702718.
20. Bailey, E.R., Matz, S.C., Youyou, W., and Iyengar, S.S. (2020). Authentic self-expression on social media is associated with greater subjective well-being. *Nature Communications* 11 (1): https://doi.org/10.1038/ s41467-020-18539-w.
21. Chapman, B.P., Fiscella, K., Kawachi, I. et al. (2013). Emotion suppression and mortality risk over a 12-year follow-up. *Journal of Psychosomatic Research* 75 (4): 381–385.
22. Lazzarelli, A., Scafuto, F., Crescentini, C. et al. (2024). Interoceptive ability and emotion regulation in mind–body interventions: an integrative review. *Behavioral Sciences* 14 (11): 1107. https://doi.org/10 .3390/bs14111107.
23. Zaid, S.M., Hutagalung, F.D., Hamid, H.S.A., and Taresh, S.M. (2025). The power of emotion regulation: how managing sadness influences depression and anxiety? *BMC Psychology* 13 (1): https://doi.org/10.1186/ s40359-025-02354-3.
24. Abler, B., Kessler, S., Kümmerle, A.M., and Preissl, H. (2013). Neural correlates of emotion regulation by reappraisal and suppression: a meta-analysis of fMRI studies. *Human Brain Mapping* 34 (11): 2898–2913. https://doi.org/10.1002/hbm.22101.
25. Kredlow, M.A., Fenster, R.J., Laurent, E.S. et al. (2022). Prefrontal cortex, amygdala, and threat processing: implications for PTSD. *Neuropsychopharmacology* 47: 247–259.
26. Barrett, L.F. (2017). *How Emotions Are Made: The Secret Life of the Brain.* Boston: Houghton Mifflin Harcourt.

27. Hökkä, P.K., Räikkönen, E., Ikävalko, H. et al. (2022). Emotional agency at work: the development and validation of a measure. *Frontiers in Education* 7: https://doi.org/10.3389/feduc.2022.852598.

28. Masuda, A., Twohig, M.P., Stormo, A.R. et al. (2010). The effects of cognitive defusion and thought distraction on emotional discomfort and believability of negative self-referential thoughts. *Journal of Behavior Therapy and Experimental Psychiatry* 41 (1): 11–17. https://doi.org/10.1016/j.jbtep.2009.08.006.

29. Greenberg, L.S. and Goldman, R.N. (2008). *Emotion-Focused Therapy: Coaching Clients to Work Through Their Feelings*. Washington, DC: American Psychological Association.

30. Bruner, J. (1990). *Acts of Meaning*. Cambridge, MA: Harvard University Press.

31. Jamieson, J.P., Crum, A.J., Goyer, J.P. et al. (2018). Optimizing stress responses with reappraisal and mindset interventions: an integrated model. *Anxiety, Stress, & Coping* 31 (3): 245–261. https://doi.org/10.1080/10.15806.2018.1442615.

32. Shum, C., Dockray, S., and McMahon, J. (2024). The relationship between cognitive reappraisal and psychological well-being during early adolescence: a scoping review. *The Journal of Early Adolescence* 45 (1): 104–133. https://doi.org/10.1177/02724316241231918.

33. Siegel, D.J. and Bryson, T.P. (2012). *The Whole-Brain Child: 12 Revolutionary Strategies to Nurture Your Child's Developing Mind*. New York: Random House.

34. Barrett, L.F. (2017). *How Emotions Are Made: The Secret Life of the Brain*. Boston: Houghton Mifflin Harcourt.

35. van der Kolk, B. (2014). *The Body Keeps the Score: Brain, Mind, and Body in the Healing of Trauma*. New York: Viking.

36. Zeitlen, D.C., Gasper, K., and Beaty, R.E. (2024). Mood regulation as a shared basis for creativity and curiosity. *Behavioral and Brain Sciences* 47: https://doi.org/10.1017/s0140525x23003461.

37. Siegel, D.J. (2010). *Mindsight: The New Science of Personal Transformation*. New York: Bantam Books.

38. Tsujimoto, M., Matsuzaki, Y., Yamaya, N., and Kawashima, R. (2023). Brain activation and functional connectivity of reappraisal and acceptance for anxious events. *eNeuro* 10 (6): https://doi.org/10.1523/eneuro.0033-23.2023.

39. Kong, Y. (2022). Are emotions contagious? A conceptual review of studies in language education. *Frontiers in Psychology* 13: 1048105. https://doi.org/10.3389/fpsyg.2022.1048105.

Chapter 5

1. Patwardhan, B., Warude, D., Pushpangadan, P., and Bhatt, N. (2005). Ayurveda and Traditional Chinese Medicine: A Comparative Overview. *Evidence-Based Complementary and Alternative Medicine* 2 (4): 465–473. https://doi.org/10.1093/ecam/neh140.

2. Carona, C., Ramos, K., and Salvador, C. (2022). Psychotherapy by Reciprocal Inhibition: Wolpe's Unique Legacy to the Evolution of Cognitive–Behavioural Therapy. *BJPsych Advances* 29 (3): 218–222. https://doi.org/10.1192/bja.2022.75.

3. Burklund, L.J., Creswell, J.D., Irwin, M.R., and Lieberman, M.D. (2014). The Common and Distinct Neural Bases of Affect Labeling and Reappraisal in Healthy Adults. *Frontiers in Psychology* 5: https://doi.org/10.3389/fpsyg.2014.00221.

4. Torre, J.B. and Lieberman, M.D. (2018). Putting Feelings into Words: Affect Labeling as Implicit Emotion Regulation. *Emotion Review* 10 (2): 116–124. https://doi.org/10.1177/1754073917742706.

5. Mehling, W.E., Wrubel, J., Daubenmier, J.J. et al. (2011). Body Awareness: A Phenomenological Inquiry into the Common Ground of Mind-Body Therapies. *Philosophy, Ethics, and Humanities in Medicine* 6 (1): 6. https://doi.org/10.1186/1747-5341-6-6.

6. Harris, L.R., Carnevale, M.J., D'Amour, S. et al. (2015). How Our Body Influences Our Perception of the World. *Frontiers in Psychology* 6: https://doi.org/10.3389/fpsyg.2015.00819.

7. Brebner, J.S., Loconsole, M., Hanley, D., and Vasas, V. (2024). Through an Animal's Eye: The Implications of Diverse Sensory Systems in Scientific Experimentation. *Proceedings of the Royal Society B: Biological Sciences* 291 (2027): https://doi.org/10.1098/rspb.2024.0022.

8. Eagleman, D. (2011). *Incognito: The Secret Lives of the Brain*. New York: Pantheon Books.

9. Schwartz, S., Vuilleumier, P., Hutton, C. et al. (2004). Attentional Load and Sensory Competition in Human Vision: Modulation of FMRI Responses by Load at Fixation during Task-Irrelevant Stimulation in the Peripheral Visual Field. *Cerebral Cortex* 15 (6): 770–786. https://doi.org/10.1093/cercor/bhh178.

10. Drew, T., Võ, M.L.-H., and Wolfe, J.M. (2013). The Invisible Gorilla Strikes Again. *Psychological Science* 24 (9): 1848–1853. https://doi.org/10.1177/0956797613479386.

11. Shimizu, Y., Umeda, M., Mano, H. et al. (2007). Neuronal Response to Shepard's Tones. an Auditory FMRI Study Using Multifractal Analysis.

Brain Research 1186: 113–123. https://doi.org/10.1016/j.brainres.2007 .09.097.

12. Safari, K., Saeed, A.A., Hasan, S.S., and Moghaddam-Banaem, L. (2018). The Effect of Mother and Newborn Early Skin-to-Skin Contact on Initiation of Breastfeeding, Newborn Temperature and Duration of Third Stage of Labor. *International Breastfeeding Journal* 13 (1): https:// doi.org/10.1186/s13006-018-0174-9.

13. Keysers, C., Hartmann, H., Packheiser, J. et al. (2024). A Systematic Review and Multivariate Meta-Analysis of the Physical and Mental Health Benefits of Touch Interventions. *Nature Human Behaviour* 8 (4): 326–342.

14. Efe, Y.S., Erdem, E., Caner, N., and Güneş, T. (2022). The Effect of Gentle Human Touch on Pain, Comfort and Physiological Parameters in Preterm Infants during Heel Lancing. *Complementary Therapies in Clinical Practice* 48: 101622. https://doi.org/10.1016/j.ctcp.2022.101622.

15. Proske, U. and Gandevia, S.C. (2012). The Proprioceptive Senses: Their Roles in Signaling Body Shape, Body Position and Movement, and Muscle Force. *Physiological Reviews* 92 (4): 1651–1697. https:// doi.org/10.1152/physrev.00048.2011.

16. Sainburg, R.L., Poizner, H., and Ghez, C. (1993). Loss of Proprioception Produces Deficits in Interjoint Coordination. *Journal of Neurophysiology* 70 (5): 2136–2147. https://doi.org/10.1152/jn.1993.70.5.2136.

17. Winter, L., Huang, Q., Sertic, J.V., and Konczak, J. (2022). The Effectiveness of Proprioceptive Training for Improving Motor Performance and Motor Dysfunction: A Systematic Review. *Frontiers in Rehabilitation Sciences* 3: https://doi.org/10.3389/fresc.2022.830166.

18. Schmalzl, L., Crane-Godreau, C., and Payne, P. (2014). Movement-Based Embodied Contemplative Practices: Definitions and Paradigms. *Frontiers in Human Neuroscience* 8: 205.

19. Chen, W.G., Schloesser, D., Arensdorf, A.M. et al. (2021). The Emerging Science of Interoception: Sensing, Integrating, Interpreting, and Regulating Signals within the Self. *Trends in Neurosciences* 44 (1): 3–16. https://doi.org/10.1016/j.tins.2020.10.007.

20. Khalsa, S.S., Adolphs, R., Cameron, O.G. et al. (2018). Interoception and Mental Health: A Roadmap. *Biological Psychiatry: Cognitive Neuroscience and Neuroimaging* 3 (6): 501–513. https://doi.org/10.1016/j.bpsc .2017.12.004.

21. Craig, (Bud) A.D. (2015). *How Do You Feel? An Interoceptive Moment with Your Neurobiological Self*. Princeton, NJ: Princeton University Press.

22. Wang, X., Wu, Q., Egan, L. et al. (2019). Anterior Insular Cortex Plays a Critical Role in Interoceptive Attention. *eLife* 8: https://doi.org/10.7554/elife.42265.

23. Terasawa, Y., Shibata, M., Moriguchi, Y., and Umeda, S. (2012). Anterior Insular Cortex Mediates Bodily Sensibility and Social Anxiety. *Social Cognitive and Affective Neuroscience* 8 (3): 259–266. https://doi.org/10.1093/scan/nss108.

24. Price, C.J. and Hooven, C. (2018). Interoceptive Awareness Skills for Emotion Regulation: Theory and Approach of Mindful Awareness in Body-Oriented Therapy (MABT). *Frontiers in Psychology* 9: https://doi.org/10.3389/fpsyg.2018.00798.

25. Khalsa, S.S., Adolphs, R., Cameron, O.G. et al. (2018). Interoception and Mental Health: A Roadmap. *Biological Psychiatry: Cognitive Neuroscience and Neuroimaging* 3 (6): 501–513. https://doi.org/10.1016/j.bpsc.2017.12.004.

26. Barrett, L.F. and Simmons, W.K. (2015). Interoceptive Predictions in the Brain. *Nature Reviews Neuroscience* 16 (7): 419–429. https://doi.org/10.1038/nrn3950.

27. Ibid.

28. Porges, S.W. (2004). Neuroception: A Subconscious System for Detecting Threats and Safety. *Zero to Three* 24 (5): 19–24.

29. Morton, L., Cogan, N., Kolacz, J. et al. (2024). A New Measure of Feeling Safe: Developing Psychometric Properties of the Neuroception of Psychological Safety Scale (NPSS). *Psychological Trauma: Theory, Research, Practice, and Policy* 16 (4): 701–708. https://doi.org/10.1037/tra0001313.

30. Schmidt, N.B., Richey, J.A., Zvolensky, M.J., and Maner, J.K. (2008). Exploring Human Freeze Responses to a Threat Stressor. *Journal of Behavior Therapy and Experimental Psychiatry* 39 (3): 292–304. https://doi.org/10.1016/j.jbtep.2007.08.002.

31. Porges, S.W. (2021). *Polyvagal Safety: Attachment, Communication, Self-Regulation*. New York: W. W. Norton & Company.

32. Bonaz, B., Bazin, T., and Pellissier, S. (2018). The Vagus Nerve at the Interface of the Microbiota-Gut-Brain Axis. *Frontiers in Neuroscience* 12: https://doi.org/10.3389/fnins.2018.00049.

33. Bigbee, J.W. (2022). Cells of the Central Nervous System: An Overview of Their Structure and Function. *Advances in Neurobiology* 41–64. https://doi.org/10.1007/978-3-031-12390-0_2.

34. Murtazina, A. and Adameyko, I. (2023). The Peripheral Nervous System. *Development* 150 (9): https://doi.org/10.1242/dev.201164.

35. Bonaz, B., Bazin, T., and Pellissier, S. (2018). The Vagus Nerve at the Interface of the Microbiota-Gut-Brain Axis. *Frontiers in Neuroscience* 12: https://doi.org/10.3389/fnins.2018.00049.

36. Fitchett, A., Mastitskaya, S., and Aristovich, K. (2021). Selective Neuromodulation of the Vagus Nerve. *Frontiers in Neuroscience* 15: https://doi.org/10.3389/fnins.2021.685872.

37. Ibid.

38. Seo, D., Rabinowitz, A.G., Douglas, R.J., and Sinha, R. (2019). Limbic Response to Stress Linking Life Trauma and Hypothalamus-Pituitary-Adrenal Axis Function. *Psychoneuroendocrinology* 99: 38–46. https://doi.org/10.1016/j.psyneuen.2018.08.023.

39. Alshami, A.M. (2019). Pain: Is It All in the Brain or the Heart? *Current Pain and Headache Reports* 23 (12): https://doi.org/10.1007/s11916-019-0827-4.

40. McCraty, R. (2022). Following the Rhythm of the Heart: Heartmath Institute's Path to HRV Biofeedback. *Applied Psychophysiology and Biofeedback* 47 (4): 305–316. https://doi.org/10.1007/s10484-022-09554-2.

41. Dicks, L.M. (2022). Gut Bacteria and Neurotransmitters. *Microorganisms* 10 (9): 1838. https://doi.org/10.3390/microorganisms10091838.

42. Strandwitz, P. (2018). Neurotransmitter Modulation by the Gut Microbiota. *Brain Research* 1693: 128–133. https://doi.org/10.1016/j.brainres.2018.03.015.

43. Kennedy, P.J. (2014). Irritable Bowel Syndrome: A Microbiome-Gut-Brain Axis Disorder? *World Journal of Gastroenterology* 20 (39): 14105. doi: 10.3748/wjg.v20.i39.14105.

44. Kabat-Zinn, J. (2013). *Full Catastrophe Living: Using the Wisdom of Your Body and Mind to Face Stress, Pain, and Illness*, Revisede. New York: Bantam Books.

45. Murtazina, A. and Adameyko, I. (2023). The Peripheral Nervous System. *Development* 150 (9): https://doi.org/10.1242/dev.201164.

46. Ghasemi, F., Beversdorf, D.Q., and Herman, K.C. (2024). Stress and Stress Responses: A Narrative Literature Review from Physiological Mechanisms to Intervention Approaches. *Journal of Pacific Rim Psychology* 18: https://doi.org/10.1177/18344909241289222.

47. Sapolsky, R.M. (2004). *Why Zebras Don't Get Ulcers: The Acclaimed Guide to Stress, Stress-Related Diseases, and Coping*, 3e. New York: Holt Paperbacks.

48. Hartman, A.J. and Liebenson, C. (2016). Rest, Resiliency, and Retuning the Body. *Journal of Bodywork and Movement Therapies* 20 (3): 610–613. https://doi.org/10.1016/j.jbmt.2016.06.013.

49. McCorry, L.K. (2007). Physiology of the Autonomic Nervous System. *American Journal of Pharmaceutical Education* 71 (4): 78. https://doi.org/10.5688/aj710478.

50. Siegel, D.J. and Drulis, C. (2023). An Interpersonal Neurobiology Perspective on the Mind and Mental Health: Personal, Public, and Planetary Well-Being. *Annals of General Psychiatry* 22 (1): https://doi.org/10.1186/s12991-023-00434-5.

51. Siegel, D.J. (2012). *The Developing Mind: How Relationships and the Brain Interact to Shape Who We Are*, 2e. New York: Guilford Press.

52. Kearney, B.E. and Lanius, R.A. (2022). The Brain-Body Disconnect: A Somatic Sensory Basis for Trauma-Related Disorders. *Frontiers in Neuroscience* 16: https://doi.org/10.3389/fnins.2022.1015749.

53. Ibid.

54. Bentley, T.G., D'Andrea-Penna, G., Rakic, M. et al. (2023). Breathing Practices for Stress and Anxiety Reduction: Conceptual Framework of Implementation Guidelines Based on a Systematic Review of the Published Literature. *Brain Sciences* 13 (12): 1612. https://doi.org/10.3390/brainsci13121612.

55. Levine, P.A. (2010). *In an Unspoken Voice: How the Body Releases Trauma and Restores Goodness*. Berkeley, CA: North Atlantic Books.

56. BIOSPHERE2. Accessed April 5, 2025. https://biosphere2.org/sites/default/files/2021-08/B21216_Press_02_DiscoverO2lo.pdf.

57. Davidson, R.J. (2003). Affective Neuroscience and Psychophysiology. Toward a Synthesis. *Psychophysiology* 40 (5): 655–665. https://doi.org/10.1111/1469-8986.00067.

58. Zou, L., Sasaki, J.E., Wei, G.-X. et al. (2018). Effects of Mind–Body Exercises (Tai Chi/Yoga) on Heart Rate Variability Parameters and Perceived Stress: A Systematic Review with Meta-Analysis of Randomized Controlled Trials. *Journal of Clinical Medicine* 7 (11): 404. https://doi.org/10.3390/jcm7110404.

59. Feldman, R. (2007). Parent–Infant Synchrony and the Construction of Shared Timing; Physiological Precursors, Developmental Outcomes, and Risk Conditions. *Journal of Child Psychology and Psychiatry* 48 (3-4, 354): 329. https://doi.org/10.1111/j.1469-7610.2006.01701.x.

60. Paley, B. and Hajal, N.J. (2022). Conceptualizing Emotion Regulation and Coregulation as Family-Level Phenomena. *Clinical Child and Family Psychology Review* 25 (1): 19–43. https://doi.org/10.1007/s10567-022-00378-4.

61. Rekutina (2020). Mythology and Reality of Olympic Agon of Ancient Greece in the Roman Era. *Science and Sport: Current Trends* 8 (2): 44–51. https://doi.org/10.36028/2308-8826-2020-8-2-44-51.

62. Krystal, M. (2012). *Indigenous Dance and Dancing Indian: Contested Representation in the Global Era.* University Press of Colorado.
63. Silverman, M. (2017). I Drum, I Sing, I Dance: An Ethnographic Study of a West African Drum and Dance Ensemble. *Research Studies in Music Education* 40 (1): 5–27. https://doi.org/10.1177/1321103x17734972.
64. Friedlander, S. (1992). *The Whirling Dervishes: Being an Account of the Sufi Order Known as the Mevlevis and Its Founder the Poet and Mystic Mevlana Jalalu'ddin Rumi.* Albany, NY: State University of New York Press.
65. Suzuki, S. (1970). *Zen Mind, Beginner's Mind.* New York: Weatherhill.
66. Shurpin, Y. "Shuckling: Why Do Jews Rock While Praying?" *Chabad.org.* Accessed April 23, 2025. https://www.chabad.org/library/article_cdo/aid/702209/jewish/Shuckling-Why-Do-Jews-Rock-While-Praying.htm.
67. Dael, N., Mortillaro, M., and Scherer, K.R. (2012). Emotion Expression in Body Action and Posture. *Emotion* 12 (5): 1085–1101. https://doi.org/10.1037/a0025737.
68. Hansen, S. (2015). *Inside-Out: The Practice of Resilience.* Resilience Institute.
69. Mendelsohn, A.I. (2019). Creatures of Habit: The Neuroscience of Habit and Purposeful Behavior. *Biological Psychiatry* 85 (11): https://doi.org/10.1016/j.biopsych.2019.03.978.
70. Ibid.
71. Wiseman, H. (2022). The Japanese Arts and Meditation-in-Action. *Zygon®* 57 (3): 744–771. https://doi.org/10.1111/zygo.12806.
72. Gupta, A.D. (2021). On the Bodily Basis of Human Cognition: A Philosophical Perspective on Embodiment. *Frontiers in Human Neuroscience* 15: https://doi.org/10.3389/fnhum.2021.745095.
73. Hill, D., Conner, M., Bristow, M., and O'Connor, D.B. (2023). Daily Stress and Eating Behaviors in Adolescents and Young Adults: Investigating the Role of Cortisol Reactivity and Eating Styles. *Psychoneuroendocrinology* 153: 106105. https://doi.org/10.1016/j.psyneuen.2023.106105.
74. Mendelsohn, A.I. (2019). Creatures of Habit: The Neuroscience of Habit and Purposeful Behavior. *Biological Psychiatry* 85 (11): https://doi.org/10.1016/j.biopsych.2019.03.978.
75. Oppenheim, C.E. (2012). Nelson Mandela and the Power of Ubuntu. *Religions* 3 (2): 369–388. https://doi.org/10.3390/rel3020369.
76. Pawelski, J.O. (2022). *Foundations of Positive Interventions.* lecture. Philadelphia, PA: University of Pennsylvania.
77. Van Dyk, G. (2021). A Tale of Two Boycotts: Riot, Reform, and Sugar Consumption in Late Eighteenth-Century Britain and France. *Eighteenth-Century Life* 45 (3): 51–68. https://doi.org/10.1215/00982601-9272999.

78. Glennon, R.J. (1991). The Role of Law in the Civil Rights Movement: The Montgomery Bus Boycott, 1955–1957. *Law and History Review* 9 (1): 59–112. https://doi.org/10.2307/743660.

79. Ibid.

80. Mendelsohn, A.I. (2019). Creatures of Habit: The Neuroscience of Habit and Purposeful Behavior. *Biological Psychiatry* 85 (11): https://doi.org/10.1016/j.biopsych.2019.03.978.

81. Sloshower, J., Zeifman, R.J., Guss, J. et al. (2024). Psychological Flexibility as a Mechanism of Change in Psilocybin-Assisted Therapy for Major Depression: Results from an Exploratory Placebo-Controlled Trial. *Scientific Reports* 14 (1): https://doi.org/10.1038/s41598-024-58318-x.

82. Dupuis, D. (2021). Psychedelics as Tools for Belief Transmission: Set, Setting, Suggestibility, and Persuasion in the Ritual Use of Hallucinogens. *Frontiers in Psychology* 12: 730031. https://doi.org/10.3389/fpsyg.2021.730031.

83. National Center for Complementary and Integrative Health. "Psilocybin for Mental Health and Addiction: What You Need To Know." Last modified April 2024. https://www.nccih.nih.gov/health/psilocybin-for-mental-health-and-addiction-what-you-need-to-know.

84. Maté, G. (2008). *In the Realm of Hungry Ghosts: Close Encounters with Addiction.* Toronto: Knopf Canada.

85. U.S. Department of Health and Human Services (2016). *Facing Addiction in America: The Surgeon General's Report on Alcohol, Drugs, and Health.* Washington, DC: U.S. Department of Health and Human Services.

86. Linehan, M.M. (2015). *DBT Skills Training Manual,* 2nde. New York: Guilford Press.

87. Kashdan, T.B. and Rottenberg, J. (2010). Psychological Flexibility as a Fundamental Aspect of Health. *Clinical Psychology Review* 30 (7): 865–878. https://doi.org/10.1016/j.cpr.2010.03.001.

88. Clear, J. (2018). *Atomic Habits: An Easy & Proven Way to Build Good Habits & Break Bad Ones.* New York: Avery.

89. Ibid.

Chapter 6

1. Ge, B.H. and Yang, F. (2023). Transcending the Self to Transcend Suffering. *Frontiers in Psychology* 14: https://doi.org/10.3389/fpsyg.2023.1113965.

2. Dollahite, D.C., Marks, L.D., Witting, A.B. et al. (2020). How Relationship-Enhancing Transcendent Religious Experiences during Adversity Can Encourage Relational Meaning, Depth, Healing, and Action. *Religions* 11 (10): 519. https://doi.org/10.3390/rel11100519.

3. Siegel, E. "Why We Still Don't Know How Many Stars Are in the Milky Way." Big Think, April 2, 2025. https://bigthink.com/starts-with-a-bang/how-many-stars-milky-way/.

4. Sagan, C. (1994). *Pale Blue Dot: A Vision of the Human Future in Space.* New York: Random House.

5. Romain, W.F. (2018). Solstice Alignments at Angkor Wat and Nearby Temples: Connecting to the Cycles of Time. *Journal of Skyscape Archaeology* 4 (2): 176–200. https://doi.org/10.1558/jsa.35712.

6. Keltner, D. (2023). *Awe: The New Science of Everyday Wonder and How It Can Transform Your Life.* New York: Penguin Press.

7. Jung, C.G. (1973). *Synchronicity: An Acausal Connecting Principle.* Translated by R.F.C. Hull. Princeton, NJ: Princeton University Press.

8. James, W. (1902). *The Varieties of Religious Experience: A Study in Human Nature.* New York: Longmans, Green, and Co.

9. Stace, W.T. (1960). *The Teachings of the Mystics.* New York: New American Library.

10. Tang, Y.-Y., Hölzel, B.K., and Posner, M.I. (2015). The Neuroscience of Mindfulness Meditation. *Nature Reviews Neuroscience* 16 (4): 213–225. https://doi.org/10.1038/nrn3916.

11. Brown, R.P. and Gerbarg, P.L. (2005). Sudarshan Kriya Yogic Breathing in the Treatment of Stress, Anxiety, and Depression. *The Journal of Alternative and Complementary Medicine* 11 (4): 711–717. https://doi.org/10.1089/acm.2005.11.711.

12. Griffiths, R.R., Richards, W.A., McCann, U., and Jesse, R. (2006). Psilocybin Can Occasion Mystical-Type Experiences Having Substantial and Sustained Personal Meaning and Spiritual Significance. *Psychopharmacology* 187 (3): 268–283. https://doi.org/10.1007/s00213-006-0457-5.

13. Yaden, D.B., Haidt, J., Hood Jr, R.W. et al. (2017). The Varieties of Self-Transcendent Experience. *Review of General Psychology* 21 (2): 143–160. https://doi.org/10.1037/gpr0000102.

14. Frankl, V.E., Winston, C., and Winston, R. (2019). *The Doctor and the Soul: From Psychotherapy to Logotherapy.* New York: Vintage Books, a division of Penguin Random House LLC.

15. Vu, M.C. and Tran, T. (2019). Trust Issues and Engaged Buddhism: The Triggers for Skillful Managerial Approaches. *Journal of Business Ethics* 169 (1): 77–102. https://doi.org/10.1007/s10551-019-04273-x.

16. Steger, M.F. (2011). Meaning in Life. In: *Encyclopedia of Adolescence* (ed. R.J.R. Levesque), 1000–1008. New York: Springer https://doi.org/10.1007/978-1-4419-1695-2_316.

17. Camus, A. (1991). *The Myth of Sisyphus,* translated by Justin O'Brien, 119–123. New York: Vintage Books.

18. Chödrön, P. (1997). *When Things Fall Apart: Heart Advice for Difficult Times*, 7. Boston: Shambhala Publications.
19. Meling, D. (2021). Knowing Groundlessness: An Enactive Approach to a Shift from Cognition to Non-Dual Awareness. *Frontiers in Psychology* 12: https://doi.org/10.3389/fpsyg.2021.697821.
20. Yousafzai, M., and Lamb, C. (2013). *I Am Malala: The Girl Who Stood Up for Education and Was Shot by the Taliban*. New York: Little, Brown and Company.
21. Goldsmith, B. (2005). *Obsessive Genius: The Inner World of Marie Curie*, 64–67. New York: W.W. Norton.
22. Multiple Sclerosis (MS), Mayo Clinic, accessed April 25, 2025, https://www.mayoclinic.org/diseases-conditions/multiple-sclerosis/symptoms-causes/syc-20350269.
23. Gschwandtner, C.M. (2021). Faith, Religion, and Spirituality: A Phenomenological and Hermeneutic Contribution to Parsing the Distinctions. *Religions* 12 (7): 476. https://doi.org/10.3390/rel12070476.
24. Anderson, J. et al. (2016). Religious Experience Activates Brain Reward Regions. *Social Neuroscience* 11 (6): 1–9.
25. Vogel, E.A., Rose, J.P., Roberts, L.R., and Eckles, K. (2014). Social Comparison, Social Media, and Self-Esteem. Psychology of Popular Media Culture 3 (4): 206–22. https://doi.org/10.1037/ppm0000047.
26. U.S. Department of Health and Human Services (2023). *Our Epidemic of Loneliness and Isolation: The U.S. Surgeon General's Advisory on the Healing Effects of Social Connection and Community*, 9. Washington, DC: U.S. Department of Health and Human Services.
27. Ollerton, J., Winfree, R., and Tarrant, S. (2011). How Many Flowering Plants Are Pollinated by Animals? Oikos 120 (3): 321–26. doi: https://doi.org/10.1111/j.1600-0706.2010.18644.x.
28. Gorzelak, M.A., Asay, A.K., Pickles, B.J., and Simard, S.W. (2015). Inter-plant Communication through Mycorrhizal Networks Mediates Complex Adaptive Behaviour in Plant Communities. *AoB Plants* 7 (plv050). doi: https://doi.org/10.1093/aobpla/plv050.
29. Wohlleben, P. (2016). *The Hidden Life of Trees: What They Feel, How They Communicate—Discoveries from a Secret World*, 9–12. Vancouver: Greystone Books.
30. Ma, Z., Zuo, T., Frey, N., Rangrez, A.Y., et al. (2024). A Systematic Framework for Understanding the Microbiome in Human Health and Disease: From Basic Principles to Clinical Translation. *Signal Transduction and Targeted Therapy* 9: 237. https://doi.org/10.1038/s41392-024-01946-6

31. Yong, E. (2016). *I Contain Multitudes: The Microbes Within Us and a Grander View of Life*, 1–6. New York: Ecco.
32. Sender, R., Fuchs, S., and Milo, R. (2016). Revised Estimates for the Number of Human and Bacteria Cells in the Body. *PLoS Biology* 14 (8): e1002533. https://doi.org/10.1371/journal.pbio.1002533.
33. Ibid.
34. deGrasse Tyson, N. (2017). *Astrophysics for People in a Hurry*, 32–33. New York: W.W. Norton & Company.
35. Orzechowska-Licari, E.J., LaComb, J.F., Giarrizzo, M. et al. (2022). Intestinal Epithelial Regeneration in Response to Ionizing Irradiation. *Journal of Visualized Experiments* (185): https://doi.org/10.3791/64028.
36. Thiagarajan, P., Parker, C.J., and Prchal, J.T. (2021). How Do Red Blood Cells Die? *Frontiers in Physiology* 12: https://doi.org/10.3389/fphys.2021.655393.
37. Bolamperti, S., Villa, I., and Rubinacci, A. (2022). Bone Remodeling: An Operational Process Ensuring Survival and Bone Mechanical Competence. *Bone Research* 10 (1): https://doi.org/10.1038/s41413-022-00219-8.
38. Rogers, S. and Lew, V.L. (2021). PIEZO1 and the Mechanism of the Long Circulatory Longevity of Human Red Blood Cells. *PLoS Computational Biology* 17 (3): https://doi.org/10.1371/journal.pcbi.1008496.
39. Lim, H.L. (2022). Mindfulness and Motivation in Self-Transformation: Thich Nhat Hanh's Teachings on the Interbeing. *MANUSYA: Journal of Humanities* 24 (3): 334–354. https://doi.org/10.1163/26659077-24030004.
40. Wilson, A.C. (2010). Dakota Wiconi (Way of Life) Mitákuye Owás'i (All My Relatives). In: *Aboriginal Policy Research Series*, vol. 6 (ed. J.P. White, E. Anderson, and D. Beavon), 191–206. London, ON: Thompson Educational Publishing https://ir.lib.uwo.ca/aprci/vol6/iss1/13.
41. Jomaa, K.A. (2022). Ummah: A New Paradigm for a Global World. *Journal of Islamic Studies* 33 (3): 437–441. https://doi.org/10.1093/jis/etac013.

Chapter 7

1. Keator, D.B., Salgado, F., Madigan, C. et al. (2024). Adverse Childhood Experiences, Brain Function, and Psychiatric Diagnoses in a Large Adult Clinical Cohort. *Frontiers in Psychiatry* 15: https://doi.org/10.3389/fpsyt.2024.1401745.
2. Crane, S.A. (2006). Historical Subjectivity: A Review Essay. *The Journal of Modern History* 78 (2): 434–456. https://doi.org/10.1086/505803.

3. Bryant, F.B. and Veroff, J. (2007). *Savoring: A New Model of Positive Experience*, 2–6. Mahwah, NJ: Lawrence Erlbaum Associates.
4. Lacy, J.W. and Stark, C.E. (2013). The Neuroscience of Memory: Implications for the Courtroom. *Nature Reviews Neuroscience* 14 (9): 649–658. https://doi.org/10.1038/nrn3563.
5. Baumeister, R.F., Bratslavsky, E., Finkenauer, C., and Vohs, K.D. (2001). Bad Is Stronger than Good. *Review of General Psychology* 5 (4): 323–370. https://doi.org/10.1037/1089-2680.5.4.323.
6. Contractor, A.A., Banducci, A.N., Jin, L. et al. (2020). Effects of Processing Positive Memories on Posttrauma Mental Health: A Preliminary Study in a Non-Clinical Student Sample. *Journal of Behavior Therapy and Experimental Psychiatry* 66: 101516. https://doi.org/10.1016/j.jbtep.2019.101516.
7. van der Kolk, B.A. (2014). *The Body Keeps the Score: Brain, Mind, and Body in the Healing of Trauma*, 280–282. New York: Viking.
8. Levine, P.A. (1997). *Waking the Tiger: Healing Trauma*, 34–37. Berkeley, CA: North Atlantic Books.
9. Schacter, D.L. (2001). *The Seven Sins of Memory: How the Mind Forgets and Remembers*, 9–15. Boston: Houghton Mifflin.
10. Camina, E. and Güell, F. (2017). The Neuroanatomical, Neurophysiological and Psychological Basis of Memory: Current Models and Their Origins. *Frontiers in Pharmacology* 8: https://doi.org/10.3389/fphar.2017.00438.
11. Schacter, D.L. (1996). *Searching for Memory: The Brain, the Mind, and the Past*, 170–175. New York: Basic Books.
12. Jung, C.G. (1916). *Analytical Psychology* (ed. C.E. Long). London: Longmans, Green and Co.
13. Bowlby, J. (1982). *Attachment and Loss, Volume 1: Attachment*. New York: Basic Books.
14. Ainsworth, M.D., Salter, M.C., Blehar, E.W., and Wall, S. (1978). *Patterns of Attachment: A Psychological Study of the Strange Situation*. Hillsdale, NJ: Erlbaum.
15. Levine, A. and Heller, R.S.F. (2010). *Attached: The New Science of Adult Attachment and How It Can Help You Find—and Keep—Love*. New York: TarcherPerigee.
16. Ibid.
17. Main, M. and Solomon, J. (1986). Discovery of an Insecure-Disorganized/Disoriented Attachment Pattern. In: *Affective Development in Infancy* (ed. T.B. Brazelton and M.W. Yogman), 95–124. Norwood, NJ: Ablex Publishing.

18. Park, C.L. (2022). Meaning Making Following Trauma. *Frontiers in Psychology* 13: https://doi.org/10.3389/fpsyg.2022.844891.

19. Maté, G. (2022). *The Myth of Normal: Trauma, Illness, and Healing in a Toxic Culture*. New York: Avery.

20. Straussner, S.L. and Calnan, A.J. (2014). Trauma through the Life Cycle: A Review of Current Literature. *Clinical Social Work Journal* 42 (4): 323–335. https://doi.org/10.1007/s10615-014-0496-z.

21. Herman, J.L. (2015). *Trauma and Recovery: The Aftermath of Violence—from Domestic Abuse to Political Terror*. New York: Basic Books.

22. McEwen, B.S. (2007). Physiology and Neurobiology of Stress and Adaptation: Central Role of the Brain. *Physiological Reviews* 87 (3): 873–904. https://doi.org/10.1152/physrev.00041.2006.

23. Ressler, K.J., Berretta, S., Bolshakov, V.Y. et al. (2022). Post-Traumatic Stress Disorder: Clinical and Translational Neuroscience from Cells to Circuits. *Nature Reviews Neurology* 18 (5): 273–288. https://doi.org/10.1038/s41582-022-00635-8.

24. van der Kolk, B. (2000). Posttraumatic Stress Disorder and the Nature of Trauma. *Dialogues in Clinical Neuroscience* 2 (1): 7–22. https://doi.org/10.31887/dcns.2000.2.1/bvdkolk.

25. "Reid Robison, MD." Reid Robison. Accessed April 22, 2025. https://www.reidrobison.com/.

26. Masten, A.S. (2014). *Ordinary Magic: Resilience in Development*, 4–9. New York: Guilford Press.

27. Park, C.L. and Blake, E.C. (2020). Resilience and Recovery Following Disasters: The Meaning Making Model. *Positive Psychological Approaches to Disaster* 9–25. https://doi.org/10.1007/978-3-030-32007-2_2.

28. Tanasugarn, A. "Hyper-Independence: Is It a Trauma Response?" Psychology Today. Accessed April 20, 2025. https://www.psychologytoday.com/us/blog/understanding-ptsd/202306/hyper-independence-is-it-a-trauma-response.

29. Johnson, S. (2008). *Hold Me Tight: Seven Conversations for a Lifetime of Love*. New York: Little, Brown and Company.

30. Simpson, J.A. and Rholes, W.S. (2017). Adult Attachment, Stress, and Romantic Relationships. *Current Opinion in Psychology* 13: 19–24. https://doi.org/10.1016/j.copsyc.2016.04.006.

31. Hill, A.P., Hall, H.K., and Appleton, P.R. (2011). The Relationship between Multidimensional Perfectionism and Contingencies of Self-Worth. *Personality and Individual Differences* 50 (2): 238–242. https://doi.org/10.1016/j.paid.2010.09.036.

32. Brown, B. (2010). *The Gifts of Imperfection: Let Go of Who You Think You're Supposed to Be and Embrace Who You Are.* Center City, MN: Hazelden.

33. Zarzycki, M. and Morrison, V. (2021). Getting Back or Giving Back: Understanding Caregiver Motivations and Willingness to Provide Informal Care. *Health Psychology and Behavioral Medicine* 9 (1): 636–661. https://doi.org/10.1080/21642850.2021.1951737.

34. Walker, P. (2013). *Complex PTSD: From Surviving to Thriving.* Berkeley, CA: Azure Coyote Publishing.

35. Simione, L. and Gnagnarella, C. (2023). Humor Coping Reduces the Positive Relationship between Avoidance Coping Strategies and Perceived Stress: A Moderation Analysis. *Behavioral Sciences* 13 (2): 179. https://doi.org/10.3390/bs13020179.

36. Maté, G. (2011). *When the Body Says No: Exploring the Stress-Disease Connection.* Hoboken, NJ: John Wiley & Sons.

37. Šoková, B., Greškovičová, K., Halamová, J., and Baránková, M. (2025). Breaking the Vicious Cycles of Self-Criticism: A Qualitative Study on the Best Practices of Overcoming One's Inner Critic. *BMC Psychology* 13 (1): https://doi.org/10.1186/s40359-024-02250-2.

38. Lollar, K. (2015). Strategic Invisibility: Resisting the Inhospitable Dwelling Place. *Review of Communication* 15 (4): 298–315. https://doi.org/10.1080/15358593.2015.1116592.

39. Walker, P. (2013). *Complex PTSD: From Surviving to Thriving.* Berkeley, CA: Azure Coyote Publishing.

40. Park, C.L. (2022). Meaning Making Following Trauma. *Frontiers in Psychology* 13: https://doi.org/10.3389/fpsyg.2022.844891.

41. Tedeschi, R.G. and Calhoun, L.G. (2004). Posttraumatic Growth: Conceptual Foundations and Empirical Evidence. *Psychological Inquiry* 15 (1): 1–18. https://doi.org/10.1207/s15327965pli1501_01.

42. Ibid.

43. Keulemans, G. (2016). The Geo-Cultural Conditions of *Kintsugi*. *The Journal of Modern Craft* 9 (1): 15–34. https://doi.org/10.1080/17496772.2016.1183946.

44. Angelou, M. (1969). *I Know Why the Caged Bird Sings.* New York: Random House.

45. Tedeschi, R.G. and Calhoun, L.G. (2004). Posttraumatic Growth: Conceptual Foundations and Empirical Evidence. *Psychological Inquiry* 15 (1): 1–18. https://doi.org/10.1207/s15327965pli1501_01.

46. Tedeschi, R.G. and Calhoun, L.G. (2018). *Posttraumatic Growth: Theory, Research, and Applications*. New York: Routledge.

47. Ibid.

48. Tedeschi, R.G., Moore, B.A., and Calhoun, L.G. (2018). *Posttraumatic Growth in Clinical Practice*. New York: Routledge.

Chapter 8

1. Killingsworth, M.A. and Gilbert, D.T. (2010). A wandering mind is an unhappy mind. *Science* 330 (6006): 932. https://doi.org/10.1126/science.1192439.

2. Keng, S.-L., Smoski, M.J., and Robins, C.J. (2011). Effects of mindfulness on psychological health: a review of empirical studies. *Clinical Psychology Review* 31 (6): 1041–1056. https://doi.org/10.1016/j.cpr.2011.04.006.

3. Davidson, R.J. and Goleman, D. (2017). *Altered Traits: Science Reveals How Meditation Changes Your Mind, Brain, and Body*. New York: Avery.

4. Brewer, J.A., Worhunsky, P.D., Gray, J.R. et al. (2011). Meditation experience is associated with differences in default mode network activity and connectivity. *Proceedings of the National Academy of Sciences* 108 (50): 20254–20259. https://doi.org/10.1073/pnas.1112029108.

5. Lazar, S.W., Kerr, C.E., Wasserman, R.H. et al. (2005). Meditation experience is associated with increased cortical thickness. *NeuroReport* 16 (17): 1893–1897. https://doi.org/10.1097/01.wnr.0000186598.66243.19.

6. Pascoe, M.C., Thompson, D.R., Jenkins, Z.M., and Ski, C.F. (2017). Mindfulness mediates the physiological markers of stress: systematic review and meta-analysis. *Journal of Psychiatric Research* 95: 156–178. https://doi.org/10.1016/j.jpsychires.2017.08.004.

7. Kabat-Zinn, J. (2005). *Wherever You Go, There You Are: Mindfulness Meditation in Everyday Life*. New York: Hyperion.

8. James, W. (1890). *The Principles of Psychology*. New York: Henry Holt and Company.

9. Crouse, K. "Phelps's Epic Journey Ends with 8th Gold Medal." *New York Times*, August 17, 2008. https://www.nytimes.com/2008/08/17/sports/olympics/17phelps.html.

10. Csikszentmihalyi, M. (1990). *Flow: The Psychology of Optimal Experience*. New York: Harper & Row.

11. Ibid.

12. Hopkins, M. "Miles Davis: Selling the Dark Prince." JazzTimes, September 6, 2024. https://jazztimes.com/features/profiles/miles-davis-selling-the-dark-prince/.
13. Kierkegaard, S. (1959). *The Journals of Søren Kierkegaard* (trans. D. Alexander). New York, Harper Torchbooks.
14. Mercer, J.A. (2023). On cultivating a beginner's mind for teaching and learning in religious education. *Religious Education* 118 (1): 1–3. https://doi.org/10.1080/00344087.2023.2175510.
15. Kolman, J.M. and Miller, S.M. (2018). Six values never to silence: Jewish perspectives on Nazi medical professionalism. *Rambam Maimonides Medical Journal* 9 (1): https://doi.org/10.5041/rmmj.10327.
16. Barks, C., trans. (2004). *The Essential Rumi: New Expanded Edition*. New York: HarperOne.
17. Nhất Hạnh, T. (2011). *True Love: A Practice for Awakening the Heart*. Boston: Shambhala Publications.
18. Confucius (1979). *The Analects* (trans. D.C. Lau). London: Penguin Books.
19. Lun, J., Kesebir, S., and Oishi, S. (2008). On feeling understood and feeling well: the role of interdependence. *Journal of Research in Personality* 42 (6): 1623–1628. https://doi.org/10.1016/j.jrp.2008.06.009.
20. Barraza, J.A. and Zak, P.J. (2009). Empathy toward strangers triggers oxytocin release and subsequent generosity. *Annals of the New York Academy of Sciences* 1167 (1): 182–189. https://doi.org/10.1111/j.1749-6632.2009.04504.x.

Chapter 9

1. Seligman, M.E.P., Railton, P., Baumeister, R.F., and Sripada, C. (2016). *Homo Prospectus*. New York: Oxford University Press.
2. Suddendorf, T., Addis, D.R., and Corballis, M.C. (2009). Mental time travel and the shaping of the human mind. *Philosophical Transactions of the Royal Society B: Biological Sciences* 364 (1,521): 1317–1324. https://doi.org/10.1098/rstb.2008.0301.
3. Kellogg, R.T., Chirino, C.A., and Gfeller, J.D. (2020). The complex role of mental time travel in depressive and anxiety disorders: an ensemble perspective. *Frontiers in Psychology* 11: 1465. https://doi.org/10.3389/fpsyg.2020.01465.
4. Bulley, A., Henry, J.D., and Suddendorf, T. (2017). Thinking about threats: memory and prospection in human threat management. *Consciousness and Cognition* 49: 1–9. https://doi.org/10.1016/j.concog.2017.01.008.

5. Baumeister, R.F., Vohs, K.D., and Oettingen, G. (2016). Pragmatic prospection: how and why people think about the future. *Review of General Psychology* 20 (1): 3–16. https://doi.org/10.1037/gpr0000060.

6. Takeuchi, K., Elmqvist, T., Hatakeyama, M. et al. (2014). Using sustainability science to analyse social–ecological restoration in NE Japan after the great earthquake and tsunami of 2011. *Sustainability Science* 9 (4): 513–526. https://doi.org/10.1007/s11625-014-0257-5.

7. Ibid.

8. Bulley, A. and Irish, M. (2018). The functions of prospection – variations in health and disease. *Frontiers in Psychology* 9: 2328. https://doi.org/10.3389/fpsyg.2018.02328.

9. Mullainathan, S. and Shafir, E. (2013). *Scarcity: Why Having Too Little Means So Much*. New York: Times Books.

10. Harari, Y.N. (2015). *Sapiens: A Brief History of Humankind*. New York: Harper.

11. Covey, S.R. (1989). *The 7 Habits of Highly Effective People: Powerful Lessons in Personal Change*. New York: Free Press.

12. Curry, O.S., Rowland, L.A., Van Lissa, C.J. et al. (2018). Happy to help? A systematic review and meta-analysis of the effects of performing acts of kindness on the well-being of the actor. *Journal of Experimental Social Psychology* 76: 320–329. https://doi.org/10.1016/j.jesp.2018.02.014.

13. Lu, R. (2025). Set it in stone: Patagonia and the evolution toward stakeholder governance in social enterprise business structures. *SSRN Electronic Journal* 57 (4): 587–631. https://doi.org/10.2139/ssrn.5179548.

14. Ibid.

15. Tedeschi, R.G. and Calhoun, L.G. (1996). The posttraumatic growth inventory: measuring the positive legacy of trauma. *Journal of Traumatic Stress* 9 (3): 455–471. https://doi.org/10.1007/BF02103658.

16. McManus, J. "Hamilton an Icon of Resilience." ESPN, July 1, 2013. https://www.espn.com/espnw/athletes-life/summer-of-w/story/_/id/9442763/espnw-surfer-bethany-hamilton-icon-resilience.

17. Masten, A.S. (2001). Ordinary magic: resilience processes in development. *American Psychologist* 56 (3): 227–238. https://doi.org/10.1037/0003-066X.56.3.22.

18. Wang, S. and Bhargava, P. (2021). Understanding the psychology of failure: failing is an essential prerequisite for success. *Journal of the American College of Radiology* 18 (3): 528–530. https://doi.org/10.1016/j.jacr.2020.09.036.

19. Carol, S. (2006). *Dweck, Mindset: The New Psychology of Success*. New York: Random House.

20. Wilson, T.D. and Gilbert, D.T. (2005). Affective forecasting: knowing what to want. *Current Directions in Psychological Science* 14 (3): 131–134. https://doi.org/10.1111/j.0963-7214.2005.00355.x.

21. Dunn, E.W., Wilson, T.D., and Gilbert, D.T. (2003). Location, location, location: the misprediction of satisfaction in housing lotteries. *Personality and Social Psychology Bulletin* 29 (11): 1421–1432. https://doi.org/10.1177/0146167203256867.

22. Kashdan, T.B. and Rottenberg, J. (2010). Psychological flexibility as a fundamental aspect of health. *Clinical Psychology Review* 30 (7): 865–878. https://doi.org/10.1016/j.cpr.2010.03.001.

23. Pyszkowska, A. and Rönnlund, M. (2021). Psychological flexibility and self-compassion as predictors of well-being: mediating role of a balanced time perspective. *Frontiers in Psychology* 12: 671746. https://doi.org/10.3389/fpsyg.2021.671746.

24. Kiluange, F., Rouco, C., and Silva, A.P. (2024). Military leadership in a VUCA environment and Bani scenario: a systematic literature review. *European Conference on Management Leadership and Governance* 20 (1): 649–660. https://doi.org/10.34190/ecmlg.20.1.3044.

25. Joonas, K., Mahfouz, A.Y., and Hayes, R.A. (2023). Strategy for growth and market leadership: the Netflix case. *AIMS International Journal of Management* 17 (2): 87–102. https://doi.org/10.26573/2.23.17.2.2.

26. Ibid.

27. Seligman, M.E.P., Railton, P., Baumeister, R.F., and Sripada, C. (2013). Navigating into the future or driven by the past. *Perspectives on Psychological Science* 8 (2): 119–141. https://doi.org/10.1177/1745691612474317.

28. Charles, R. (1994). *Snyder, The Psychology of Hope: You Can Get There from Here*. New York: Free Press.

29. Valle, M.F., Scott Huebner, E., and Suldo, S.M. (2006). An analysis of hope as a psychological strength. *Journal of School Psychology* 44 (5): 393–406. https://doi.org/10.1016/j.jsp.2006.03.005.

30. Snyder, C.R. (1994). *The Psychology of Hope: You Can Get There from Here*. New York: Free Press.

31. Hanssen, M.M., Vancleef, L.M., Vlaeyen, J.W. et al. (2014). Optimism, motivational coping and well-being: evidence supporting the importance of flexible goal adjustment. *Journal of Happiness Studies* 16 (6): 1525–1537. https://doi.org/10.1007/s10902-014-9572-x.

32. Seligman, M.E.P. (2006). *Learned Optimism: How to Change Your Mind and Your Life*. New York: Vintage Books.

33. Ibid.

34. Ibid.

35. Conversano, C., Rotondo, A., Lensi, E. et al. (2010). Optimism and its impact on mental and physical well-being. *Clinical Practice & Epidemiology in Mental Health* 6 (1): 25–29. https://doi.org/10.2174/174501 7901006010.25.
36. Gordon, R.A. (2008). Attributional style and athletic performance: strategic optimism and defensive pessimism. *Psychology of Sport and Exercise* 9 (3): 336–350. https://doi.org/10.1016/j.psychsport.2007.04.007.
37. Girma, H. (2019). *Haben: The Deafblind Woman Who Conquered Harvard Law*. New York: Hachette Books.
38. Girma, H. "Disability & Innovation: The Universal Benefits of Accessible Design." Haben Girma, June 28, 2016. https://habengirma.com/2016/06/28/disability-innovation-the-universal-benefits-of-accessible-design-by-haben-girma-apple-wwdc-2016/.
39. Frank, A. (1995). *The Diary of a Young Girl: The Definitive Edition* (ed. O.H. Frank and M. Pressler) (trans. M. Susan). New York: Doubleday.
40. Deci, E.L. and Ryan, R.M. (2006). Hedonia, eudaimonia, and well-being: an introduction. *Journal of Happiness Studies* 9 (1): 1–11. https://doi.org/10.1007/s10902-006-9018-1.
41. Ryan, R.M. and Deci, E.L. (2001). On happiness and human potentials: a review of research on hedonic and eudaimonic well-being. *Annual Review of Psychology* 52: 141–166. Palo Alto, CA: Annual Reviews.
42. Ryan, R.M., Huta, V., and Deci, E.L. (2008). Living well: a self-determination theory perspective on eudaimonia. *Journal of Happiness Studies* 9 (1): 139–170.
43. Wilkes, J., Garip, G., Kotera, Y., and Fido, D. (2022). Can Ikigai predict anxiety, depression, and well-being? *International Journal of Mental Health and Addiction* 21 (5): 2941–2953. https://doi.org/10.1007/s11469-022-00764-7.
44. Buffett, W. "Go to Work for Whomever You Admire the Most." Speech, Terry College of Business, University of Georgia, Athens, GA, July 18, 2001. https://speakola.com/corp/warren-buffett-university-of-georgia-2001.

Chapter 10

1. Gallagher, W. (2007). *The Power of Place: How Our Surroundings Shape Our Thoughts, Emotions, and Actions*. New York: Harper Perennial.
2. Saxbe, D.E. and Repetti, R.L. (2010). No place like home: home tours correlate with daily patterns of mood and cortisol. *Personality and Social Psychology Bulletin* 36 (1): 71–81. https://doi.org/10.1177/0146167209352864.

3. Augustin, S. (2009). *Place Advantage: Applied Psychology for Interior Architecture.* Hoboken, NJ: Wiley.
4. Roy, B., and Prabhu, M. (2022). "Yale Experts Explain Collective Well-Being." Yale Sustainability. Accessed April 25, 2025. https://sustainability.yale.edu/explainers/yale.experts-explain-collective-well-being
5. Sapolsky, R.M. (2017). *Behave: The Biology of Humans at Our Best and Worst.* New York: Penguin Press.
6. Lyubomirsky, S. (2008). *The How of Happiness: A New Approach to Getting the Life You Want.* New York: Penguin Press.
7. Kings, C., Moulding, R., Yap, K. et al. (2021). Measuring possessions as extensions of self and links to significant others in hoarding: the possessions as others and self inventory. *Journal of Psychopathology and Behavioral Assessment* 43 (2): 441–453. https://doi.org/10.1007/s10862-020-09858-9.
8. Kellett, S.C., Greenhalgh, R., Beail, N., and Ridgway, N. (2010). Compulsive Hoarding: An Interpretative Phenomenological Analysis. *Behavioural and Cognitive Psychotherapy* 38 (2): 197–213.
9. Frost, R.O. and Steketee, G. (2010). *Stuff: Compulsive Hoarding and the Meaning of Things.* Boston: Houghton Mifflin Harcourt.
10. Alone. Season 1, episode 1, "And So It Begins." Produced by Leftfield Pictures. Aired June 18, 2015, on History Channel. https://www.history.com/shows/alone.
11. Stewart, J.B. "Looking for a Lesson in Google's Perks." The New York Times, March 15, 2013. https://www.nytimes.com/2013/03/16/business/at-google-a-place-to-work-and-play.html.
12. Li, Q. (2009). Effect of forest bathing trips on human immune function. *Environmental Health and Preventive Medicine* 15 (1): 9–17. https://doi.org/10.1007/s12199-008-0068-3.
13. American Society of Interior Designers. "ASID Releases Comprehensive Research Study on the Impact of Design in the Workplace." ASID, July 2017. https://www.asid.org/news/asid-releases-comprehensive-research-study-on-the-impact-of-design-in-the-workplace.
14. Guendelsberger, E. (2019). *On the Clock: What Low-Wage Work Did to Me and How It Drives America Insane.* New York: Little, Brown and Company.
15. Triandis, H.C. (1994). *Culture and Social Behavior.* New York: McGraw-Hill.
16. Brown, B. (2012). *Daring Greatly: How the Courage to Be Vulnerable Transforms the Way We Live, Love, Parent, and Lead.* New York: Gotham Books.
17. Carson, R. (1962). *Silent Spring.* Boston: Houghton Mifflin.
18. Klein, N. (2019). *On Fire: The (Burning) Case for a Green New Deal.* New York: Simon & Schuster.

19. Crenshaw, K. (1991). Mapping the margins: intersectionality, identity politics, and violence against women of color. *Stanford Law Review* 43 (6): 1241–1299.
20. World Economic Forum (2023). *Global Gender Gap Report 2023*. Geneva: World Economic Forum https://www.weforum.org/reports/global-gender-gap-report-2023/.
21. Amin, S.N. and Alizada, N. (2020). Alternative forms of resistance: Afghan women negotiating for change. *Journal of International Women's Studies* 21 (6): Article 23. https://vc.bridgew.edu/jiws/vol21/iss6/23/.
22. Barton, B. (2012). *Pray the Gay Away: The Extraordinary Lives of Bible Belt Gays*. New York: New York University Press.
23. United Church of Christ. "Open and Affirming Coalition: UCC LGBTQIA+ Advocacy." Accessed April 25, 2025. https://openandaffirming.org/.
24. Clark, P. and Kaufman, Z.D. (ed.) (2009). *After Genocide: Transitional Justice, Post-Conflict Reconstruction, and Reconciliation in Rwanda and Beyond*. New York: Columbia University Press.
25. Corrales, J. and Penfold, M. (2015). *Dragon in the Tropics: Venezuela and the Legacy of Hugo Chávez*, 2e. Washington, DC: Brookings Institution Press.
26. Williams, C.D., Bravo, D.Y., Umaña-Taylor, A.J. et al. (2020). Intergenerational transmission of cultural socialization and effects on young children's developmental competencies among Mexican-origin families. *Developmental Psychology* 56 (2): 199–207. https://doi.org/10.1037/dev0000859.
27. Gutiérrez, I.T., Menendez, D., Jiang, M.J. et al. (2019). Embracing death: Mexican parent and child perspectives on death. *Child Development* 91 (2): https://doi.org/10.1111/cdev.13263.
28. Nour, N.M. (2009). Child marriage: a silent health and human rights issue. *Reviews in Obstetrics and Gynecology* 2 (1): 51–56.
29. Tutu, D. (1999). *No Future Without Forgiveness*. New York: Doubleday.
30. Wierzbicka, A. (1999). *Emotions Across Languages and Cultures: Diversity and Universals*. Cambridge: Cambridge University Press.
31. Philbin, M.M., Parker, C.M., Flaherty, M.G., and Hirsch, J.S. (2018). Public libraries: a community-level resource to advance population health. *Journal of Community Health* 44 (1): 192–199. https://doi.org/10.1007/s10900-018-0547-4.
32. Festini, S.B. (2022). Busyness, mental engagement, and stress: relationships to neurocognitive aging and behavior. *Frontiers in Aging Neuroscience* 14: https://doi.org/10.3389/fnagi.2022.980599.

33. Maslach, C. and Leiter, M.P. (2022). *The Burnout Challenge: Managing People's Relationships with Their Jobs.* Cambridge, MA: Harvard University Press.

34. Bullard, R.D. (ed.) (2005). *The Quest for Environmental Justice: Human Rights and the Politics of Pollution.* San Francisco: Sierra Club Books.

35. Kaplan, R. and Kaplan, S. (1989). *The Experience of Nature: A Psychological Perspective.* Cambridge: Cambridge University Press.

36. Corrales, J. (2018). *Fixing Democracy: Why Constitutional Change Often Fails to Enhance Democracy in Latin America.* New York: Oxford University Press.

37. Llano, S.M. "In Chávez's Venezuela, Crime Flourishes." Christian Science Monitor, December 3, 2008. https://www.csmonitor.com/World/Americas/2008/1203/p06s01-woam.html.

Acknowledgments

To YOU, READER, thank you for choosing to dedicate your time to this book. I know your attention and energy are precious, and I am honored you've chosen to spend some of them here, exploring these ideas with me. My greatest hope is that within these pages you discover something new, something meaningful, something useful, and perhaps even something transformative. Your willingness to engage with these words is itself a powerful step toward thriving.

To my coaching clients, whose courage, vulnerability, strength, flexibility, and commitment continue to inspire and teach me each day. Your openness to grow through challenge and your dedication to discovering what it truly means to thrive are a constant source of inspiration. Thank you for trusting me to walk alongside you.

Adriana, my wife and life partner, embodies the strength and resilience that inspired much of this journey and these pages. Her support grounded me at every turn and offered clarity when the writing felt overwhelming, and perspective when I needed it most. She willingly dove deep into the ideas alongside me, tirelessly sharpening the manuscript with her keen editorial eye. This book owes its heart to her extraordinary presence in my life. To my sons, Charles and Jacques, your love and kindness infused meaning into every step of this process and reminded me of the why behind this project.

I'm deeply grateful to my niece Nicole, whose commitment and attention to detail throughout the research process helped ensure that the ideas in this book accurately reflect the science. To my niece Anael, thank you for offering encouragement during moments when the writing felt most uncertain. My sister Sofia supported me and helped translate early concepts into the visual direction that became the cover. To my mother, Felicitas, thank you for introducing me to many of the concepts in this book at a young age. Your belief in me gave me the courage to go back to school, and your love helped bring this book to life.

Laurel Harris, my coach, started me on this path nearly nine years ago, long before the first words appeared on these pages. Her wisdom and willingness to explore ideas created a space where growth became possible. Laurel's unique ability to create a safe container and steady encouragement to stay curious helped inform the heart of my approach to thriving. I'm grateful for her support, presence, and the gentle provocations that helped bring this book into being.

To Lara Merriken, whose partnership throughout this journey has been deeply transformative, thank you for adding your voice to this project with such a touching Foreword. Our daily conversations while bringing Anther to life provided me with the space to explore these ideas in depth. Lara's intuition, her ability to sense what truly connects with others, and her gift for communication helped refine these concepts in ways that resonate with readers. I'm also grateful to her husband, Bill Nelson, whose incisive feedback and encouragement to lean fully into the AIR methodology sharpened both my thinking and the manuscript.

Kathryn Britton, editor extraordinaire and the driving force behind the Theano Writers' Workshops, generously offered the gift of clarity, structure, and flow. Her careful eye and sharp feedback helped trim nearly a third of this manuscript, refining the ideas without losing their depth. Kathryn helped focus the message so the book would remain accessible to readers and played a key role in bringing the AIR methodology to life. Her thoughtful questions and challenges encouraged greater authenticity in my writing, and her insightful approach not only strengthened these pages but also deepened my own understanding of what thriving means.

I'm also grateful to the Theano Writers' Workshop reviewers, Anil Kale, Jan Stanley, Neal Moore, Elaine O'Brien, and Kim Wimmer, for their openness to exploring these ideas with me, their generous feedback, thoughtful questions, and belief in this work.

To the extraordinary MAPP team, James Pawelski, Leona Brandwene, Laura Taylor, Virginia Millar, Aaron Boczkowski, Jayden Gibison, Abby Quirk, Nicole Stottlemyer, and Marty Seligman, thank you. My gratitude extends equally to all lecturers and the vibrant alumni community, especially members of MAPP 18 and fellow assistant instructors. Your commitment to building a life-changing program on a foundation of connection, knowledge, compassion and science has left a profound impact on my life. Without you, I wouldn't even know how to define thriving, much less how to embody it.

To the Georgetown Institute for Transformational Leadership, my sincere gratitude for the invaluable lessons and enduring friendships formed during my time there. Your teachings expanded my understanding of how effective leadership can create the conditions for thriving. I'm equally grateful for the exceptional community I found, where shared purpose is continually cultivated through meaningful connection.

To the facilitators, interns, volunteers, and my entire cohort in the Compassionate Inquiry Professional Training Program, thank you for creating a space of courageous exploration. Your presence offered powerful tools and insights into what it means to meet others and ourselves with compassion. The experience continues to shape how I listen, how I support, and how I write about thriving.

To the Wiley team, Brian Neill, Gabriela Mancuso, Julie Kerr, Sangeetha Suresh, Alyssa Benigno, Deborah Williams, Philo Antonie Mahendran, Matthew Kissner, and everyone else who touched this project, thank you for believing in me and in my vision for this book. Your guidance and tireless efforts transformed these ideas into reality. Collaborating with such a dedicated team has been an extraordinary privilege.

To Rimjhim Dey, Andrew DeSio, Jessica Zagacki, Skye Levine, and the exceptional team at DEY, thank you for your creativity. Your guidance in sharing the book's message with a broader audience through thoughtful storytelling and media engagement has been instrumental. I'm grateful for your commitment and deep care in helping introduce these ideas to the world with integrity. Working with you has been a wonderful and joyful learning experience.

To Carine Redmond from Carine Redmond Pubic Relations and Janine Allen, Jennifer Farr, and the team at Kaiser Partners, thank you for your support in sharing the message of this book within Canada. Your guidance and vision helped ensure these ideas reached the right audiences. I'm grateful for your partnership and for the vital role you played in helping this work find its way into the world.

To Salomon Resler, whose creative vision and helped translate the ideas in this book into a message that could ripple beyond its pages. You helped bring these concepts to life and your work expanded the reach of this message as an open invitation for others to thrive.

To Eliot Johnson and his team at AGNTCY, and to Oliver Galang, Amal Sembhi, Carolyn Chow, and the team at Off Guard Marketing, whose creativity and expertise in marketing the book have been invaluable. Your work on my website and your guidance in leveraging new technologies helped amplify the ideas in this book far beyond what I imagined. I'm grateful for your vision and for your role in making these concepts more accessible to those who may benefit from them.

To Jeremy Cammy, thank you for your unwavering support in launching this book and ensuring it reaches the hands of those who can benefit from its message the most. Your expertise in storytelling transformed the launch into a meaningful experience, and I'm deeply grateful for your positivity and contagious energy.

To Molly Tuttle, thank you for bringing the heart of this book to life in such a vibrant cover and in the design of the Elements of Thriving map. Your creativity perfectly captured the essence of thriving. I'm deeply grateful for your ability to express visually what words alone cannot.

Without technology, this book might never have existed. I'm grateful to those whose work makes new tools possible, allowing us to create in ways previously unimaginable. As part of the writing process, I used artificial intelligence to support research and refine the narrative. Grammarly and Perplexity provided writing suggestions and assisted in summarizing research. I also worked with large language models like ChatGPT and Claude, which became thought partners when I felt stuck. While these new technologies provided valuable support, the words on these pages reflect a deeply human process, enhanced but not defined by technology.

To everyone who generously offered their endorsements for this book, thank you. Your willingness to lend your voice has been humbling. Each of your words gave me encouragement and reinforced the importance of this message.

Writing this book, I'm standing on the shoulders of giants, the thinkers, scientists, and traditions whose insights expanded my understanding of what it means to thrive. My gratitude extends to all whose ideas, recorded or unrecorded, have found their way into these pages, including those whose names may not appear but whose impact is deeply felt. Your collective wisdom forms the foundation upon which this exploration of human thriving rests.

This book didn't come into being alone. From family, friends, colleagues, teachers, mentors, and advisors to every passing conversation that sparked a new insight, I want to extend my deepest gratitude to the constellation of people who made this journey possible. Although my name appears on the cover, this book is the result of many voices, minds, bodies, hearts, and souls: Abimbola Tschetter, Ainur Alpys, Alan Vaisberg, Alberto Wolstein, Alejandra Moreno, Alejandra Gonzalez, Alejandro Katz, Alejandro Kuperschmidt, Alexa Bernal, Alim Esmail, Alison Lawler-Dean, Allen Fay, Aman Gohal, Amira Leifer, Ana Gabriela Viso, Andre Souroujon, Andrea Pesate, Andrea Limbardi, Andrew Soren, Anie Peguero, Ann Parthemore, Ann Vanichkachorn, Anne Pereira, Antonio Sosa, Arie Bernal, Ariel Siller, Ava Shahi, Avi Davidovits, Azmin Gowa, Bernadette Reichel, Beth Correia, Bhumi Trivedi, BJ Jones, Bo Parizadeh, Carla Keown, Carlos Belozercovsky, Carly Guberman, Caroline Adams Miller, Caroline Desrochers, Carter Jennigan, Cesar Ibrahim Indriago, Chad Aboud, Charles Rosemberg Rimeris Z"L, Charlie Friedman, Chenaniah Henderson, Cheryl Cheng, Chris Brockbank, Chris Hamley, Christina Cheuk, Colleen Finnerty, Corinne Kneis, Craig Loudon, Courtney Gehl, Cyrelle Freeman, Damien Catani, Damien Liddle, Dana Emanuel, Danica Oldford, Daniel Benhamu, Daniel Benhayon, Daniel Breve, Daniel Carles, Daniel Levy, Daniel Melul, Daniel Sensel,

Daniel Simkins, Danielle Tarbutt, Danny Fung, Dan Tomasulo, Danny Wang, Daphne Robertson, Darcie Richler, Darlene Marshall, David Waich, David Yaden, Deanne McKenzie Davis, Dengting Boyanton, Derek Applebaum, Devon Fetrow Tomasulo, Diana Mosher, Diego Moreno Z"L, Drew Dutton, Elena Rodighiero, Elias Nahum, Elliot Shiffman, Elizabeth Jennings, Emily Esfahani Smith, Emmy Shiffman, Emmy Weisman, Emy Flores, Eric Wittmann, Ernesto Spira, Esther Benhamu, Esther Joaquin, Esther Yoo, Eugene Tee, Ezequiel Salama, Ezer Chiqui Benaim, Faisal Khan, Faisal Khan, Frank Jackson, Gady Blitz, Gail Banack, Geoff Suares, Glain Roberts-McCabe, Gloria Prieto, Graham Wong, Harry Gray, Harris Krofchick, Heather Reisman, Heather Zaorki, Heindrik Bernabe, Helen Shafer, Henry Richardson, Howard Weinerman, Isaac Peckel, Isabelle Dingemans, Ivan Favreau, Jacqueline Hazan, Jacques Miodownik, Jacques Simkins, Jaime Garzon, Jamie Sun Chung, Jarret Stewart, Jason Godley, Javier Pinedo, Javier Rattia, Jennifer Liu, Jennifer Spencer, Jer Clifton, Jeremy Ehrlich, Jerome Peeters, Jessica Hart, Jessica Kim, Jessica Srikantia, Jill Schulman, Jodi Wellman, Joel Treisman, Joel Vaiser, Joel Wardinger, Jonathan Freeman, Jonathan Gheller, Jonathan Greer, Jonathan Horsford, Jonathan Suchar, Jordan Jacob, Jordan Leslie, Jordana Cole, Jose Panero, Josey Murray, Julia King Pool, Julie Munroff, Karim Hemani, Kate Adajar, Kate Beckett, Katie McClure, Katy Sine, KC White, Kerianne Smith, Kerry O'Neill, Kim Lancaster, Kirsten Calloway, Kirsten Chapman, Klaudio Leshjani, Kris Rumano, Kristen Lessig Schenerlein, Kristina Shea, Kristy Bates, Kwesi Redwood, Kym Baum, Laura Garrison-Brook, Lauren Thompson, Lea Bottoni, Leigh Lampert, Leo Jaegerman, Leon Cohen, Lisa Sansom, Liz Sutton, Lizzie Lee, Lori Legaspi Moores, Louis Alloro, Louisa Jewell, Lucy Li, Luis Moreno Z"L, Maicky Koenig, Maks Ezrin, Mandy Walters, Manuel Diaz-Granados, Mariah DuBose, Mariangela Rodriguez, Mario Basso, Marisela Cuellar, Mark Ang, Marlene Jaegerman, Martina Steiger, Maritza Jackson Sandoval, Martin Blank, Masha Rosemberg Z"L, Mary Sinnott, Matthew Chee, Michael Joseph Groark, Michael Kolesa, Michael Konig, Michael Tan, Michel Weiss, Michelle Krofchick, Michelle Hintz, Michelle Morrison, Mika Keener Opp, Milton Hernandez Z"L, Mindy Applebaum, Miranda Anderson, Mitch Abrams, MJ Shaar, Mona Kennedy, Montserrat Partida, Myra Resler, Naomi Fink, Natalie

Cooper, Natalie Akinin, Nathan Benaim Z"L, Nathan Williams, Neil Bhagat, Neil Christopher, Nicole Perez Cueter, Niels Gott, Niki Daines, Nissim Levy, Noelle Ybarra, Pablo Hyman, Patricia Panero, Patricia Rosas Godoy, Patrick Givelas, Paul Budovitch, Prakriti Pax Tandon, Payton Nyquvest, Pierre Garcia, R.C. Edwards, Rachel Wainer, Rafael Jimenez, Rafael Rosemberg Z"L, Rania Husseini, Reid Robison, Rephael Houston, Ricardo Kort Z"L, Roberta Saffels, Roberto Rimeris, Robyn Wilson, Roger DeWitt, Rosalinda Ballesteros, Rosana Gutierrez, Sady Benzaquen, Samantha Taylor, Sara Benaim, Sara Prieto, Sarah Koning, Sarah Van Dyck, Sarah Wilson, Scout Sanders, Sebastian Mizrahi, Selma Sadzak, Sharon Feldman Danzger, Sharona Weinerman, Shaye Haver, Sheri Fisher, Sherry Lixian Xie, Simon Tache, Sofia Kort Gobel Z"L, Sonya Looney, Soraya Senosier, Stacey Schultz, Stella Iordanidi, Steve Thayer, Steve Cooper, Sunet Terblanche, Suzanne Kort, Sven Greve, Tamara Myles, Tanya Hughes, Taylor Parker, Tessa Virtue, Tom Rotelli, Tracy Wallach, Tzvi Sytner, Valerie Averia, Vanessa Cooper, Virginia Millar, Vivian Souroujon, Yair Szarf, Yoel Rosenheck, Yolanda Morell, Yosef Lynn, Zhenya Evans, and all those whose names escape these pages but not my gratitude.

About the Author

JON ROSEMBERG EMPOWERS leaders and organizations to break free from survival mode and step boldly into thriving. He has spent more than two decades coaching Fortune 500 executives and global teams through deep transformations, demonstrating that positive change begins when we courageously reclaim our agency. Drawing on his experiences of personal and professional reinvention, Jon combines real-world business insight with cutting-edge research and practical wisdom to help others find meaning and thrive.

Jon's belief in human potential led him to co-found Anther, a firm dedicated to helping individuals and teams transform uncertainty into possibility. Previously, he held senior leadership roles at Walmart, Procter & Gamble, Indigo, and served as Chief Operating Officer at scale-up GoBolt. He holds an MBA from Cornell University, a Master of Applied Positive Psychology (MAPP) from the University of Pennsylvania, and advanced certifications in leadership, coaching, and complex negotiations.

Growing up in Caracas, Venezuela, Jon experienced adversity and loss on a journey that took him from New York and Montreal to Toronto, where he now lives with his wife, Adriana, and their two sons. Today, as co-founder of Anther and CEO of Strongpoint Group, he continues to champion growth and well-being, serving as a judge for the Canadian Workplace Well-Being Awards and as an assistant instructor in Penn's MAPP program.

Index